Icons and Iconoclasm in Japanese Buddhism

Kūkai and Dōgen on the Art of Enlightenment

PAMELA D. WINFIELD

OXFORD
UNIVERSITY PRESS

OXFORD
UNIVERSITY PRESS

Oxford University Press is a department of the University of Oxford.
It furthers the University's objective of excellence in research, scholarship,
and education by publishing worldwide.

Oxford   New York
Auckland   Cape Town   Dar es Salaam   Hong Kong   Karachi
Kuala Lumpur   Madrid   Melbourne   Mexico City   Nairobi
New Delhi   Shanghai   Taipei   Toronto

With offices in
Argentina   Austria   Brazil   Chile   Czech Republic   France   Greece
Guatemala   Hungary   Italy   Japan   Poland   Portugal   Singapore
South Korea   Switzerland   Thailand   Turkey   Ukraine   Vietnam

Oxford is a registered trademark of Oxford University Press
in the UK and in certain other countries.

Published in the United States of America by
Oxford University Press
198 Madison Avenue, New York, NY 10016

Library of Congress Cataloging-in-Publication Data
Winfield, Pamela D.
Icons and iconoclasm in Japanese Buddhism : Kūkai and Dōgen on the
art of enlightenment / Pamela D. Winfield.
pages cm
Includes bibliographical references and index.
ISBN 978-0-19-975358-1 (hardcover : alk. paper)—ISBN 978-0-19-994555-9 (pbk. : alk. paper)
1. Buddhism and art—Japan.   2. Kūkai, 774–835.   3. Dōgen, 1200–1253.
4. Meditation—Shingon (Sect)   5. Meditation—Sōtō Zen.   I. Title.
BQ4570.A7W56 2013
294.3'3670952—dc23
2012018028

ISBN 978-0-19-975358-1
ISBN 978-0-19-994555-9

Icons and Iconoclasm
in Japanese Buddhism

To my family, for their "utmost confidence"

Contents

Acknowledgments

NO WOMAN IS an island.

I would like to extend my gratitude first to my family, friends, students, and colleagues who have supported me through the many years of writing this research, first as a dissertation and then rewriting it as a book. Thanks go first to my parents, whose moral support, material sustenance, educational opportunities, and cultural gifts can never be returned fully in kind. In addition to his unswerving emotional support, Jacques Fasan provided research assistance at every level, from cleaning up my endnotes, glossary, and bibliography to asking the deeper questions that helped me to connect the dots. The Elon University students in my *Religion and Art of Asia* interdisciplinary seminars prompted me to clarify, edit, and smooth over conceptual disconnects. The attentive listeners at conferences in Japan and in the United States provided many constructive comments that helped make this a better book. Portions of this research were presented in Japanese at the International Research Center for Japanese Studies (Nichibunken) and Kobe College in 2002, and in English at Santa Clara University in 2005, the Chapel Hill Zendō, and Elon University in 2006. I am also grateful to Yoritomi Motohiro and Nichibunken for allowing me to reprint portions of chapter 2 that originally appeared in the *Seinarumono katachi to ba* (The Figure and Place of the Sacred) conference proceedings.

At the institutional level, thanks are due first to Temple University for their Russell Conwell Fellowship, Training Grant, and Dissertation Completion Grants. The Cross Cultural Institute/Kobe College Corporation's Margaret S. Foley Graduate Fellowship for Research in Japan facilitated my research under Yoritomi Motohiro at Nichibunken in Kyoto from 2001–2002. My subsequent affiliation with Temple University Japan in Tokyo opened many doors and library resources to me first as a graduate student and then as a post-doctoral fellow and occasional visiting assistant professor in the summers. A Religion and Art Fellowship from the Asian Cultural Council facilitated further research in Tokyo in 2007. I am extremely grateful to Ishii Seijun of Komazawa University for his many kindnesses while working in Tokyo during this time and for his indispensable assistance in obtaining the *shisho* copyright permission from Eiheiji monastery in 2011. A publication subvention for first-time authors from the Association for Asian Studies, and a publication assistance grant from Elon University's Faculty Research and Development Fund provided the necessary financial support to cover image reproduction costs.

I would also like to thank individually those who have been instrumental in helping me think through the issues and prepare this manuscript for publication. Whether their influence is great or small, whether their guidance has been direct or indirect, I am indebted to them all. In Philadelphia, Nagatomo Shigenori, Nancy Steinhardt, Kurt Behrendt, Ellen Zhang, Lucy Bregman, as well as Nathan Sivin and William LaFleur, helped me to first conceptualize this material and bring it to fruition as a dissertation. Mikkyō scholars Yoritomi Motohiro, Manabe Shunsho, Ryūichi Abé, Richard Payne, and Itō Naoko, as well as Zen scholars Steven Heine, Ishii Seijun, Taigen Daniel Leighton, Shohaku Okumura, Tanahashi Kazuaki, Norman Waddell, Christian Steineck, Taitaku Josho Pat Phelan, and others have all been invaluable resources for me over the years. Art historians Donald McCallum, Cynthea Bogel, Melissa McCormick, Patricia Graham, Patricia Fister, Sherry Fowler, Sonya Lee, and Winston Kyan have been encouraging, inspiring, and helpful at every turn. Scholars of Japanese Buddhism Robert Sharf, James Dobbins, Jacqueline Stone, William Waldron, Richard Jaffe, Barbara Ambros, as well as other friends and colleagues in Japan, such as Yasuo Yuasa, François Lachaud, Robert Duquesne, S. Silvio Vita, and Iwamoto Akemi were as generous with their time as with their tomes. The Kawata family in Kyoto, the Kobayashi family in Yokohama, my *sempai* and *dōkyūsei* from Temple University, former colleagues at Meredith College, and friends and colleagues at Elon University have been extremely supportive of my scholarship over the years.

In addition, I wish to acknowledge those who make our jobs possible and yet rarely expect any thanks in return, namely all the librarians at Nichibunken, Komazawa University, Kōyasan University (especially Kinoshita-san), Temple University Japan (especially Tom Boardman), the Starr Library at Columbia University (especially Noguchi Sachie), and Elon University (especially Patrick Rudd, Susan Apple, and Lynn Melchor). In addition, I wish to thank Grace Lin and Sun Lixia for their help with Chinese texts, and Hiroko Solari who checked my Japanese grammar and style for one particularly important letter of correspondence. Hillary Pedersen's assistance with all copyright permissions and photo licensing matters in Japan was indispensable. She was efficient, professional, and extremely good-natured as she established rapports with temple priests and museum curators, dealt with international banking issues and navigated Japanese legalese on my behalf. Natalie Butler provided professional help in scanning images, and Sarah Holland assisted with the index. Finally, Cynthia Read and Charlotte Steinhardt at Oxford University Press are an ideal editorial team for any author; they were patient, encouraging, informative, and creative as they shepherded this manuscript from inception to completion. I extend my thanks to them all.

Editorial Notes

1. To maintain consistency with quoted Chinese translations, Chinese terms in the text also appear according to the Wade-Giles transliteration system.
2. Except in cases of a direct quote, in which all diacriticals and italics have been left as originally published,
   - foreign terms that have entered into the American lexicon appear without diacriticals or italics (e.g., samsara, nirvana, mantra, mudra, mandala, dharma, satori, sutra, stupa).
   - other familiar Buddhist terms and proper names appear with diacriticals but no italics (e.g., Mahāyāna, Theravada, Vajrayāna [Mikkyō], Zen).
   - more technical Buddhist terms and specific sutra names appear with diacriticals and italics (e.g., *dharmakāya, dharmadhātu, dharmas, samādhi, Hua-yen, Avataṃsaka Sūtra, sokushin jōbutsu, shinjin datsuraku*).

Introduction

WE LIVE IN the age of Google images and YouTube. Our high resolution scanners, iPhone cameras, instant video streams, and satellite news feeds make images seem ubiquitous, free, open to the public, and taken for granted. But are they? Photojournalists are still routinely rounded up by authoritarian regimes intent on controlling public perception. Self-regulating television, movie, and video-gaming industries continue to rate and even censor visual content for specific media outlets. Intellectual property lawyers profit enormously from protecting and/or promoting the integrity of their clients' images. Indeed, for anyone reading the online version of this text with the occasional illustration omitted because electronic copyright was not extended, it is evident that the problem of imagery is with us still.[1] Despite Walter Benjamin's optimistic view that the work of art in the age of mechanical reproduction is democratic and freely accessible, we nevertheless still have today our own mechanisms for image-control and even image-removal.[2] Especially when it comes to religious icons, there nevertheless remains the lingering presupposition that at least some images are particularly powerful and uniquely valuable mediators of meaning. Just as *hibutsu* ("hidden Buddhas") were secreted away from view for centuries, access to some religious imagery in this book has been restricted to protect its perceived power from the cheapening maw of mass consumption, as Theodor Adorno and Max Horkheimer would argue.[3] Then, as now, inaccessibility ensures sanctity.

This presupposition lies at the heart of this study. What is it about the power of the visual? Why do people debate whether a picture is worth a thousand words or if the movie is better than the book? Which is correct, the old adage that seeing is believing, or Jesus' remark to doubting Thomas, "blessed are those who have not seen and yet believe?"[4] How does one render the invisible visible, and conversely, how does our visual thinking, to borrow Rudolf Arnheim's phrase, shape the contours for what we believe to be possible?[5] Does the concreteness of form control, contradict, or conform to our ideas of the ultimate?

These questions and others were no less pressing in the premodern era. This study approaches the problem of religious imagery by taking two great Japanese Buddhist masters and comparing their thoughts and projects related to Buddhist visual experience and expression. Certainly, there are significant historical, art historical, doctrinal, and practical differences between Kūkai (774–835), the ninth-century founder of Japan's esoteric Shingon Mikkyō sect on the one hand, and Dōgen (1200–1253), the thirteenth-century founder of Japan's Sōtō Zen sect on the other. To address these differences fully, however, would constitute a volume in itself. Kūkai's and Dōgen's respective historical, political, socioeconomic, and cultural locations will therefore be invoked only when they pertain directly to the thematic focus of this study, that is, to their ideas and projects specifically related to Buddhist imagery, image-experience, representation, form, formlessness, and the nondistinction between the two. Likewise, although it is evident that both patriarchs are inheritors of, and contributors to, Buddhism's rich religio-artistic legacy, the larger continental traditions and discourses surrounding Buddhist visual culture will only be briefly outlined here and referenced specifically when they directly relate to Kūkai's or Dōgen's oeuvres. This study is intended to be a focused and therefore necessarily selective exercise in comparative thought, not an exhaustive survey of all Buddhist art, architecture, scripture, and commentary pertaining to form. Nevertheless, the following brief survey is provided to orient beginning readers and familiarize them with key developments in Theravada, Mahāyāna, Vajrayāna (Jp. Mikkyō), and Zen Buddhist art and doctrine.

The so-called an-iconic, nonfigural phase of early classical Indian or Theravadin art advanced an iconography of absence to indicate the Buddha's complete and utter selflessness in the state of nirvana. Because Buddha had transcended all suffering and all desires in the world of samsara, by definition this also meant that he had transcended all bodily desires. His realization of no-self (*an-ātman*), therefore, was taken literally to mean no-body. The Buddha, consequently, was not depicted in any anthropomorphic form in this early period, but rather intimated only by such symbolic emblems as dharma wheels, footprints, empty thrones, or parasols over riderless horses. These nonfigural visual cues indicated his presence by his very absence.

Later Mahāyāna Buddhism, however, collapsed the philosophical divide between samsara and nirvana. This Buddhist ideal of nondualism, defined as the abrogation of any two extremes, inspired a new iconography of embodiment to indicate the Buddha's always-already enlightened nature in all the forms of the universe. As this later phase of figural Buddhist art in Gandhāra and Central Asia absorbed neighboring religious influences from the first centuries CE onward, the Greco-Roman, Zoroastrian, Manichean, and Nestorian Christian gods of light gradually became conflated with the enlightened nature of the historical Buddha.[6] As a result of this synthesis, an extended concept of a universal Buddha-body called the *dharmakāya* came to be understood as the embodiment of Great Light itself (literally, Jp. *Dainichi*, Skt. *Mahāvairocana*). Like the sun, this cosmic Buddha-monarch illumined all, equally, and resided in a palace of unimaginable brightness and wisdom called the *dharmadhātu*.

In keeping with Mahāyāna Buddhist philosophy, this palace of being ultimately was nothing other than our own world of samsara, but one had to practice the dharma in order to perceive it. Two main strains of Mahāyāna Buddhism developed throughout Asian history, namely Vajrayāna (Jp. Mikkyō) and Zen Buddhist thought and practice.[7] For early esoteric adherents like Kūkai, perceiving the *dharmadhātu* meant being initiated into the elaborate and highly symbolic practices of the quick and diamondlike path of esoteric Mikkyō Buddhism, which located Dainichi's three secrets of body, speech, and mind in mudra hand gestures, mantra sacred invocations, and mandala visual displays. For later Zen adepts like Dōgen, however, it meant "just sitting," as he believed that sitting zazen automatically manifests the realization of the original enlightenment at the heart of being.

Thus, the early classical Indian divide between samsara and nirvana promoted an iconography of absence, while the Mahāyāna collapse of this philosophical divide contributed to an iconography of embodiment. Mikkyō esoteric Buddhism (institutionalized as Shingon in Japan) later fashioned an iconography of the ultimate to unify Mahāyāna's sprawling pantheon of Buddhist deities, while Zen Buddhism promoted an iconography of engaging and the direct experience of satori instead of Mikkyō's elaborate symbol-systems. To express their detachment from even the idea of Buddhahood, therefore, Zen iconoclasts such as Tan-hsia T'ien-jan (J. Tanka Tennen 739–824), Ikkyū Sōjun (1394–1481), and others burned, urinated on, or otherwise parodied images of buddhas and patriarchs. These important discourses surrounding the philosophy of form, Buddhist artistic expression, and religious experience in specifically the Mikkyō and Zen Buddhist contexts form the background to our more focused discussion of Kūkai and Dōgen's oeuvres.

Outline of the Chapters

Chapter 1 presents the basic theoretical framework and historiographical material necessary for contextualizing this comparative and multidisciplinary project. It introduces some fundamental vocabulary for discussing Kūkai's and Dōgen's distinctly unitive or purgative kinds of religious experience, and suggests that these experiences, combined with their inherited esoteric and Zen Buddhist traditions, also correlate to their views of iconicity and iconoclasm. At the same time, however, it also qualifies these reified categories in important ways, which will further be taken up in chapters 3 and 4, dedicated to Kūkai and Dōgen, respectively.

Chapter 2 explores Kūkai's primarily spatial, and Dōgen's primarily temporal interpretations of Kegon (Ch. *Hua-yen*) doctrine. These provide the important philosophical framework for their unitive and purgative paradigms for awakening. Their primarily spatial and temporal "takes" on reality also seem to influence how they view the relationship between form and emptiness as articulated in the *Heart Sūtra*. Kūkai's spatial-reflexive reading of "form is emptiness, emptiness is form" sets him up for the experience of *kaji* and an embrace of forms *as* emptiness. By contrast, Dōgen's temporal-sequential reading sets him up for the experience of *shinjin datsuraku* and the valuation of the imageless void before the forms of the world (oneself included) are reconstituted. I further argue that Kūkai's Two World mandalas, and Dōgen's *shisho* transmission certificate, help to inform their primarily spatial and temporal outlooks, respectively.

Chapters 3 and 4 present Kūkai's and Dōgen's key philosophical writings and projects directly related to art, mental images, visuality, and perception. Chapter 3 introduces Kūkai's Two World mandalas and other mandalic projects that convey Mikkyō doctrines through a highly stylized iconographic code. By recognizing the collapse between signifier and signified in Mikkyō's symbol system, this chapter demonstrates that for Kūkai, art can be the direct expression of awakening. At the same time, however, it notes that Kūkai also deconstructed the sacred power of such exceptional images into emptiness, so that all forms are seen in the light of what I call intericonicity.

Chapter 4 focuses on key fascicles of Dōgen's *Shōbōgenzō* that elucidate his inconstant view of imagery. On the one hand, Dōgen scorns a painting of Nāgārjuna manifesting the full-moon *samādhi* (calling it nothing but a painting of a rice cake, the title of another fascicle). On the other hand, however, Dōgen avidly seeks out other Zen images, which he treats as icons. The audience he is addressing, the particular image under consideration, and the level of understanding of his interlocutors seem to be the deciding factors as to whether Dōgen approves of an image or not. His self-acclaimed possession of the True Dharma Eye (*shōbōgen*), it seems, ultimately makes him the arbiter of whether art can represent the enlightenment experience or not.

Chapter 5 provides some concluding remarks to this comparative study and tentatively offers new directions in the study of icons and iconoclasm beyond the scope of Kūkai's and Dōgen's oeuvres. The qualifier "tentatively" is used here deliberately. The space-time analytical model, the text-image methodology, and the experience-expression feedback loop advanced here may indeed have significant implications for the study of mystical experience and artistic expression in other religious traditions as well. At the same time, however, it should not be assumed that the conclusions drawn from this study are universally applicable. Kūkai and Dōgen represent two complementary poles of thought within the Japanese Buddhist tradition, which has its own philosophical presuppositions far removed, for example, from the monotheistic concerns about idolatry of the three major Abrahamic traditions. The motivations behind Buddhist iconoclasm, therefore, are completely unrelated to Jewish, Muslim, or Protestant Christian rationales for image-removal. Consequently, juxtaposing the spiritual trajectories and associated arts of other kataphatic and apophatic examples may, or may not, be illumined by a similar approach taken here.

To begin at the beginning, however, let us now focus on Kūkai and Dōgen on the art of enlightenment. As we explore how imagery relates to the experience, expression, and perception of enlightenment, we will encounter Kūkai's and Dōgen's meditative *techné*, artistic techniques, and literary technologies. These will help us to better understand and appreciate the feedback loop between religious experience and artistic expression that lie at the heart of this study.

*Icons and Iconoclasm
in Japanese Buddhism*

I

Introduction to the Art of Enlightenment

BY ITS VERY nature, the issue of icons and iconoclasm is an interdisciplinary project. It touches upon the overlapping concerns of art history as well as religious studies, material culture as well as mysticism studies. It is a rich and varied subject that engages all of one's sensibilities and faculties, for it considers both the visible and invisible dimensions of religious art and doctrine. It is a visually and conceptually compelling topic of inquiry that explores the ability of real or imagined forms to inspire—as well as to express—the ineffable insights of religious experience. In the specific context of Buddhism under consideration here, it compels one to pose some fundamental, yet heretofore unasked questions, regarding the nature and function of imagery before, during, and after awakening: Do images help or hinder the realization of Buddhahood? Does the experience of awakening involve the imagination or not? Can art ever represent the experience of enlightenment itself?

This study focuses on these questions of artistic expression and religious experience in premodern Japanese Buddhist art and doctrine. It explores how the great Buddhist masters of the Heian (794–1192) and Kamakura (1192–1333) periods understood the art of enlightenment in its fullest double sense, that is, both as an expression of, and as a method or technique for, achieving enlightenment. It specifically looks to two representative voices for and against the role of imagery in the experience of awakening. These are namely Kūkai (774–835) and Dōgen (1200–1243), the respective founders of Shingon Mikkyō and Sōtō Zen Buddhism in Japan.

Kūkai believes that highly imaginative, visualized union with deities and colorful mandala paintings are necessary for realizing one's potential

Buddhahood in this very body (*sokushin jōbutsu*). Dōgen, by contrast, believes that the moment of realization is ineffable and nonlocative, free of body and mind and not representable in any static form. At the same time, however, no sooner does Kūkai build up mandalic architectures of understanding and bodies of knowledge than does he deconstruct them into emptiness. Likewise, Dōgen is at times extremely difficult to pin down; his views on imagery seem to shift and change depending on the picture under consideration or on the audience he is addressing. Juxtaposing Kūkai's rich, vibrant iconicity (emptied of substance) with Dōgen's sparse iconoclasm (qualified by a few special Zen icons) will hopefully present a more varied, balanced, and nuanced vision of how Japanese Buddhists themselves understood the role of imagery vis-à-vis awakening.

These two eminent figures are deliberately juxtaposed here despite the historical gap between them in order to both support and subvert their constructed reputations. Since at least the early modern period, Kūkai has primarily been associated with the visuality, "aesthetic enjoyments," and "opulence" of the Heian court,[1] while Dōgen has primarily been seen as embodying the ascetic, world-denying, and "stern" samurai ideal of the Kamakura shōgunate.[2] These associations are not altogether incorrect, but require a great deal more explanation and qualification. Kūkai did indeed construct (yet also deconstruct) the importance of his visualized, sculpted, and painted esoteric images, and Dōgen did reject (yet also embrace) specific forms of Buddhahood in his own idiosyncratic manner.

Juxtaposing and nuancing the claims and counterclaims of these two eminent Japanese masters builds upon, yet also provides a necessary complement to, previous studies of the two renowned monks. Philosophers such as David Shaner and Yuasa Yasuo first established the comparability of Kūkai's and Dōgen's body-mind theories over twenty-five years ago, but Shaner's phenomenological approach and Yuasa's Jungian associations graft completely foreign Western European conceptual constructs onto their writings.[3] The present study, by contrast, looks internally to within the Buddhist tradition itself to elucidate the Kegon (Ch. *Hua-yen*) philosophy of form that most influenced Kūkai's and Dōgen's contributions, and integrates the careful study of visual and material culture into the consideration of their oeuvres. As a result, this examination of the texts and images associated with their respective projects to establish Shingon Mikkyō and Sōtō Zen in Japan will present a more balanced view of what one might call today Kūkai's and Dōgen's religio-artistic theories.

Comparing and contrasting both textual and visual materials in this way will also serve to liberate these two Japanese patriarchs from past sectarian scholarship that has primarily locked them into strictly iconographic-ritualistic or philological-philosophical categories, respectively. Moreover, the inherent interdisciplinary approach of this study will help to restore the historical symbiosis between visuality and religion (either in its affirmative or negative sense) and further contribute to bridging the text-image gap that has formed the basis for many of the turf wars between the academic disciplines of art history and religious studies. This study, therefore, seeks to provide a broad conceptual approach to the problem of imagery and experience in Japanese Buddhism, and selects these two archetypal figures who model opposing yet complementary paradigms for enlightenment with and without images. For both Kūkai and Dōgen believed that awakening in the present lifetime was possible and that it was somehow intimately connected with imagery (whether in a positive enhancing way or as something from which one needed to "break through"). Their individual experiences studying abroad in China provide a case in point.

The Problem

When the esoteric master Kūkai returned to Japan in 806 after two years of study in T'ang dynasty China, he arrived laden with hundreds of texts, images, and ritual accoutrements for propagating his new esoteric doctrines in Japan. Kūkai's *Catalogue of Imported Items* (*Shōrai mokuroku*) records that he imported from China over two hundred scriptures and commentaries, eighteen ritual implements, eight precious objects (i.e., relics), five mandala paintings, and five patriarch portraits. It asserts that all of the iconic imagery and ritual paraphernalia associated with his new Mikkyō esoteric teachings can hasten the initiate along the quick path of awakening, and that the mandalas in particular condense all of Buddha's teachings into visual form and can "enlighten the beholder in a single glance" (*itto jōbutsu*).[4] When the governor of Sanuki province consequently praised Kūkai fifteen years later in a letter dated 821, he extolled, "He studied abroad to seek the Way; he went empty-handed and returned fully-equipped" (*kyoō jikki*).[5]

By contrast, when the Sōtō Zen master Dōgen returned to Japan in 1227 from his four years abroad in Sung dynasty China, he turned the ancient governor's statement on its head. He declared that he too went abroad to seek the Way, but that he proudly "returned empty-handed" from the continent (*kūshu genkyō*).[6] On one level, Dōgen's counterclaim can be understood to mean simply that he carried back relatively few Chinese scriptures and pictures, but on a deeper level it suggests in typically minimalist Zen fashion that he carried nothing other than the experiential realization of emptiness, the definition of enlightenment itself. Dōgen thus reaffirms Kūkai's notion that enlightenment can occur in the present lifetime, but implicitly critiques Mikkyō's old elaborate visual displays and ritual procedures for doing so. He thus radically differentiates himself from his acquisitive predecessor, overturns the expectations of those anticipating a new influx of imported Buddhist materials from the continent, challenges their predilection for all things Chinese, and valorizes this very lack of materials in a quintessentially Zen sentiment of less-is-more.

It is certainly also possible that more mundane and pragmatic matters may have influenced Kūkai's and Dōgen's views on imagery. They were operating on radically different budgets in their respective eras, and Dōgen's empty-handed return may well have been making a virtue of necessity since he had nowhere near the resources Kūkai had. In fact, Kūkai had in only two years managed to spend his entire twenty-year Japanese government stipend on his treasure trove of painted silks and scriptures. He used Japan's state funds to commission Li Chen and approximately a dozen Chinese painters to paint ten scrolls: five patriarch portraits, three copies of the Womb World mandala (Jp. *taizōkai*), and two copies of the Diamond World mandala (Jp. *kongōkai*).[7] These visual materials were not the only things Kūkai spent his money on; twenty scribes copied 216 sutras and commentaries in 461 fascicles, and the bronzesmith Chao Wu was commissioned to cast fifteen of the eighteen ritual implements that Kūkai brought back.[8]

On the other hand, Dōgen was but an independent seeker traveling abroad in search of the true dharma with his companion Myōzen (1184–1225). As a foreigner in China lacking even the most basic of ranks, he possessed neither the economic nor the clerical capital to acquire the kind of dharma treasures Kūkai was able to obtain. Nevertheless, in addition to carrying back the relics of his former companion, Dōgen did return home with a small "collection of Zen mementos" given to him by his master Tendō Nyojō (Ch. T'ien t'ung Ju-ching 1163–1228).[9] Dōgen reportedly returned with the *chinzō* portrait of his master Nyojō, his *shisho* certificate confirming the authenticity of his dharma transmission, the then 109-year-old dharma robe of his sixth-generation predecessor, the Chinese patriarch Fu-jung Tao-kai (1043–1118), and two Sōtō doctrinal texts.[10] Such pragmatic financial considerations, however, do not negate the fact Kūkai and Dōgen understood the power and importance of religious imagery in very different ways.

All of Kūkai's imported visual and ritual paraphernalia were an indispensable part of his new Mikkyō method for obtaining enlightenment, a process that he formulated as "becoming a Buddha in this very body" (*sokushin jōbutsu*). This concise doctrinal soubriquet not only indicated that one could obtain liberation quickly in the present lifetime, but also that the locus of one's enlightenment was necessarily in and with the form of one's physical body. Dōgen, by contrast, subsequently plays on Kūkai's by then well-known motto and cleverly writes a fascicle in 1239 entitled not *sokushin jōbutsu* (即身成仏) but rather *sokushin zebutsu* (即心是仏) or "This Very Mind is Buddha."[11] In so doing, Dōgen again reaffirms Kūkai's claim that enlightenment is possible in this lifetime, but his pun on the homonyms *shin* 身 (body) and *shin* 心 (mind) shifts the locus of enlightenment from the corporeal to the mental. He concurrently collapses the potentiality of Mikkyō into the immediacy of Zen with great rhetorical effect, and effectively recasts the Mikkyō maxim for Zen doctrinal emphasis. From Dōgen's perspective, elaborate visual and ritual procedures may well lead to one eventually becoming a Buddha in this very body, but as Dōgen further riffs in the *Bendōwa* fascicle, *sokuza jōbtusu* "[by] just sitting zazen, one becomes a Buddha."[12] That is, for Dōgen, just sitting (*shikan taza*) in Zen meditation automatically actualizes one's inherent Buddha nature so that the practitioner instantaneously grasps that this very mind—already, right now—is Buddha. For this reason, instead of requiring initiation into Mikkyō's secret path of *mantrayāna* and its three secrets of body (mudra), speech (mantra), and mind (mandala), Dōgen simply states in his *Secret Words* (*Mitsugo*) fascicle that truly secret practice is just knowing oneself.[13]

The metaphorical significance of coming home either "fully equipped" or "empty-handed" thus extends into larger doctrinal issues in East Asian Buddhism. These issues touch upon the difference between potential and acquired enlightenment, gradual and sudden awakening, the relationship between practice and realization, and enlightenment with or without the form of the physical body (Kūkai insists on using mudra hand gestures and literally becoming a Buddha in this very body, while Dōgen claims the body eventually drops off with the mind in Zen meditation). Taken together, Kūkai and Dōgen thus highlight two poles of thought regarding the role that imagery and image experience play in the practical philosophies of Buddhism. They are both undeniably Buddhist masters, yet they understand the nature and method of Buddhist awakening and its relationship to form in fundamentally different ways.

Unitive and Purgative Experience

Kūkai and Dōgen construct two equally valid, yet distinct paradigms for the experience and expression of enlightenment. These can be identified as:

1. UNITIVE MODEL: A mutual, nondual union of two entities, established especially between the practitioner and Mikkyō's main deity Dainichi Buddha. Such a unitive model requires an open, unobstructed space within which these two beings can come together in deity yoga. Kūkai's imagistic religious experience of *kaji* or mutual empowerment between practitioner and Buddha represents the highest expression of this non-dual union in unobstructed space. This spatial orientation embraces forms *as* emptiness, the body *as* Buddha, and art *as* enlightenment. They are all considered to be nothing other than Dainichi's cosmic self-expressions.

2. PURGATIVE PROCESS: A threefold sequential movement that
   a. asserts the everyday existence of self vs. other;
   b. negates self-and-other in a moment of absolute cessation;
   c. finally reaffirms the self by virtue of other existents rushing back in to the field of contemplative awareness and confirming the provisional self as but an interconnected and coconditioning one of many. Such a process for enlightenment requires unobstructed time within which the pivotal second movement of absolute cessation can occur. Dōgen's moment of "dropping off body-mind of self and other" (*shinjin dat-suraku*) represents the pivotal moment when everyday form drops away, to be later reaffirmed by all forms and thus seen in a transformed light.[14] This temporal orientation disallows representing the ineffable moment of emptiness in any fixed form, hence static, pictorial arts are routinely deconstructed.

In other words, Kūkai fundamentally envisions enlightenment as a recip-rocal union of self and world (as personified by Dainichi) in unobstructed space, whereas Dōgen fundamentally experiences Buddhahood as a sequential assertion, negation, and reaffirmation of the self and world in unobstructed time. Kūkai sees enlightenment as a nondual union of the body, speech, and mind of the self and the visualized deity. Here, the deity Dainichi, the Great Sun Buddha, is concretely visualized as a distinctly luminous mental object in the sphere of the meditator's imagination. By contrast, Dōgen sees enlight-enment as a complete eradication of all mental objects, including even the awareness of one's own body-mind complex in the realm of the imagination.

Dōgen advocates completely dropping off body-mind (*shinjin datsuraku*) in meditation, and then reconstituting the form of one's identity only by virtue of, and in radical codependence with, all the myriad other existents in the world. To put it more succinctly, Kūkai's unitive model indicates the state of oneness that occurs when self and world unify ($1 + 1 = 1$). Dōgen's purgative process outlines a state of oneness that occurs when self, and then the loss of that self, ultimately and intimately unifies one with the world ($1 + 0 = 1$).

Their unitive and purgative experiences help to inform their general attitudes toward form and emptiness, and particularly the artforms *of* emptiness. In Kūkai's case, this refers to the Two World Mandalas that depict the phenomenal and noumenal aspects of Dainichi Buddha, the personification of emptiness and the cosmic world-body of universal Buddhahood. In Dōgen's case, this refers to all natural forms in their constant flux and change, though particular Zen icons, such as his *shisho* transmission certificate, are exceptional since they express and authenticate the realization of emptiness in fixed form. If such divergent religious experiences may account for Kūkai's and Dōgen's views on imagery, the subject of this study, then it behooves us to look more closely at the experience itself.

Active and Passive Meditation

Various typologies for categorizing mystical experience have been proposed by scholars in the past, but none seem particularly well suited to analyzing Kūkai's and Dōgen's unitive and purgative forms of religious experience. Rudolf Otto contrasts mysticisms of unifying vision vs. introspection, and Evelyn Underhill presents a promising typology of lover vs. ascetic, but Otto associates unifying vision with a Eurocentric conception of God, and Underhill turns the lover trope into a discussion of medieval European marriage and the ascetic trope into an analysis of alchemy.[15] Max Weber overgeneralizes by proposing world-affirming vs. world-denying mystics,[16] though Livia Kohn's enstatic/embodied vs. ecstatic/disembodied categories[17] are helpful in conceptualizing Kūkai's unitive vs. Dōgen's purgative paradigms for enlightenment.

By contrast, there seems to be some neurological evidence to account for these two basic kinds of religious experience. Psychological studies have shown that the posterior parietal lobe, the area of the brain responsible for orienting oneself in space, tends to shut down either partially or completely in deep meditation.[18] The level of neurological blockage, called deafferentiation, in this orientation area may help to explain those accounts by myriad mystics throughout history who either describe the kataphatic (*via positiva*) feelings of divine union and/or the apophatic (*via negativa*) feelings of absolute selflessness in the void. Some of the methods used in these recent studies of neurotheology have fallen under scrutiny, and their conclusions have been critiqued as being overly reductionistic since brain states do not necessarily correspond to mind states.

That being said, however, some interesting indications have emerged from brain scans of Christian contemplatives and Buddhist practitioners while engaged in meditation. In a series of experiments conducted at the University of Pennsylvania in the late 1990s, neurologists d'Acquili and Newberg monitored the brain states of advanced Christian and Buddhist practitioners. They fitted them with electrodes, automatically injected chemical tracers into their brains, and obtained freeze-frame brain scans of the moment they indicated their meditative climax. The results of these studies distinguished two basic kinds of contemplation, which d'Acquili and Newberg labeled either active or passive meditation. In active meditation, one focuses one's attention on a real or imagined object and one experiences feelings of divine union. In passive meditation, one attempts to shut the mind down completely of all thoughts, perceptions, and emotions, and one experiences a moment of complete and utter selflessness.[19] These two paradigms indeed seem to correlate to Kūkai's and Dōgen's respective arts of enlightenment.

In active meditation, one begins by intentionally focusing one's attention on a real or imagined object such as the *ajikan* disk depicting Dainichi's seed syllable. Neurologically speaking, this means that the brain's right attention association area (AAA) engages those parts of the brain responsible for visual perception and spatiality. It also signals the hypothalamus (which controls the body's arousal or quiescent functions) to activate an ergotrophic or aroused response. Sustained concentration on the visual image creates a feedback loop between the AAA and the hypothalamus, so that the meditator enjoys "a mildly pleasant state of excitation."[20] Usually for survival reasons, one's quiescent functions are blocked when the hypothalamus goes into arousal mode, but under certain conditions, neurologists have noted a "spillover effect."[21] When the hypothalamus reaches an extreme point of excitation, it actually "rebounds"[22] and sends out neural signals for extreme quietude as well. This may help to explain numerous accounts of profound calm in the midst of highly charged prayer or meditation. At this point, one's cerebral circuits are being overloaded by the explosion of neural signals for both excitement and quietude. The entire system thus goes into overdrive, which enhances the AAA's ability to focus on the real or imagined object even further. This overdrive mode ultimately affects the orientation association area (OAA) of the brain as well. The right orientation area in the parietal lobe, which controls one's sense of spatiality, receives nothing but the video-stream of the AAA's idée fixe, so the image seems to take up the whole of space. Simultaneously, the left orientation area, which controls the sense of one's own body, completely shuts down so that one's bodily boundaries seem to blur and fade. Taken together, one's sense of self seems to melt into the image. D'Acquili and Newberg conclude that as a result of this active meditation on a mental image, "the mind would experience a startling perception that the individual self had been mystically absorbed into the transcendent reality of [the deity]. In this fashion, neurology could explain the *Unio Mystica*—the Mysterious Union with God."[23] In the esoteric Buddhist context, it could equally explain Kūkai's unitive model of *kaji* with Dainichi Buddha.

Passive meditation, by contrast, attempts to shut the mind down completely of all thoughts, images, and emotions. This form of meditation also begins in the brain's right attention association area (AAA), the seat of willed actions. Instead of deliberately setting the intention to focus on an image, however, the passive meditator engages it to clear the mind. It engages the thalamus and hippocampus, which controls the flow of neural input to various parts of the brain, and these two brain structures gradually deprive the brain's orientation area of information (OAA deafferentiation). This triggers the hypothalamus to signal further quiet and calm. As the feedback loop of neural input flows, it fosters a trophotrophic response and "deeper and deeper levels of meditative calm [are reached] with every pass."[24] When the hypothalamus reaches its deepest quiescent level, however, the so-called "spillover" effect occurs and triggers the opposite arousal response as well. The flood of signals for both quiescence and arousal surge through the brain's circuits, and this overdrive mode of heightened activity in the brain again forces the AAA to operate at its highest level. This time, however, "the deafferenting effect that the attention area is directing toward the orientation area becomes supercharged, and in milliseconds, the deafferentation of the orientation area becomes complete."[25]

It is important to note here that this sudden and radical sense of selflessness occurs in a matter of milliseconds; the right and left orientation areas controlling the sense of one's own body and its location in the world shut down completely and utterly in a mere nanosecond. Whereas active meditation on a mental object seems to involve a gradual and total self-absorption into a visualized spatial entity, passive meditation seems to result in a sudden and complete rupture, an instantaneous flick of the switch that utterly evaporates one's sense of self-awareness in space. This fleeting moment of what d'Acquili and Newberg term "Void-Consciousness" or "Absolute Unitary Being"[26] seems to correspond with Dōgen's purgative model for *shinjin datsuraku*, the moment of completely "dropping off body and mind" of self and other.

These two active and passive meditative paradigms are helpful to our present discussion of Kūkai's and Dōgen's unitive and purgative meditative ideals in space and time. D'Acquili and Newberg err, however, by ascribing the former active meditation only to theistic Christianity and passive meditation to nontheistic Buddhism, as if both active and passive strains were not present in both religious traditions. D'Acquili and Newberg also speculate that active meditation may be a lower level meditative experience than passive meditation, since the orientation area is only partially deafferented in active meditation and wholly deafferented in passive meditation. This suggests an implicit bias against imagistic meditation experience; a theme that will be taken up in the next section. Nevertheless, their neurological insights are significant, and helpful to our more general discussion of the Buddhist philosophies of form and the art of enlightenment.

Visualized Union and Contentless Experience

There is still a widely held belief especially amongst those Euro-American scholars still influenced by D. T. Suzuki, that Zen's contentless, imageless experience is necessarily higher or somehow better than Mikkyō's highly imagistic experience. For Suzuki, all of the historical developments and religious struggles of Buddhist history culminated in Zen. As a result, he claimed that Zen is "the most essential factor in [Buddhism]" and that the Zen tradition "gradually bring[s] to light the hidden implications of the original faith and enrich[es] it in a manner undreamed of in the beginning."[27] This implicit superiority of contentless experience is usually traced back to early Buddhism, which codified Hindu meditative techniques into nine hierarchical *dhyana* states rising up through the realms of desire and pure form to finally reach the ultimate realm of formlessness (Skt. *arūpadhatu*). The last four meditative states in the realm of formlessness before the realization of nirvana were awareness of infinite spatiality, infinite consciousness, nothingness, and neither thought nor non-thought.

From the Mikkyō perspective, however, privileging the realm of Formlessness does not recognize the fundamentally enlightened nature of forms just as they already are (Skt. *tathatā*). To Mikkyō adepts, the contentless state of "no mind, no thought" (Jp. *munen musō*, Skt. *āsphānaka samādhi*), also known as "no-consciousness no-body *samādhi*" (Jp. *mushikishin sanmai*) or "unmoving *samādhi*" (Jp. *mudō sanmai*), is considered to be a low-level exoteric stage that doesn't fully understand the always embodied nature of emptiness/suchness.[28] The *Kongōchōkyō* (Skt. *Vajraśekhara Sūtra*), for example, states that the Buddha himself abandoned the extremely ascetic *āsphānaka samādhi* in favor of deliberately mobilizing the imagination in meditation. According to this seventh-century esoteric scripture, Buddha became enlightened when he visualized a vajra unifying with a moon disk, symbolizing the union of his seed of potential Buddhahood with fully realized Buddhahood.[29] As the esoteric patriarch Amoghavajra (Ch. Pu-k'ung Ching-kang, Jp. Fukū kongō, 705–774) further clarifies in his *Kongōchō giketsu* commentary:

> In the esoteric mantra teaching…this [*āsphānaka*] samadhi is not dwelt in. This is because this samadhi is a void samadhi that denies all forms and phenomena, whereas from the standpoint of the esoteric mantra teaching, all forms and phenomena are, just as they are, truth.…The attitude that shuns forms and phenomena and delights in empty samadhi is a deluded attitude that does not realize the use of true wisdom.[30]

Mikkyō's alternative standpoint that repopulates meditative experience with forms thus serves as a foil to Zen's reputedly pure imageless state. It is for this reason that Kūkai himself ranks contentless meditation as but the fifth of ten stages of mind in his *Precious Key to the Secret Treasury* (*Hizō hōyaku*). Disparaging the early pratyekabuddha ideal of low-level "Hinayāna" Buddhism, Kūkai condescendingly comments, "upon complete cessation of their body and mind, they believe they enter Nirvana," but they immediately detach from this delusion and convert to Mahāyāna as soon as their karmic merit, the Buddha's grace, and expedient means provide the opportunity.[31] If Kūkai had the opportunity to meet Dōgen, he might well rank Dōgen's experience of "dropping off body-mind of self and other" along with the early pratyekabuddhas, whom he says, "are of small and inferior wisdom."[32]

In all fairness to Zen, however, one should acknowledge that both imagistic and nonimagistic strains of Buddhist meditation existed from the start in classical Indian Buddhism. According to Buddhaghosa's fifth-century *Visuddhimagga* manual of meditation, visualized union with colored disks called *kasiṇa maṇḍalas*, for example, constituted an important preliminary practice in śamatha calm meditation.[33] In this practice, one focused and stabilized the mind on a physical or mental image of a colored circle until one eventually had the sensation of merging with it. Also, according to the *Visudhimagga*, one could reach the other early classical meditative ideal of absolute cessation of all mental cognitions (Skt. *nirodha samāpatti*) with the addition of vipassanā insight meditation.[34] Its added insights into the radical impermanence and insubstantiality of self and world could lead to ultimate wisdom or *prajñā*, defined as the realization of selflessness. The combination of these two image-filled and imageless meditative techniques lead to a curious double standard: in later Mahāyāna Buddhism, the word for wisdom itself, *prajñā*, could equally indicate either a state of unified consciousness or the complete eradication of all cognitive activity.[35] Kūkai and Dōgen tend to favor the former or the latter strain of this shared legacy, respectively.

This discussion of Buddhist meditative techniques also raises the issue of space and time, the focus of chapter 2. Because images are fundamentally spatial in nature, and the workings of the mind are active and temporally dynamic, the presence or absence of mental images in meditation indicates a relatively spatial or temporal mode of awareness. By their very nature, śamatha contemplations on colored disks are spatially oriented, while vipassanā meditations are more temporally oriented as they focus the mind on the passing nature of every sensation and fleeting thought. These two techniques are therefore designed to lead to a feeling of nondual union in unobstructed meditative space, or a moment of absolute cessation in unobstructed meditative time, respectively. These two meditative goals, as well as their reciprocal vs. sequential ideals for religious experience, are inherited legacies from the past that influenced Kūkai's and Dōgen's respective views of imagery. Their prototypical models and inherited religious ideals as expressed in both text and image were fundamentally shaped by a *relative* emphasis on space or time and were present in varying forms and to varying degrees from the very inception of Buddhism.

In other words, Kūkai's textual and visual expressions of spatialized time reflect and inform his meditative ideal of *kaji*'s nondual union. His visualized unification of self with deity could not have been formulated without the precedent of some early śamatha visualization practices with *kasiṇa maṇḍalas*, a spatial and reflexive understanding of form and emptiness, *bodhimaṇḍa* ritual enclosures, and Mikkyō's generally synthetic character. As explained further in chapters 2 and 3, these factors allowed Kūkai to embrace form *as* empty, and hence construct and deconstruct numerous interresonating architectures of understanding.

By contrast, Dōgen's textual-visual expressions of temporalized space reflect and inform his ideal meditative moment of absolute cessation in *shinjin datsuraku*. Dōgen could not have advanced the notion of temporarily forgetting and then reconstituting the self without being heir to the early Buddhist ideals of cessation (*nirodha samāpatti*) brought about by vipassanā's insight into impermanence. As we shall see in chapter 2, the threefold sequential understanding of form and emptiness structures his enlightenment experience through unobstructed time, as it did for his predecessors Bhāvaviveka (Ch. Ch'ing pien, Jp. Shōben 490–570), Seigen (Ch. Ch'ing-yüan 660–740), and other readers of the *Diamond Sūtra* before him. Other factors, such as the Zen-Taoist concern for time, realization as practice in time, and an overwhelming preoccupation with the transhistorical transmission of what he calls the True Dharma Eye, all contributed to shape Dōgen's inconstant view of imagery. Dōgen navigates an extremely fine line in determining which or what kinds of images are amenable to whom, and why some are incompatible with his overarching concern for practice-realization in, through, and as time.

Deconstructing Contentless Experience

Despite the fact that both imagistic and nonimagistic meditative ideals have been in the Buddhist toolbelt from the very beginning, nevertheless, for over a century of academic scholarship in religious studies, the early Indian model of ineffability persisted as the "normative ideal"[36] against which later, image-oriented Mahāyāna movements in East Asia were unfavorably compared. Mikkyō's iconic systems thus constituted the decadent "decline"[37] or pathological "disease"[38] of true Buddhism, and Zen's contentless experience and iconoclastic minimalism reconstituted the faithful return to and final culmination of Buddha's original teaching.

Zen's superiority complex particularly resonated with the presuppositions of Western or Western-trained scholars, who were largely primed by a Judeo-Protestant animus against idolatry.[39] Such Protestant rhetoric was primarily aimed against the Roman Catholic Church for corrupting the supposedly pure teachings of Jesus and Paul. It targeted superstitious image veneration, relic worship, magical but meaningless rituals, ecstatic visions as proof of faith, and all the other ostensibly fruitless paths to salvation.

This Protestant bias against imagery, which itself is currently being deconstructed by scholars such as David Morgan and Jess Hollenbach,[40] extended into Buddhist scholarship as well. Historians tended to construct parallels between Mikkyō and Roman Catholic thought on the one hand, and Zen and Protestant thought on the other. These scholars noted Mikkyō's love of ritual, icons, mandala diptychs, and *juzu* beads for mantra recitations, and associated them all with the smells and bells of Roman Catholic ceremony, its statuary, its Renaissance triptych altarpieces, and its rosary beads for Hail Mary recitations. They likewise noted the parallels between Dōgen or Shinran (1173–1262) and Luther's charismatic reform movements within their established orthodoxies. They correlated Zen's emphasis on *jiriki* or self-powered personal illumination with the Protestant emphasis on the individual as the agent of his own salvation (as opposed to relying on intermediary priests). The lavish displays of esoteric ritual among the effeminate Heian courtiers was contrasted with the militant Zen ascetic ideal among the Spartan samurai warriors of the Kamakura period, and this easily recalled the decadent displays of wealth, power, and prestige of the Medici popes vs. the disciplining wars of Reformation for which Luther wrote hymns such as "A Mighty Fortress Is Our God."

As a result of such Protestant concerns in Euro-American scholarship, the historical and pan-Asian reality of Buddhist image and relic worship was either wholly neglected or explained away as merely expedient means (*upāya*) for the dull-witted masses. Other scholars simply tried to mitigate the perceived power of images at the time. For example, Hakeda's often-quoted translation of Kūkai's *Catalogue of Imported Items* displays this Protestant anxiety about possibly sounding too idolatrous. To soften Kūkai's powerful claims for his newly imported esoteric mandalas and to downplay the immanence of the images, Hakeda inserts an expression of doubt into his translated phrase "the sight of the [mandalas] *may well* enable one to attain Buddhahood."[41] However, as Robert Sharf has correctly pointed out, the classical Chinese unequivocally asserts that the mandalas simply, directly, and emphatically have the remarkable ability to do nothing other than "enlighten in a single glance (*itto jōbutsu*)."[42] This unambiguous declaration was made in the promotional context of Kūkai trying to market his new sutras and visual aids to the Heian court, where he was competing against his predecessor Saichō (767–822). If anything, therefore, the sense of Kūkai's sales pitch is to overstate the mandalas' efficacy, not to understate it as Hakeda did.

It was in the context of this so-called Protestantization of Buddhism in nineteenth- and twentieth-century Euro-American scholarship that D. T. Suzuki first introduced Rinzai Zen Buddhism to the West. While he worked with Paul Carus in the 1890s and while teaching at Columbia University after World War II, Suzuki cast Zen primarily as a mystical tradition premised on self-negation, not a religious faith involving elaborate rituals and a rich artistic heritage in its own right. He tended to privilege Zen's extralinguistic, extra-imagistic, spaceless, timeless experience of supranormal consciousness, saying, "Zen may lose all its literature, all its monasteries, and all its paraphernalia; but as long as there is satori in it it will survive to eternity."[43] As a result of his efforts, an entire cottage industry comparing Japanese-Christian mysticism cropped up, with the usual suspects limited to the Western-trained but Zen-influenced philosophers Nishida and Nishitani on the one hand and Meister Eckhart or other mystics of the *via negativa* on the other.

In the current climate of scholarship fueled by the hermeneutic of suspicion, however, scholars of mysticism studies have compensated for this normative paradigm either by trying to resurrect the role of images in mystical experience or by denying the existence of such contentless experiences altogether. Steven Katz, for example, in 1978 writes in his seminal *Language, Epistemology and Mysticism*:

> There are *no* pure (i.e., unmediated) experiences...patterns and symbols of established religious communities...[are] at work before, during and after the experience.[44]

For Katz, religious experience is fundamentally a self-fulfilling prophecy, for the linguistic and ideational content of any religious system is always present, even during the experience itself. Mysticism is socially constructed and conditioned; there is nothing pure or unmediated about it. Consequently, for Katz, there can be no claims to absolute cessation whatsoever, since that supposedly contentless state is itself the content for which one has been primed during years of rigorous religious training. The very notion of *nirodha samāpatti* or *shinjin datsuraku* or the very aspiration to dropping off body-mind itself mediates the moment.

The ramifications of Katz's argument are significant to this study, since they indicate that all mystical experiences always already involve language or, by extension, the prelinguistic visual vocabulary of images. This argument will be reinvoked in chapters 3 and 4 when we look more closely at Kūkai's and Dōgen's view of imagery. Given Shingon's iconic and Zen's iconoclastic reputations, one might expect that Katz's central point would be proved by Kūkai and disproved by Dōgen, that is, that mental mandala images are necessary and present when one experiences *kaji*, and that mental images are eradicated at the moment of *shinjin datsuraku*. Paradoxically, however, the opposite is the case. Sharf has already pointed out that Mikkyō's Two-World mandalas are not actively meditated upon and that they do not serve as visual aids for ritualized deity yoga.[45] Furthermore, in the Zen context, there are examples in which visual cues and the recollection of specific images, such as the *shisho* certificate, are key to understanding Dōgen's statements about the ineffable moment of mind-to-mind transmission.[46] Closely looking at Kūkai's and Dōgen's views, therefore, not only supports and subverts the received knowledge about their respective schools; it also occasions a re-evaluation of the secondary scholarship on Buddhism itself.

Critics of Katz charge that his stance could only come out of a deconstructionist milieu in which "the author is dead." For them, Katz construes his own reader-response as a better criterion for knowing what all the dead mystics meant but didn't say, claimed but could not have really realized. In response to Katz's contextualist argument, which essentially chalks all experience up to nurture, other scholars look to nature and basic human brain functions to account for mystical experience, regardless of religious training or cultural influences. Neuropsychologists, such as Davidson and d'Acquili and Newberg mentioned earlier, have accordingly approached the problem of mystical experience from a more scientific-empirical angle.

Thus, one need not throw the baby out with the bathwater, so to speak. Rather, one may strike a balance between the pendular swings of academe by acknowledging the validity and importance of both imagistic and nonimagistic experience and expression. One might be able to affirm the equal value of both unitive and purgative tendencies of Japanese Buddhism (and other religions for that matter), provided that one carefully nuance not only the absolute ineffability of supposedly contentless experience, but also the over-reified significance of imagistic experience as well.

Resurrecting Visual Experience

Now that the Protestant bias in Euro-American scholarship has been called out into the open and seen for being the colonial appropriation of the Other that it was, Zen no longer can be called the Protestant reform movement to Catholic Mikkyō. Japanese and American scholars have consequently gone to great lengths to deconstruct Zen's wholesale iconoclasm and to reconstruct interest in Mikkyō art and doctrine.

At last, serious consideration is again being given to the significance of image experience, that is, those mental images or thought-forms arising from the unconscious into consciousness through intentional or unintentional imagination and/or meditative experience. Following Katz's lead, revisionist scholars from the 1980s to the early 2000s have deconstructed the notion of Zen's "pure experience" altogether. Bernard Faure has contributed much to deconstructing the antinomian cast of Suzuki Zen, while T. Griffith Foulk and Robert Sharf have effectively demonstrated that images served as powerful "doubles" for departed Ch'an masters in medieval China.[47] Seminal works, such as Richard Payne's *Re-visioning Kamakura Buddhism* and Sharf's *Living Images,* have done much to resuscitate the visual field of Zen Buddhism during Japan's medieval period, as has the ill-defined yet still helpful notion of the Zen "imaginaire" in Bernard Faure's *Visions of Power.* Taigen Daniel Leighton's *Visions of Awakening* has demonstrated Dōgen's usage of the *Lotus Sūtra's* most fantasmagorical imagery, and Duncan Williams has uncovered *The Other Side of Zen*, namely, its social and cultural milieux, not just its philosophical and doctrinal positions.

This shift in focus and attention to the material and visual dimensions of religious history has led to some turf wars with art historians, whose traditional domain has always focused on images. The Sōtō Zen historian Bernard Faure, for example, attempted to stake out a claim and legitimate his discussion of religious imagery by stating, "Art historians…overlook and make others overlook—for lack of the ability to think about it—the ritual nature and the invisible part of every religious image."[48] Predictably, this statement only ended up provoking the wrath of many art historians, but the storm resulting from it has died down and some important collaborations between art historians and religion scholars have come about as a result. Robert and Elizabeth Horton Sharf's work is a case in point. At their cosponsored symposium at McMaster University, "religion scholars were asked to focus on images, rather than texts, and art historians were asked to attend to the ritual or institutional dimensions of their objects."[49] The reciprocal interest in each other's traditional domain has helped to break down the artificial and wholly modern disciplinary boundaries that have kept these interrelated fields from joining forces.

Art History and Religious Studies—A Call for Détente

The rigors of deconstruction in the 1980s helped to reveal and dismantle the philological logocentrism that first shaped the nineteenth-century German *Wissenschaft* of religious studies. As a result, the disciplinary contours artificially separating image-based art history and text-based religious studies shifted and blurred.[50] Religion scholars consequently began to look to image, space, ritual performance, and material culture to complement and qualify some of the prescriptive scholasticism that they found in the scriptural texts. Pedagogically speaking, as well, many scholars of religious studies began to discover what art historians had known for decades, that sensory reinforcement of ideas tends to "lock them in," especially in the case of this visually primed generation of learners.

This academic division of labor between textual and visual studies of course was misdirected from the start.[51] Both the art of language and the language of art are equally capable of expressing religious ideas and doctrines, even those ineffable ones, such as nirvana or emptiness. For some, nonfigural images of empty thrones and riderless horses convey the message of nirvana as clearly as the scholastic Abhidharma literature analyzing it and space as the only unconditioned existents in a sea of seventy-two other kinds of *dharma* existents. The bubblelike form of a Zen *ensō* circle, to one primed to its significance, can communicate the interpenetration of form and emptiness just as effectively as the vast literature of the *prajñāpāramitā sūtras* and commentaries. Yet, from the traditional value-laden religious studies perspective, it was believed that "higher" contentless experience generates texts that either explain meditative states postexperientially (descriptive) or recommend meditative methods for getting there (prescriptive). These texts were the domain of religious studies scholars. Conversely, it was presumed that "lower" image experience generates art (illustration) or is generated by the process of doing art (improvisation). These products of the imagination were traditionally the domain of art history scholars.

According to this admittedly sweeping overgeneralization, scholars of religious studies presupposed that language and texts were somehow closer to the ineffable than art. It was more abstract, invisible, and a less material medium than real images, the philologists thought, though they usually soon realized that the limits of language were as definite as those of stone. Moreover, these early scholars tended to forget about the imagery of experience altogether, privileging instead the "higher" realms of formless meditation as Hinduism and early classical Indian Buddhism dictated. Meanwhile, most art historians tended to forget about the experience of imagery, taking art as a given, forgetting about the artist's original inspiration or meditative creativity in order to privilege the analysis of composition, style, technique, materials, iconography, influence, provenance, patronage, politics, and gender. Scholars of religious studies disregarded image experience in order to get at "the ultimate" invisible sphere of immateriality, which they thought they could somehow find best in the texts. Art historians, conversely, tended to disregarded image experience in order to focus on the visible sphere of materiality. Put another way, scholars of religion were inclined to search for the ineffable prior to creation; art historians leaned toward investigating the products, not the process of creation.

Image experience was thus the neglected middle term that both camps tended to ignore. The founding citizens of both camps of religious studies and art history, however, undervalued this common denominator in the interests of privileging their own theoretical agendas. Nevertheless, the division of labor worked extremely well for about a century. Both sides benefited greatly from specialization in the history and analysis of textual and visual material.

The time is ripe, however, for a reassessment of this traditional arrangement. Scholars of religion are beginning to realize their own logocentrism after the rigors of Derrida's deconstructionism, and conversely, art historians are beginning to ask the more philosophical questions about art. In addition to identifying the who, what, where, when, and how of an image, art historians are also beginning ask "Why religious art in the first place?" "What religious purpose or function does it serve?" "What soteriological or eschatological ideals motivate the donors and the worshipers?" "Where does this remarkable religious imagery *come* from?"

There is a presupposition that idea precedes image and that the text must therefore dictate artistic illustration. This is indeed the case with scriptural sanctions for figural representations of the Buddha's body, which predate the emergence of anthropomorphic images by one or two centuries. The opposite, however, can also be the case: art can and indeed often does precede text. In some cases, the so-called an-iconic or more properly called nonfigural depictions of the Buddha were already being produced several centuries before the appearance of scriptural bans against making anthropomorphic images of Buddha. Thus, texts often simply codified or legitimated what people were already doing on the ground and what kinds of images they were already worshiping at a given place and time. For example, according to the Pali scriptures, webbed fingers and toes are marks of Buddhahood (*lakṣana*), but such scriptural accounts probably derive from or reflect the technical exigencies of carving or casting Buddha statues with digits that would not break off.

Thus, the scripted or sculpted forms of ideas should be seen as symbiotic partners in the mysterious project of religious inspiration. Sometimes ideas precede image, and sometimes image precedes idea. That is, sometimes language and images express pre-existing religious ideas (especially the case with Shingon's codified religious iconography), and sometimes the creative use of language and images can generate new religious ideas. This is especially the case with Dōgen, whose wordplays, for example, reinterpret Buddha Nature (*busshō*) to be a quality indistinguishable from all existence, not an attribute that all sentient beings possess. Together, the generative symbiosis of idea and textual-visual expression construct Buddhism's philosophies of form. These philosophies in turn influence meditative experiences, which in turn influence new philosophies of form. This feedback loop explaining the interdependence of text and image, idea and expression, philosophy and experience all account for innovation within tradition. Thus, scholars of art history and religious studies alike need to consider how philosophies of form, visual traditions, and different meditation techniques *together* constitute an inherited religious tradition. Such traditions influence whether one has an image experience or a supposedly contentless one, and they influence to what extent one's textual, visual, or practical expression of that experience reinforces, revises, or extends the tradition into new territory.

The result of these developments and general trends within religious studies is that many scholars of religion have now become interested once more in investigating the visual and material culture of Japanese Buddhism. This sea change has led to a resurgence of interest in Mikkyō, as evidenced by the publications of some important edited volumes, as well as other monographs.[52] The consequence of these contributions is that Mikkyō's reputation as a decadent decline of original Buddhism is being corrected and that Zen's reputation for wholesale iconoclasm is now being qualified. Of course, no one can deny Mikkyō's overwhelming complexity of iconography and symbolism, and there are infamous stories of antinomian, iconoclastic Zen antics. However, now one is in a position to reconsider both of these assumptions and look closely at both the texts and the images of Shingon and Zen in order to adjust and update our vision of Buddhist art and experience in Japan's premodern age.

The present study of Kūkai's and Dōgen's religio-artistic theory and practice builds upon this recent trend and attempts to restore the fundamental concern of religion with art and art with religion. Investigating issues of iconicity and iconoclasm brings the artificially separated academic disciplines of art history and religious studies back together again in their historically inseparable symbiosis. Historically speaking, it is evident that artists were monks and monks were artists. Doctrinally speaking as well, it is evident that Kūkai and Dōgen both believed that fully realizing Buddhahood within this lifetime was possible, given their methods, affirming yet emptying form on the one hand, and negating yet reconstituting form on the other. This study seeks to bridge the altogether modern, artificial, and somewhat arbitrary academic division of labor between art history and religious studies, and their attendant offspring of material culture and mysticism studies. It is in this spirit that the following chapters attempt to explicate both Kūkai's and Dōgen's views of imagery vis-à-vis religious experience.

2

Mikkyō Space, Zen Time

OUR OBSERVATIONS IN the Introduction and chapter 1 regarding Buddhist philosophies of form were sweeping and general. They provided a broad overview of the major schools of thought, modes of expression, and kinds of meditative experiences that helped set the stage for Kūkai and Dōgen as both inheritors of, and contributors to, Buddhism's philosophies of form. Now we turn directly to the literary output and material culture of both Kūkai and Dōgen.

To help make sense of Kūkai's and Dōgen's religio-artistic theories, the organizing principles of unobstructed space and time are indispensable to this study. These terms do not refer to volumetric square footage or to chronometric clock time, nor do they refer to the architectural mimesis of Henry Corbin's *imago templi* or Mircea Eliade's return to a primordial time *in illo tempore*.[1] In Buddhism, there is neither any one archetypal building to reconstruct nor any one primordial moment to return to ritually. To do so would be to affix artificial essence to both. Rather, given the interpenetrating worldview of Buddhism, and especially of Kegon Buddhism discussed more fully in this chapter, unobstructed space can be any place, which by extension means all places. Unobstructed time can be anytime, hence always. Both are empty of fixed essence. The where and when of one's enlightenment by necessity must be understood within this expanded definition of space and time.

In addition, it should be recalled at the outset that both Kūkai and Dōgen do in fact discuss space and time together. It is impossible to have the one without the other. Indeed, Ryūichi Abé has pointed out the temporal aspects of Kūkai's art and doctrine, and Taigen Dan Leighton has studied the spatial images that Dōgen derived from the *Lotus Sūtra*.[2] However, in terms of a *relative* emphasis, and in terms of how they put Kegon theory into practice, a compelling textual and visual case can be made for the fact that Kūkai principally envisioned emptiness spatially, whereas Dōgen experienced it temporally. As a result, Kūkai envisions enlightenment as a reciprocal union of self and Buddha in unobstructed space (*kaji*), whereas Dōgen experiences Buddhahood as a sequential assertion, negation (*shinjin datsuraku*), and reaffirmation of the self in unobstructed time. Distinguishing between these two kinds of unitive and purgative mysticisms in this expanded sense of space and time may help to explain their respective iconic and iconoclastic views, to be discussed in further detail in chapters 3 and 4. It is hoped that juxtaposing the thought of Kūkai and of Dōgen in this way may provide a wider perspective on the forms of emptiness in Japanese Buddhism.

The Problem

When one considers the nature of form, one usually thinks in terms of material substances that create and occupy physical space. Alternately, one sometimes thinks of forms in terms of their duration, or as events that unfold in and through time. No form can be said to be wholly spatial or temporal in nature, but in terms of relative emphasis, we use nouns and verbs to linguistically express how we perceive the way objects and events abide in the spatio-temporal matrix. The goal of Buddhist enlightenment is to see and personally experience the emptiness of these primarily spatial or temporal forms.

What then, one might ask, is the form of the enlightenment experience itself? Where or when does the realization of emptiness take place? How did Buddhist practitioners themselves understand the place or the time of their enlightenment? This chapter focuses on the thought of Kūkai and of Dōgen in an attempt to address this question from a comparative point of view. Certainly, ancient Indian notions of *bodhimaṇḍa* and Chinese geometric ideals influenced Shingon, while Taoist process-oriented philosophy influenced Zen. What then, is the common denominator for considering them together?

It is the thesis of this chapter that the common inheritance of Kegon cosmology can be the basis for a fruitful comparison of Kūkai's and Dōgen's thought. It is important to establish this common denominator linking their worldviews, otherwise one risks comparing apples to oranges. In addition, it is important to find this common ground from within the Buddhist tradition itself, otherwise one runs the risk of colonizing Buddhism with Western European phenomenological or Jungian-inspired categories. Certainly, a shared Kegon worldview does not erase the very different historical and social contexts in which Kūkai and Dōgen operated. However, looking to Kegon thought does provide the essential Buddhist link enabling this associative and comparative project in the first place.

The first part of this chapter argues that Kūkai primarily understood the Kegon worldview spatially, whereas Dōgen placed particular emphasis on its temporal aspects. It will describe Kegon's vision of universes within universes and times within times by using the terms "holographic" and my own neologism "holochronic." Both make reference to the photographic technology that enables a single part to contain a whole three-dimensional image; "holochronic" simply adapts this metonymic principle to *chronos* or time.[3]

The second half of the chapter will demonstrate how Kūkai's and Dōgen's philosophical understandings may have influenced their practical experiences of the forms of emptiness. Kūkai mainly stressed Kegon's spatial metaphors, hence his enlightenment experience is envisioned as a reciprocal energy exchange between the body, speech, and mind of Buddha and the practitioner in unobstructed space (*kaji*). This visualized exchange in imagined space further reinforces Kūkai's reflexive understanding of form and emptiness that will become important for his claims about art. By contrast, Dōgen chiefly emphasized Kegon temporality, hence his enlightenment experience follows a sequential assertion, negation (*shinjin datsuraku*), then reaffirmation of the body-mind in unobstructed time. Experiencing this alternation between form, emptiness, and then form again, likewise will impact Dōgen's inconstant views on imagery, as his views on art and imagery tend to shift and change depending on whether he is adopting a pre- or post-enlightened standpoint. The foundation legends of both sects are an appropriate starting point to discuss their two distinct paradigms.

Legends of the Rise and Fall: Obtaining Enlightened Wisdom in Space and Time

Mythologically speaking, the foundation legends of Mikkyō and Zen help to reconstruct and reinforce Kūkai's basic spatial and unitive, and Dōgen's temporal and purgative enlightenment paradigms.

According to Mikkyō lore, the founder of the esoteric lineage is Dainichi Buddha (Skt. *Mahāvairocana*), who entrusted the esoteric teachings to the bodhisattva Kongōsatta (Skt. *Vajrasattva*) in an iron tower (*nanten tettō*) in southern India until humanity was ready for his advanced teachings.[4] In the unobstructed space of the iron tower, and in the company of the one thousand buddhas of the past, present, and future who are eternally housed within, the first human patriarch Nāgārjuna receives two esoteric sutras from the bodhi-sattva Vajrasattva (fig. 2.1). He specifically obtains the *Dainichikyō* (Skt. *Mahāvairocana sūtra*) and the *Kongōchōkyō* (Skt. *Vajraśekhara sūtra*). These two foundational texts are then eventually illustrated as the all-important Womb and Diamond World mandalas, respectively, to be analyzed in icon-ographic detail later in this chapter. From Shingon's ultimate point of view, these two foundational strains of textual and visual authority are said to be nondual. This Mikkyō myth of origins thus provides a normative template for understanding its ideal for acquiring wisdom. It clearly indicates that a supra-normal space is required for the exchange of esoteric knowledge between Buddhist deities and human patriarchs, as well as for the synthesis of two sutras and two paradigmatic mandalas.

It is true that later clerics, such as Tokuitsu (781?–842?), questioned the transmission of both scriptures at the iron tower, and that the Hossō priest Shinkō (934–1004) ultimately separated the lineage into two separate scrip-tural transmissions.[5] More specifically, Shinkō speculated that Nāgārjuna only received the *Kongochōkyō* in the iron tower and that it was the esoteric master Śubhākarasiṃha who received the *Dainichikyō* scripture at Kaniṣka's five-story pagoda in northern India. Shinkō's two-transmission theory was later illus-trated by Fujiwara Munehiro (active mid-twelfth century), who created a famous pair of polychrome panels for Eikyūji temple in 1136. However, of the two, only the Nāgārjuna image is pictured here, as Shinkō's theory contravenes Kūkai's original thought as expressed in his commentary on the *Kongōchōkyō* called the *Kyōōkyō kaidai*. Kūkai writes, "this *sūtra* [the *Kongōchōkyō*] and the *Dainichikyō* are together the essence of the Tathāgata's Secret Repository which Nāgārjuna Bodhisattva discovered in the Iron Tower of South India."[6]

By contrast, the legendary foundation of Zen's dharma lineage is estab-lished not by the cosmic Mahāvairocana Buddha, but rather by the his-torical Śakyamuni Buddha. In the Zen narrative, Śakyamuni's disciple Mahākaśyapa immediately becomes enlightened when the Buddha simply and silently holds up a flower. This mysterious mind-to-mind transmission of the dharma also extends to Nāgārjuna, whom Zen recognizes as its four-teenth patriarch.[7] However, instead of ascending the towering *tahōtō* many-jeweled pagoda above ground, in Zen lore Nāgārjuna descends to the deepest ocean-floor negations undercutting the sea of conceptual dualisms. He obtains the *Prajñāpāramitā sūtras* from the dragon king's palace at the bot-tom of the sea and resurfaces as the enlightened holder of the perfection of wisdom. Nāgārjuna's symbolic path thus follows a tripartite sequential par-adigm. This involves a progression from everyday awareness on the surface,

Figure 2.1. Nāgārjuna receiving esoteric scriptures from Vajrasattva in the iron tower, southern India (*Ryobu daikyō kantokuzu - Ryūmyō*). Fujiwara Munehiro, c. 1136, National Treasure, Fujita Museum of Art, Osaka. Used with permission.

Figure 2.2. Detail from the *Kegon engi emaki:* Gisho receiving the *Kegonkyō* at the dragon king's palace at the bottom of the sea. Before 1253, Kamakura Period, Kōzanji, Kyoto. Used with permission.

to a psycho-existential "drowning" or "great death" in the meditative depths below, followed by a reemergence and renewed life as one reborn with the transformed vision of perfect wisdom at the end. In the Zen tradition, it is a process, not a place, that bestows enlightened knowledge, and Nāgārjuna's journey is marked by the assertion, negation, and final reaffirmation of self and other in and through time.

To this author's knowledge, there is no extant illustration of Nāgārjuna's episode in Chinese or Japanese art history, but other sects modeled their own scriptural origins on it. One example comes from the Kegon school's illustrated *emaki* hand scroll, which narrates the miraculous journey that the Korean monk Gisho undertook to acquire Kegon's principal scripture (fig. 2.2). In this image, a guide reassures Gisho not to be afraid of the passing *makara* sea creatures as they float down to the dragon king's palace, whose corner roof eaves can be seen emerging through the parting waves.[8] The fact that this Kamakura-period hand scroll dates to before 1253, and is therefore contemporaneous with Dōgen's lifetime, speaks to the popularity of this motif in his day. Moreover, as a student of both Tendai and Zen, it is highly likely that Dōgen was familiar with the legendary hagiography of Nāgārjuna, as both Tendai and Zen debated his place in the lineage history *Fuhōzō innen-den* (Ch. *Fu fa-tsang yin yüan-chuan*) dated to 1004 CE.[9]

Thus, in the Mikkyō myth, time is contained within space since the eternal buddhas are contained within the iron pagoda; but in the Zen myth, space is contained within the matrix of time, for the dragon king's palace lies along the path of the *prajñā*-seeking pilgrim. One can therefore speak in general of spatialized time in Kūkai's paradigm, and temporalized space in Dōgen's.

Kegon Philosophy and Holographic Spatiality in the Writings of Kūkai

Kūkai clearly understood the micro-macrocosmic nature of Kegon space and time, but tended to emphasize its spatial aspects, especially when advancing his new esoteric doctrine in Japan.

Kegon Buddhism derives its namesake from the *Flower Garland Sūtra* (Jp. *Kegonkyō*, Ch. *Hua-yen jing*, Skt. *Avataṃsaka-sūtra*), a fifth- or sixth-century text most probably of central Asian origin. The Gaṇḍavyūha section of the sutra chronicles the adventures of the young pilgrim Sudhana, who visits fifty-two (or fifty-four) spiritual friends depending on the translation. As Sudhana journeys along the path to enlightenment, he meets each dharma friend in his or her own specific environment.[10] Chinese artists throughout the ages have typically depicted these Buddha-fields in architectonic terms; that is, by showing each spiritually advanced being housed within its own pagoda or palatial complex.[11] When Sudhana's journey ends, however, he arrives at a particularly extraordinary place. Here, he sees a magnificent holographic vision of Maitreya's tower, which is described in the following manner,

> The interior of the Tower reveals itself as being as wide as the sky.... Moreover within the tower there are hundreds of thousands of towers, each one as exquisitely adorned... and each one, while preserving its individual existence, at the same time offering no obstruction to the rest.... In one particularly high, spacious and exquisitely decorated tower, of incomparable beauty, he sees at one glance the entire trichiliocosm.[12]

This holographic vision of multiverses is further amplified by the image of Indra's Net, which Fa-tsang (643–712) describes in his *Treatise of the Golden Lion*, a commentary on the sutra. This image likens the entire universe to a vast latticework of interlaced existents, which are represented by a jewel at every knot of every node in this infinite netscape of being. Every jewel has multiple facets, and every facet of every jewel reflects every facet of every other jewel in the entire universe without obstruction. This sentiment of nonobstruction

Figure 2.3. Birushana Buddha. Tōshōdaiji, Nara, c. 759. Used with permission.

between thing and thing (*jijimuge*) is the hallmark of Kegon's most enlightened Buddha realm (*dharmadhātu*).

Kūkai was probably first exposed to Kegon-inspired imagery after he moved
to the capital of Nagaoka (ca. 791) to attend college. Nearby in the old capital of Nara, Kūkai may have encountered the impressive Birushana Buddhas
of Tōshōdaiji and Tōdaiji, either as a student or as a wandering *shidosō* self-
ordained priest. Commonly described as the cosmic Buddha, Birushana (Skt.
Vairocana) images preceded Kūkai's introduction of Mahāvairocana imagery
in the ninth century. Also known as Dainichi or the "Great Sun" Buddha
in Japan, Mahāvairocana is directly equated with the *dharmakāya* (the universal body of Buddhist teaching) in the *Dainichikyō* and Kūkai's extensive
writings.

Tōshōdaiji's eighth-century dry-lacquer Birushana figure (fig. 2.3), for
example, measures over three meters tall and is framed by a magnificent gilt
bronze aureole of one thousand baby buddhas (*senbutsuko*). These miniature
figures, as well as miniature historical buddhas on each petal of its lotus base,
are understood to be unobstructed aspects of Birushana's universally enlightened and enlightening body. The cosmic monumentality and refracted iter-
ation of buddhas in this sculptural complex gives form to Kegon teachings
about the holographic nature of the *dharmakāya*.

Figure 2.4. Birushana Buddha's lotus base (detail), Tōdaiji, Nara, 752. Photograph by the author.

In addition, the lotus base for the monumental Birushana at Tōdaiji Temple in Nara (fig. 2.4) could have given Kūkai another first lesson in Kegon cosmology.[13] Cast and consecrated in 752 by Emperor Shōmu (701–756), each lotus petal displays interpenetrating *bhumi* lands, multiple world-systems and overlapping heavens minimized to horizontal bands in the upper register.

It is quite probable therefore, that Kūkai saw these images in the 790s. However, Kūkai's first concrete textual reference to Kegon thought only appears after he returned from T'ang China in 806. In his *Catalogue of Newly Imported Items (Shōrai mokuroku)*, Kūkai says that his Sanskrit master Prajñā entreated him to carry back to Japan his new translation of the *Avataṃsaka sūtra*, the scriptural foundation for Kegon philosophy. Kūkai then quotes and comments on this sutra in *The Meaning of Sound, Word and Reality (Shōji jissōgi)*, written ca. 817–818. Kūkai quotes:

It is said in a sutra that "the Body of the Buddha is supra-rational in that all lands are in it" or that "[the Buddha, of whom] each hair contains many lands as vast as oceans, pervades the entire World of Dharma," or that "in a follicle of [the Buddha's] hair, there are unimaginable lands as many as particles of dust, in each of which Vairocana Buddha is present, revealing the sublime Dharma in the midst of an assembly; [that] even in a particle of dust of each land there are many small and large lands as numerous as particles of dust, in all of which without exception Buddha resides."[14]

Kūkai then comments on the holographic interpenetration of buddhas, bodies, lands, and other spatial entities:

> It is evident from these passages that [the manifestations of] the Body of the Buddha and the bodies of sentient beings are manifold in size. The Body of the Buddha can be regarded as having the magnitude of the World of Dharma, as vast as infinite space, or as having ten Buddha lands or one Buddha land, or as having the size of a particle of dust. Thus the Body of the Buddha, the body of each sentient being, and each land, small and large, are interrelated and interdependent.[15]

Kūkai's selection of sutra citations and his preoccupation with the size and number of *bhumi* lands and Buddha bodies also helped him explain the holographic spatial system of his newly imported Diamond and Womb World mandalas. This pair of mandalas depicts the *dharmadhātu* realm of enlightenment in two aspects, which Kūkai maintains are actually nondual and nondistinct from oneself. Specifically, Kūkai samples Kegon metaphors and phraseology to explain that Dainichi's myriad but ultimately unified aspects—as depicted in the Two World mandalas—are nothing other than one's own being. In *The Precious Key to the Secret Treasury* (Jp. *Hizō hōyaku*) Kūkai writes,

> Buddhas as numerous as particles of dust are the Buddhas of our Mind. He who is of the Diamond and Matrix realms, and who is one and many at once like drops of sea water is our Body.[16]

Kūkai also obliquely equates the physical and mental infinitude of the Two World mandalas with the immensity of ultimate reality in *The Meaning of the Word Hum (Unji gi)*.

> The form [i.e., the phenomenal Womb World]
> and mind [i.e., the noumenal Diamond World]
> of that One [i.e., the *dharmakāya*, Mahāvairocana, Dainichi] are immeasurable;
> Ultimate reality is vast and boundless.[17]

Furthermore, in his 817 treatise, *Becoming a Buddha In This Very Body* (*Sokushin jōbutsugi*), Kūkai goes on to emphasize the spatiality of the *dharmakāya* by employing the Kegon terminology of nonobstruction amongst phenomena. He writes:

> "The ground of great space" is the Dharmakāya Buddha. He is analogous to great space; he is eternal,[18] being unobstructed, and embraces in himself all phenomena. That is why he is compared to great space. Grounded in him, all things exist; therefore, the term "ground" is used.[19]

It is interesting to note that Kūkai primarily selects Kegon's spatial metaphors when he is intent on establishing, or literally grounding, his new spatial system in a new land. Kūkai wrote his first very spatial comments on the *Kegonkyō* shortly after he petitioned Emperor Saga in 816 to establish a monastic center at Kōyasan. In short order, Kūkai then successfully transplanted his imported Mikkyō teachings into new ground in many places: at Kōyasan (816), at Nara where he copied the eighty-fascicle version of the *Kegonkyō* and performed a dedication rite to it (820), at Tōdaiji where he built a Shingon chapel (822), at Tōji where he outfitted the main hall with sculpted mandala figures (823), and ultimately, at the Shingon'in chapel within the inner sanctum of the Imperial Palace itself (835). In these major centers and throughout the *kokubunji* system that Kūkai had overseen as Tōdaiji's administrative superintendent or *bettō* from 810–813, Kūkai literally grounded his new teachings in the spatial art and architectures of his new system.

It is further interesting to note that Kūkai's later comments on the Kegon scriptures become more temporal, or at least more balanced, toward the end of his career after Mikkyō has taken root in Japan. In the *Ten Stages of Mind* written toward the end of his career in 830, Kūkai places Kegon theory in the ninth stage of mind surpassed only by Shingon Mikkyō practice. In the ninth stage he outlines the Essentials of the *Kegonkyō* and writes:

> [Vairocana] taught that infinite time is in one moment and that one moment is in infinite time; that one is in many and that many is in one, that is, that the universal is in particulars and that the particulars are in the universal. He illustrated this infinitely interdependent relationship of time and space with the simile of Indra's net and with that of the interfusion of the rays of lighted lamps…(he taught that) one must ascend the Five Ranks of Development of Bodhisattvahood[20]…and that since the attributes and the essence are nondual, the Ten Bodies of the Buddha are to be returned equally to Vairocana Buddha. These are the essentials of the *Avataṃsaka sūtra*.[21]

From these comments, we can see that Kūkai ultimately recognized Kegon's theory of interdependent and interpenetrating space and time, but that he emphasized Kegon spatiality when he was preoccupied with advancing Mikkyō's new doctrinal system in Japan. Kegon philosophy continued to inform his thought even into his sixties, as he wrote in *The Secret Key to the Heart Sūtra* (*Hannya shingyō hiken*) in 834, the year before his death:

> Form and emptiness are nondual from the beginning;
> Particulars and the universal have always been identical.
> Without any obstacles the three [interpenetrations] are interfused.
> The simile of water or gold explains the main tenet.[22]

Naturally, like any religion, the Mikkyō system is not entirely spatial in nature. Mikkyō practitioners actively move through the Shikoku pilgrimage every year, and Shingon's elaborate eighteen-step ritual performances are fundamentally time-oriented. Time does, in fact, figure prominently in Mikkyō's discourse regarding its role as the quick-as-lightning, clear-and-hard-as-diamonds vehicle to enlightenment. This point in particular is worthy of further consideration, since it supports Kūkai's claim that the Mikkyō practitioner can attain Buddhahood with the present body instead of reincarnating through multiple *kalpas* or incalculable measurements of time.

Closer inspection of this claim, however, reveals that the Mikkyō discourse of speedy enlightenment is fundamentally spatialized, for as the Japanese philosopher Yuasa Yasuo says, time often becomes envisioned as "a quantity and a volume."[23] The reason the Mikkyō practitioner can rapidly realize Buddhahood in Kūkai's scheme is because it condenses and compacts all time within its clearly delineated and specially consecrated spaces. Engage with that space, and the practitioner engages with all times, everywhere, in true Kegon fashion. Undergoing the *abhiṣeka* initiation ceremony within a *kanjōdō* initiation hall, for example, encapsulates Nāgārjuna's legendary esoteric dharma transmission within the iron tower in southern India, which itself encapsulates Dainichi's universal palace where resident buddhas of the past, present, and future assist in the perpetual preaching of the dharma. As Kūkai explains by quoting Vajrabodhi's commentary on the *Kongōchōkyō*,

> Nāgārjuna looked inside the stūpa...he immediately realized that inside the tower was Mahāvairocana's universal palace. Samantabhadra and Mañjuśri and all the other great Buddhas and bodhisattvas of the past, present and future abided within the stūpa. Thereupon,

Figure 2.5. Central Perfected Body Assembly, Diamond World mandala. 855–89 Tōji, Kyoto. Courtesy Benrido.

Nāgārjuna was granted Vajrasattva's abhiṣeka, received his empowerment [in the three mysteries], and upheld the scriptures of the secret Dharma to promulgate it to the world.[24]

By enfolding and encapsulating the past, present, and future within micromacrocosmic architectural constructions (e.g., initiation halls, iron towers, and universal palaces), Mikkyō subsumes temporal awareness under spatial boundaries and localizes time on physical, mythological, and cosmological planes. This general tendency in Mikkyō to spatialize time is visually made explicit in the central Perfected Body Assembly Hall of Dainichi's palatial Diamond World mandala. Here, the one thousand buddhas of past, present, and future are depicted in six concentric layers of miniature faces within (fig. 2.5).

Now that we have demonstrated how Kūkai *tends* to spatialize time, let us take a closer look at how his esoteric system envisions the realm of enlightenment in spatial terms.

Spatializing Buddhahood: Iconography of the Two World Mandalas

The Diamond World mandala (fig. 2.6a) explicitly illustrates the adamantine wisdom of the *dharmadhātu* realm in all its aspects, whereas the Womb World mandala (fig. 2.6b) iconographically encodes the compassionate method for arriving at this enlightened realm. Taken together, the Diamond and Womb World mandalas depict both the ends and means of Dainichi's perfectly enlightened wisdom and potentially enlightening method. It should be recalled, however, that ultimately Mikkyō's ontological Diamond wisdom (*chi*) and Womblike soteriological principle (*ri*) are nondual (*richi funi*).

Figure 2.6 (a) The Diamond World mandala, c. 855–89. Tōji, Kyoto. Courtesy of Benrido.

In analyzing these images, it is important to recall that they are designed primarily to describe and diagram the way things are; they are not actively meditated upon to lead the adept to a state of enlightenment as in the later, fully developed Tibetan mandala tradition. As examples of middle-period tantra, these two ninth-century Chinese mandalas are merely spatialized blueprints for perfect mandala palaces. The Womb and Diamond World mandalas are architectural floorplans that lay out what the realm of enlightenment looks like before and after enlightenment, respectively. They are descriptive ontological diagrams of the *dharmadhātu* as it appears to the aspiring or accomplished adept. They do not function as mental props for visualizing

Figure 2.6 (b) Womb World mandala, c. 855–89. Tōji, Kyoto. Courtesy Benrido.

and thereby becoming one with Buddha; they do not function as prescriptive soteriological aids for one's own personal awakening, as does the *ajikan* disk to be discussed in chapter 3. Rather, as Robert Sharf argues, the Two World mandalas' fundamentally spatialized mapping of enlightenment serves an important ritual function: they condense and channel Dainichi's macrocosmic power into the ritual hall, microcosmically make his palatial environment present in the space, automatically transform it into a pure land, and hence anyone in its vicinity into a Buddha.[25] It is for this reason that Kūkai claimed that one glance at them could enlighten.

It should further be noted that in Shingon temples, the Womb World mandala is usually displayed to the right of the Diamond World mandala.

Given the Sino-Japanese convention of reading from right to left, the Shingon school of esoteric Buddhism usually takes the right-hand Womb World as its starting point and then progresses to the left-hand Diamond World. This hermeneutic shall be followed here.

Spatializing the Path of Awakening: Iconography of the Womb World

The Womb World mandala signals the Buddha's compassionate methods for birthing Buddhahood in the phenomenal realm. Figure 2.7 outlines its twelve concentric halls centered around the Lotus Court (1) whose striking red, eight-petaled lotus symbolizes the full flowering of potential enlightenment in this very body. Like a lotus, the esoteric path progressively cultivates the seed of enlightenment from out of the muck of materiality to blossom into the full light of enlightenment.

BUDDHA SECTION

1. The Lotus Court or Central Dais of the Eight Petals (Jp. *chūtai hachiyōin,* no Skt.)
2. Hall of Universal Knowledge (Jp. *henchiin,* no Skt.)
3. Mantra Holders Hall (Jp. *jimyōin,* Skt. *Vidyādharas*)
4. Shaka Hall (Jp. *shakain,* Skt. *Śākyamuni*)
5. Kokūzō Hall (Jp. *kokūzōin,* Skt. *Ākāśagarbha*)
6. Monju Hall (Jp. *monjuin,* Skt. *Mañjuśrī*)
7. Soshitsuji Hall (Jp. *soshitsujiin,* Skt. *Susiddhikara*)

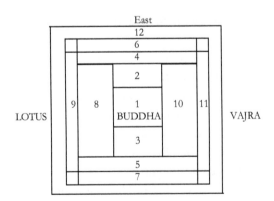

Figure 2.7. Womb World mandala

LOTUS SECTION

8. Kannon Hall (Jp. *kannonin*, Skt. *Avalokiteśvara*)
9. Jizō Hall (Jp. *jizōin*, Skt. *Kṣitigarbha*)

VAJRA SECTION

10. Kongōshū Hall (Jp. *kongōshuin*, Skt. *Vajrapāṇi*)
11. Jōkaishō Hall (Jp. *jōkaishōin*, Skt. *Sarvanivāraṇaviṣkambhin*)
12. External Vajra Section (Jp. *gekongōbu*, Skt. *vajravali*)

The 278 figures residing in these twelve halls personify forces necessary for achieving enlightenment in this very body. They can be grouped concentrically or perceived in the round in three or four layers, depending on whether one adopts Amoghavajra or Śubhākarasiṃha's commentary of the *Dainichikyō*. This discussion of the Womb World layout, however, will follow the traditional tripartite grouping of halls. This organizing rubric spatially maps out the path of awakening into three main groups: the seven halls of the central capital I-shaped Buddha section personify aspects of one's innate Buddha potential, the two halls of the Lotus section to the viewer's left exhibit aspects of benign compassion, and the two halls of the Vajra section to the viewer's right house aspects of adamantine wisdom.

Seven Buddha halls in the center, top, and bottom of the mandala form the capital I-shaped core of the Womb World (1-7). Specifically, above and below the central Eight-Petaled Lotus Court (1), serene Buddha-mothers in Hall 2 and wrathful, yet compassionate Wisdom Kings below in Hall 3 give birth to bodhisattvas residing in the flanking Lotus and Vajra sections. Atop this core Buddha section resides Sakyamuni and his retinue in Hall 4, and below in Kokūzo's Hall 5 reside the multi-armed emanations of Kannon, symbolizing compassion, and Kongōshū, symbolizing wisdom. Hall 6 above personifies as Monju the wisdom that all sentient beings inherently possess; Hall 7 below represents the *susiddhi* fruits of actualizing that innate wisdom through the realization of emptiness. Halls 8 and 9 to the viewer's left comprise the Lotus Section, which houses Kannon and Jizō's retinue of compassionate bodhisattvas. Halls 10 and 11 to the viewer's right comprise the Vajra Section, which houses Kongōshū and Jōkaishō's retinue of adamantine wisdom bodhisattvas. The whole is surrounded by a peripheral hall (12) populated by guardians and celestial deities in the realm of Pure Form. It even makes a gesture to the realm of Formlessness here at the limits of the Womb World of Desire.

Figure 2.8. Four psycho-heavenly realms of Formlessness (*Arūpadhātu-caturdevāḥ*) pictured as stupas. External Vajra Section of the Womb World mandala, Tōji. Courtesy Benrido.

Four stupas in the upper left-hand corner of Hall 12 represent the four formless *dhyana* states of infinite spatiality, infinite consciousness, nothingness, and neither thought nor nonthought (fig. 2.8). This gesture to the triple world of desire, form and formlessness will iconographically resonate with the last two halls of the Diamond World mandala, where Dainichi wrathfully manifests as Gōsanze in and as the triple world. As a result, the two mandalas complement each other in expressing Dainichi's universal presence.

Spatializing the Realm of Enlightenment: Iconography of the Diamond World

Unlike the Womb World, which maps out the means to enlightenment in the phenomenal realm, the Diamond World mandala presents a picture of the ultimate end, that is, a vision of perfected (not potential) enlightenment in the noumenal realm. Figure 2.9 shows the Diamond World mandala's 3 x 3 grid of nine mini-mandalas or palatial assembly halls for courtly retinues of enlightened figures to gather in.

Traditionally, the vision of this nine-hall palace is exegeted by beginning at the center square, descending down, turning left, and spiraling clockwise

5. Shiine (1-4)	6. Ichiine (1-5)	7. Rishue
4. Kuyōe (1-3) All Actions (Karma-mandala)	1. Jōjinne Body (Mahā-mandala) 6 elements	8. Gōsanze
3. Misaie Speech (Dharma-mandala)	2. Samayae Mind (Samaya-mandala)	9. Gōsanze-Samayae

Figure 2.9. Diamond World mandala

up, around, and down until one reaches the bottom right-hand corner.[26] This mandala can be analyzed according to three major categories:

1. Halls 1-4 display a kaleidoscopic explosion of buddhas and bodhisattvas that refract Dainichi's adamantine wisdom. The first four halls depict the four mandalas (*shimandara*) or perfect worlds of Daincihi's physical, verbal, mental, and actional aspects (i.e., Dainichi's three secrets of body, speech, and mind, plus their fourth summation). These four modes of Dainichi's self-expression are the four ways in which Dainichi, the personification of emptiness, expresses himself as world-forms, world-sounds, world-thoughts, and the total collection of all world-actions or karmas.[27] Specifically, they are:

   a. Perfected Body Assembly Hall (Jp. *Jōjinne*, Skt. *Vajradhātu-mahāmaṇḍala*) represents the mahā-mandala associated with Dainichi's perfect universal body. It is comprised of the six esoteric elements of earth, water, fire, air, space, and consciousness. The latter element of consciousness is indicated by the presence of five wisdom buddhas to be discussed in the section detailing the center of the grid. This hall provides the template for the first six mini-mandalas in the Diamond World.

   b. Samaya Assembly Hall (Jp. *Sammayae*, Skt. *Vajradhātu-guhya-dhāraṇī-maṇḍala* or *samaya-maṇḍala*) reiterates the above hall but in the form of the samaya-mandala associated with Dainichi's second secret of mind. Here each deity appears as a sign or mind-seal symbolizing its original vow (e.g., vajra, banner, sword).

    c. Subtle Assembly Hall (Jp. *Misaie*, Skt. *Vajrdhātu-sūkṣma-maṇḍala*) also reiterates the above, but in the form of the dharma-mandala or Dainichi's secret of speech. Figures here hold three-pronged vajras to convey the subtle power of their mantras.

    d. Offerings Assembly Hall (Jp. *Kuyōe*, Skt. *Vajradhātu-karmapūjā-maṇḍala*). This hall reiterates all the aspects and activities of Dainichi's body, mind, and speech, summarized as his collective karmic activities.

2. In Halls 5-6 there is a progressive condensation of these kaleidoscopic deities into the single figure of Dainichi at the top center. Like a Russian doll, the myriad deities of the first four halls are sequentially telescoped into ever-simpler metonymies until the sixth and top center square, which displays the single figure of Dainichi. Specifically, these halls are:

    a. The Four Seals Asssembly Hall (Jp. *Shiine*, Skt. *Vajradhātu-catur-mudrā-maṇḍala*) represents the condensation of the first four mandalas.

    b. The One Seal Assembly Hall (Jp. *Ichiine*, Skt. *Vajradhātu-ekamudrā-maṇḍala*) presents the single metonymic figure of an imperially clad Dainichi as the embodiment of the entire Diamond World mandala. His distinctive wisdom-fist *chiken-in* mudra, in which the right index finger is enclosed in the left-hand fingers, implies the unity of all dualisms, such as vajra and lotus, one and many, acquired wisdom and the principle of realizing Buddhahood through compassionate method.

3. Halls 7-9 depict how this singularity of Dainichi's solar illumination instantiates in the triple world. Later Tendai versions of the Diamond World mandala indicate only the first six halls,[28] but the Diamond World mandala that Kūkai brought back from China in 806 has nine halls.[29] Specifically, these include:

    a. The deities of the seventh Rishu Assembly Hall (Jp. *Rishue*, Skt. *Naya-maṇḍala*) center around Kongōsatta (Skt. *Vajrasattva*) who embodies the guiding principle that the passions are nondual with enlightenment.

    b. The eighth Gōsanze Assembly Hall (Jp. *Gōsanzee*, Skt. *Trailokyavijaya-maṇḍala*) presents the wrathful aspect of Kongōsatta and his retinue to indicate his conquest over the three worlds (*trailokyavijaya*) of desire, form, and formlessness, or alternately anger, greed, and ignorance.

    c. The ninth Gōsanze-samaya Assembly Hall repeats this latter hall only in samaya form.[30] This discussion of the principle of Dainichi's presence in the phenomenal world complements our previous discussion of the Womb World mandala.

Detailing the Center of the Two Worlds

The central halls of the Womb and Diamond World mandalas iconographically encode Daincihi's material and mental aspects, which are said to interfuse throughout the cosmos. In the Womb World, the material elements are represented by the central court's rainbow band of colors, which encloses the five wisdom buddhas and helping bodhisattvas who symbolize the universal principle of potential realization. In the Diamond World, material elements are symbolized by anthropomorphic figures in each corner of the central Perfected Body Assembly Hall, while the element of perfect mind is represented by the five wisdom buddhas and auxiliary bodhisattvas. Ultimately, these two images are seen as nondual, and their buddhas iconographically match when displayed together.

Figure 2.10 outlines the Lotus Court or Central Dais of the Eight Petals at the epicenter of the Womb World mandala. The whole lotus court is enclosed by a square five-colored band representing the five material elements. The sixth immaterial element of consciousness is represented at the four corners of the band in the form of four jewel vases symbolizing Dainichi's four virtues: his mind of compassion, his mind of awakening, his ability to use expedient means, and his unsurpassed view.[31] From each vase emerge a lotus and a vajra. They indicate that the vessel of esoteric teachings contains the principle of

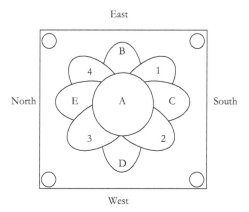

Figure 2.10. Womb World mandala detail: Central Lotus Court

Directions	5 Wisdoms	Diamond Names	Womb Names of Buddhas
A. Center	total	Dainichi in *chiken-in* (*Mahāvairocana*)	Dainichi in *jō-in* (Skt. *Mahāvairocana*)
B. East	mirror	Ashuku (*Akṣobhya*)	Hōdō (Skt. *Ratnaketu*) "Jewel Pennant"
C. South	equality	Hōshō (*Ratnasambhava*)	Kaifukeō (Skt. *Saṃkusumitaraja*) "Flower Opening King"
D. West	observation	Muryōju/Amida (*Amitābha*/*Amitāyus*)	Muryōju (Skt. *Amitābha*/*Amitāyus*) "Immeasurable Life/Light"
E. North	action	Fukūjōju (*Amogasiddhi*)	Tenkuraion (Skt.*Divya-dundubbhi-megha-nirghoṣa*) "Heavenly Drum's Thunder Sound"

Figure 2.11. Diamond and Womb World mandala Correlations

compassionate method (lotus) to actualize innate wisdom (vajra).[32] The eight lotus petals in the central court are also punctuated by three-pronged vajra spikes, again indicating the intimate interconnection of matter and mind, practice and attainment, principle (*ri*) and wisdom (*chi*).

The imperially clad Dainichi at the center of the Womb World (A) is distinguished from his Diamond World counterpart principally by his *jō-in* mudra of meditation, the Buddha's method par excellence. Moreover, the Womb World's five buddhas (A-E) appear in their phenomenal aspects, though they will iconographically mirror the five wisdom buddhas of the Diamond World as outlined above (fig. 2.11). The layout of this diagram follows the visual logic of the conventional Two World mandala display, and lists the Womb World deities to the right of the lefthand Diamond World counterparts.

These five wisdom buddhas of the Womb World mandala are assisted by four attendant bodhistattvas at the ordinal directions (1-4). They embody the four immeasurables that first awaken the mind of enlightenment and that with practice, can eventually develop into fully enlightened figures.[33] As such, they emphasize process over product and Buddha's enlightening practice over enlightened perfection (fig. 2.12).

Figure 2.13 details the center of the Diamond World. Personified figures of the material elements of earth, water, fire, and air appear in the four corners,[34] while the element of space is implied in the center by Dainichi and by the entire mandala itself. The sixth immaterial element of mind is also already implied in this court by the totality of five wisdom buddhas listed below (A-E). It is

Directions	Four Immeasurables	[Diamond Names]	Womb Names of Bodhisattvas
1. SE	equanimity	[Various *Pāramitā,* Great,	Fugen "Universal Wisdom" (*Samantabhadra*)
2. SW	joy	Inner, Outer and Attraction	Monju "Wondrous Felicity" (*Mañjuśrī*)
3. NW	compassion	Bodhisattvas]	Kanjizai/Kannon "Freely Contemplating" (*Avalokiteśvara*)
4. NE	love		Miroku "Benevolent" (*Maitreya*)
○ □			Four jewel vases of lotuses & vajras Band of five elements

Figure 2.12. Womb World Auxiliary Bodhisattvas

also implied by the four *pāramitā* bodhisattvas (I-IV) around Dainichi in the center, and the sixteen great bodhisattvas (1-16) around each wisdom Buddha in the four directions. These figures personify the kaleidoscopic refractions of Dainichi's diamondlike wisdom, and are outlined below for future reference. As we shall see in chapter 3, Kūkai will recombine select figures from these mandalas at Tōji and at Kōyasan to create new kaleidoscopic and intericonic patterns of Dainichi's wisdom in the world.

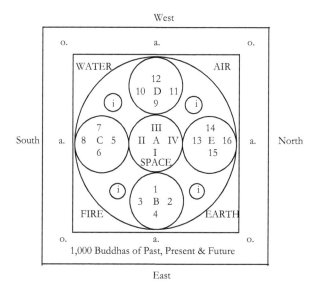

Figure 2.13. Diamond World mandala detail: Central Perfected Body Hall

CENTER

A. Dainichi (Skt. *Mahāvairocana*) in the center moon disk personifies the pure undefiled mind and perfect enlightened wisdom of the *dharmadhātu* realm (Jp. *hokkai-taishō-chi*, Skt. *āmala-vijñāna* or *dharmadhātu-svabhava-jñāna*). Dainichi Buddha is surrounded by four paramitā bodhisattvas:

I. Kongōharamitsu	(Skt. *Vajrapāramitā*)	Diamond Perfection
II. Hōharamitsu	(Skt. *Ratnapāramitā*)	Jewel Perfection
III. Hōharamitsu	(Skt. *Dharmapāramitā*)	Law Perfection
IV. Katsumaharamitsu	(Skt. *Karmapāramitā*)	Karma Perfection

DIAMOND REALM (BOTTOM-EAST)

B. Ashuku Buddha (Skt. *Akṣobhya*) below Dainichi (to the east) personifies the mirror-mind wisdom (Jp. *daienkyō-chi*, Skt. *ādarśa-jñāna*) of pure undistorted cognition. Ashuku Buddha is surrounded by four of sixteen great bodhisattvas:

1. Kongōsatta	(Skt. *Vajrasattva*)	Diamond Being
2. Kongōō	(Skt. *Vajrarāja*)	Diamond King
3. Kongōai	(Skt. *Vajrarāga*)	Diamond Love
4. Kongōki	(Skt. *Vajrasādhu*)	Diamond Joy

JEWEL REALM (LEFT-SOUTH)

C. Hōshō Buddha (Skt. *Ratnasambhava*) on Dainichi's left (to the south) personifies the equality wisdom (Jp. *byōdōshōchi*, Skt. *samatā-jñāna*) that cognizes all things with equanimity. Hōshō Buddha is surrounded by four of sixteen great bodhisattvas:

5. Kongōhō	(Skt. *Vajraratna*)	Diamond Jewel
6. Kongōkō	(Skt. *Vajratejas*)	Diamond Light
7. Kongōtō	(Skt. *Vajraketu*)	Diamond Pennant
8. Kongōshō	(Skt. *Vajrahāsa*)	Diamond Laugh

LOTUS REALM (TOP-WEST)

D. Muryōju/Amida Buddha (Skt. *Amitābha/Amitāyus*) above Dainichi (to the west) personifies the observation wisdom (Jp. *myōkan-zatchi*, Skt.

pratyavekṣanā-jñāna) that understands situations with insightful compassion, not bias. Amida Buddha is surrounded by four of sixteen great
bodhisattvas:

9. Kongōhō	(Skt. *Vajradharma*)	Diamond Dharma
10. Kongōri	(Skt. *Vajratīkṣṇa*)	Diamond Sharpness
11. Kongōin	(Skt. *Vajrahetu*)	Diamond Cause
12. Kongōgo	(Skt. *Vajrabhāṣa*)	Diamond Speech

KARMA REALM (RIGHT-NORTH)

E. Fukūjōju Buddha (Skt. *Amoghasiddhi*) on Dainichi's right (to the north)
personifies action wisdom (Jp. *jōshosa-chi*, Skt. *kṛtyānuṣṭāna-jñāna*) that
knows how to put wisdom into practice using expedient means.[35] Fukūjōji
Buddha is surrounded by four of sixteen great bodhisattvas:

13. Kongōgō	(Skt. *Vajrakarma*)	Diamond Action
14. Kongōgo	(Skt. *Vajrarakṣa*)	Diamond Protection
15. Kongōge	(Skt. *Vajrayakṣa*)	Diamond Fang
16. Kongōken	(Skt. *Vajramuṣṭi*)	Diamond Fist

All of these figures are spatially fixed but doctrinally dynamic. To the initiate, they are actually considered to be emanations of Dainichi who reveals
himself to himself as four surrounding wisdom buddhas and all the auxiliary
bodhisattvas. This process of self-multiplying self-manifestation is couched in
the language of gift exchange, as Dainichi and the other four wisdom buddhas
are said to offer one another the sixteen great bodhisattvas, the four *pāramitā*
bodhisattvas, eight inner and outer offering (*kuyō*) bodhisattvas (i, o) as well as
four attraction bodhisattvas (a) who punctuate the outer band of one thousand
buddhas of past, present, and future. As a result, the central hall of the Diamond
World is populated with all the unobstructed, self-multiplying, kaleidoscopic
emanations of Dainichi's universal body (which by definition includes mind).

In the above, we have observed just how spatial Kūkai is in his thinking. He
embodies and physically locates all the nondual aspects of Dainichi's enlightened worlds: its mind and matter, its noumena and phenomena, its ends and
means, its four mandalas and four immeasurables, its perfected wisdom, and its
principle of using compassionate method to actualize potential enlightenment.

In comparison to Kūkai's highly spatialized system, Dōgen, by contrast,
will argue that all of Kūkai's constructs of being are rather but momentary

phases of becoming. "The world of Dharma," he maintains in the *Sansuikyō* fascicle, for example, "should not always be related to measurements upward, downward, and in the four diagonals; at the same time, the four elements, the five elements, the six elements and so on, relying on the concrete place to which they go, just *momentarily* establish the four-cornered dharma world."[36] Let us now turn to Dōgen see how Sōtō Zen temporalizes space.

Kegon Philosophy and Holochronic Temporality in the Writings of Dōgen

If Kūkai emphasized Kegon's holographic space, then Dōgen emphasizes its holochronic time. If Kūkai built a micro-macrocosmic spatial system, Dōgen advances a micro-macrochronic temporal system. Kūkai describes universes within universes, Dōgen describes times within times. Kūkai literally seeks to "ground" his new esoteric teachings in Japan through visual art and architecture. By contrast, Dōgen is preoccupied with establishing Zen's lineage in Japan and extending the legacy of the True Dharma Eye beyond his own lifetime through the performing arts of neverending practice. Kūkai's mandala palaces and doctrinal tracts constantly construct and deconstruct unobstructed space in order to see the emptiness within and without the walls. Dōgen, by contrast, in his simple insistence on practice and experience, tries to blow apart three-dimensional space completely to open it up to the fourth dimension, that of time, or as he puts it: *Being-Time* (*Uji*).

When Dōgen says being-time, he means that every form is a time and that every thing is an event. In the *Being-Time* fascicle of his *Shōbōgenzō* treatise, Dōgen explains that one should consider even one's self as a time, interfused with a whole universe of times. For Dōgen, this book is a time. America is a time. You are a time and everything and everyone else is a time. This is not simply an expression of Dōgen's deep-seated awareness of impermanence, though it is certainly that. Dōgen's use of *uji* is, additionally, an expression of temporalized space, as all beings and objects occupying space become existents subsumed under the temporal mode of duration.

In advancing his fundamentally temporalized worldview, Dōgen utilizes the Kegon terminology of nonobstruction between thing and thing (*jijimuge*) but puts his own temporal "spin" on it. He advises his disciples,

> What you should do is lay out yourself sequentially and see this (i.e., yourself) to be the whole universe. Inspect each and every thing in that universe as being a time. Things not obstructing each other, parallels

times not obstructing each other.... Having laid yourself out sequentially, you indeed see yourself. In this way, you have the fact that you yourself are time.[37]

In keeping with this sequential observation of oneself as a time, one can concurrently view all being-times in two ways. There is the aspect of an instantaneous individual "just now" being-time (*nikon*), and the dynamic range or extension of being-time (*kyōryaku*). In the *Uji* fascicle, Dōgen explains the function of individual and ranging time:

> Strung out, all the beings in the whole universe are individual times. In being-time (*uji*) there is the function of ranging; (being-time) ranges from today to tomorrow, from today to yesterday, from yesterday to today, *from today to today, from tomorrow to tomorrow*. This is so because ranging itself is the function of time.[38]

It is natural to think of "the arrow of time" as unidirectional and irreversible, progressing from the past through the present and into the future.[39] However, here, Dōgen claims that time can flow both backward and forward, and even within self-same moments. That is, Dōgen's notion of time ranging "from today to today, [and] tomorrow to tomorrow" enables all individual being-times, even contemporaneous ones, to enfold within one another in holochronic fashion. These momentary and enduring aspects of time are expressed throughout Dōgen's oeuvre, but are particularly prevalent when discussing the authentic transmission of the true dharma amongst patriarchs. He borrows the phrase "buddhas alone, together with buddhas" (*yuibutsu yobutsu*, the title of another fascicle) from the *Lotus Sūtra*, to indicate that only a Buddha can know other Buddhas.[40] That is, only when an individual experiences the "just-now" moment of personal enlightenment can one "meet" or "see" the host of other Buddha ancestors and share in the transhistorical transmission of the dharma through ranging time. Ultimately, these historical and transhistorical aspects are nondual. In the *Transmission of the Robe (Den-e)* fascicle, Dōgen writes,

> (Buddhas and patriarchs)...transmit the authentic tradition from the past to the present...from the present to the future...from the present to the past...*from the past to the past...from the present to the present...from the future to the future*...from the future to the present...from the future to the past. This is the authentic transmission of buddhas alone, together with buddhas.[41]

This transmission of the dharma "from the past to the past, from the present to the present, from the future to the future" makes no sense unless one keeps a temporalized Kegon worldview in mind. Unless one abandons linear thinking and unless one understands Kegon's holochronic notion of times within times, Dōgen's assertions simply make no sense.

Dōgen differs from Kūkai, however, in that he rarely quotes or references the *Kegonkyō* directly. In contrast to Kūkai's demonstrated and pervasive reliance upon Kegon doctrines, imagery, and scripture, Dōgen's historical connection to Kegon is admittedly less direct. He inherits Kegon's sense of interpentration via the *Lotus Sūtra*, which he studied during his Tendai training on Mount Hiei as a young man. This principle Tendai scripture philosophically builds on the holographic cosmology of Kegon's *Avataṃsaka sūtra*. More specifically, the *Lotus Sūtra* teaches that all Buddhist teachings are essentially one (*ekayāna*), but that they merely differ according to the phase in which Buddha preached them. According to Tendai's formal doctrine of the Five Periods, the Buddha initially revealed Kegon's main scripture, but no one understood the fullness of his realization at the time. He consequently accommodated his message to his audiences in four subsequent phases of increasingly sophisticated teachings (i.e., the Sūtra pitaka, Mahāyāna sutras, Perfection of Wisdom literature, and finally the *Lotus* and *Nirvāṇa Sūtras*). As a result, the *Lotus Sūtra*, which Leighton has demonstrated exerted considerable influence over Dōgen's thought, constructs itself as the latest and most sophisticated reformulation of the *Kegonkyō* itself. Because it is fundamentally premised on Kegon's philosophy and imagery, it teaches, for example, that the "three-thousand worlds are present in one moment of thought."[42] This famous line not only explains how multiplicity can be contained within singularity, but also indicates how exterior reality can be contained within interior mental perception and how expansive physical space can be subsumed within one moment of time. Dōgen's discourse of temporalized space and temporal interpenetration is directly traceable to this common Kegon inheritance.

In sum, we can tentatively conclude that Kegon philosophy can been seen as the common denominator for directly juxtaposing Kūkai's and Dōgen's thought. Kūkai tends to envision its holographic message of "one in all, all in one" in terms of spatialized temporality, emphasizing universes within universes and Buddha bodies within Buddha lands. Dōgen by contrast, temporalizes space and put his own temporal spin on Kegon cosmology. He stresses times within times in what I call "holochronic time," an interpenetrating, ranging sense of time that links all sentient and insentient bodies together as impermanent being-times (*uji*). Kūkai tends to emphasize Kegon spatiality in order to become as solid and vajra-like as Dainichi's adamantine body-speech-mind, while Dōgen tends to emphasize the immediacy of Kegon temporality to awaken one's body-mind complex with a whack! of the *kyosaku* staff, itself another symbol of dharma transmission. For Kūkai, forms are spatial, but because they are empty of fixed essence, they do not obstruct one another in space. As a result, within the sphere of holographic space, forms interpenetrate one another micro-macrocosmically. For Dōgen, forms are times. Every *thing* is an *event*. Because the form of time is empty of fixed essence, times of buddhas and patriarchs interpenetrate one another in nonlinear fashion.

This common inheritance of Kegon thought helped both Buddhist founders establish their respective schools in Japan, either in its material or mental dimensions. All of Mikkyō's spatial imagery—its mandala and stupa architecture, its sculptures in the round, and its references to Dainichi's secret palace—construct a visual vocabulary of forms. They are nouns designed to open up from the microcosmic to the macrocosmic. The language of Zen, by contrast, with its predicate logic (to borrow Nishida's terminology) and its simple insistence on practice, experience, and transmitting the dharma from generation to generation, unfolds via verbs designed to open up from the instant to the eternal.

Temporalizing Buddhahood: Iconography of the Shisho

Figures 2.14a and 2.14b showing Dōgen's *shisho* or transmission certificate illustrates this point further. This key image for Sōtō priests was held in secret at Eiheiji for centuries and officially recognized as a National Treasure in 1900. Although it is most likely a medieval copy of the original, it still conforms to Dōgen's textual description of such certificates.[43] It employs a unique visual strategy that cleverly illustrates this holochronic sense of time's ranging, deconstructed of any horizontal or vertical models. As Dōgen maintains in the *Uji* fascicle, "times of past and present do not line up and accumulate, nor do they pile up on top of each other."[44] Rather, the *shisho* displays the sacred time of "the transmission of buddhas alone, together with buddhas."

Fifty patriarch names and the suffix *bodaboji* radiate in a circle around the central transliterated moniker for Śakyamuni Buddha's enlightened wisdom (*shakamuni bodaboji*). Dōgen's name (without the suffix) is located directly below this, in between the first and last Zen patriarchs. Specifically, the first Zen patriarch Mahākāśyapa (Jp. Makakashō) appears to Dōgen's

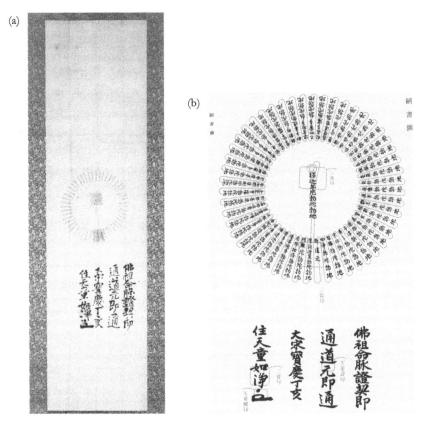

Figure 2.14. (a) Shisho transmission certificate, thirteenth century, Eiheiji Temple, Fukui Prefecture and (b) detail. Used with permission, courtesy of Ishii Seijun.

left and his own master Nyojō appears to his right, as if Dōgen is standing shoulder to shoulder with them across time. Reading the progression clockwise starting from Mahākāśyapa at the bottom of the circle, Bodhidharma (Jp. Bodaidaruma) appears slightly to the right of center above Buddha, twenty-eight generations after Mahākāśyapa. The famous sixth patriarch Hui-neng (Jp. Enō 638–713) appears six generations after Bodhidharma, at approximately the two o'clock position of the circle. Progressing clockwise, Fu-jung Tao-kai (Jp. Fuyō Dōkai), whose dharma robe Dōgen supposedly inherited, appears twelve generations after Hui-neng approximately at the four o'clock position of the circle. Dōgen's lineage grandfather Chikan (Ch. Chih-chien 1105–1192) appears sixteen generations after Hui-neng, while Nyojō appears directly after Chikan, and Dōgen naturally follows directly after Nyojō. The *shisho* can also be read counterclockwise, so that Dōgen can trace his ancestral lineage backward through the generations to the first patriarch and directly to the Buddha's enlightened mind. A thin red line out-lining the transmission weaves in and out among each and every name, but this miraculously reversible "arrow of time" ultimately meets in the center at Buddha's enlightened mind, which unifies them all.

This *kechimyaku* or surrogate bloodline for celibate dharma heirs may refer to the legends about the Sōtō lineage founder Seigen, who copied a certificate in his own blood, or a mixture of his and the sixth patriarch's blood, or a mix-ture of the first and second partriach's blood.[45] Dōgen himself comments in the *Shisho* fascicle that some certificates are written in blood from a finger or a tongue, though others write it in milk or oil.[46] Three large red *inka* seals of the monk Sanbō stamp both Buddha's and Dōgen's names in the circle and also stamp the name of Dōgen's master Nyojō, which appears at the bottom left at the end of the accompanying inscription. Master Nyojō's own name-seal appears twice in the accompanying inscription below. His real name-seal appears once over Dōgen's name and his Buddhist name-seal appears once over the last character (meaning End, I did it, or *facit*). Roughly translated, the inscription says:

> [Just as] the lifeblood passes through the buddhas and patriarchs of this certificate, [so too] does it pass through Dōgen (*Nyojō seal*).
> The Great Sung, 3rd year of Pao Ch'ing (1227)
> [signed] the living Tendō Nyojō (*Sanbō seal*).
> *Facit* (*Nyojō seal*)[47]

Describing the certificate, Dōgen says in his *Shisho* fascicle:

> Today in our lineage from Tōzan, [the way] the certificate is writ-ten is different from [the way] it is written in the Rinzai and other [lineages]."[48] ... Although he [the historical Buddha] realizes the truth on the 8th day of the 12th month thirty years after his descent and birth ... *it is the same realization of the truth shoulder to shoulder with, and in time with, the many buddhas,* it is realization of the truth before the many buddhas; and it is realization of the truth after all the many buddhas.[49]

Without this circular format in mind, Dōgen's description of patriarchs real-izing the truth shoulder to shoulder with one another (*shobutsu seiken*) in time would simply not make sense. That is, the image of all patriarch buddhas throughout history lined up in a circle side by side and shoulder to shoulder with one another helps one to understand how their minds can transhistorically "see" one another across the circle of time. It helps to explain how their minds can "meet" in a momentary *nikon* that is simultaneously nondual with that ranging circle of *kyōryaku* holochrony. It helps to explain Dōgen's claim that "there is no time that is not [the mutual transmission of] the buddhas"[50] and it helps to explain his opening line of the *Enlightened Vision* (*Ganzei*) fascicle, which states: "If *koṭis* of thousand myriad kalpas of learning in practice are gathered together into a happy circle, it will be eighty-four thousand Eyes."[51] That is, if millions and millions of infinite periods of time were gathered together, all the learning in practice that occurred therein would make up a happy circle of countless True Dharma Eyes looking across the aeons at one another. This image also helps to explain why Dōgen is so partial to his oft-quoted *Lotus Sūtra* phrase, stating that only a buddha can know other buddhas despite the centuries between them. In this way, it becomes evident that looking at Dōgen's writings in light of the important images in his life can yield significant insights that mere textual exegesis alone cannot. Thus, despite Dōgen's iconoclastic tendencies, one has to acknowledge that he nevertheless relies upon these particular kinds of Zen icons to shape and mold his thinking.

In addition, one has to acknowledge that Dōgen valorizes and reveres these images as icons that paradoxically and uniquely fix the ineffable dharma transmission in graphic form. The *Shōbōgenzō* recounts many instances when Dōgen sought out and requested special displays of *shisho* transmission certificates. Dōgen's overwhelming preoccupation with seeing and handling the actual confirmation objects of transmission rival only a present-day art historian's passion for getting access to museum storage or private collections. Dōgen's account of one particular discovery is telling. It is unclear whether this passage is written self-referentially, as Dōgen often did, or if a later hand added to it.

> Dōgen, when in Sung [China], had the opportunity to bow before certificates of succession, and there were many kinds of certificate[s]. One among them was that of the veteran master I-ichi Seido.... One day Seido said, "*Admirable old [calligraphic] traces are prized possessions of the human world. How many of them have you seen?*" Dōgen said, "*I have seen a few.*" Then Seido said, "*I have a scroll of old calligraphy in my room. It is a roster. I will let you see it, venerable brother.*" So saying, he fetched it, and I saw that it was a certificate of succession. It was a certificate of the succession of Hōgen's lineage and had been obtained

from among the robes and pātra (almsbowl) of an old veteran monk; it was not that of the venerable I-ichi himself. The way it was written is as follows: "*The first Patriarch Mahākaśyapa realized the truth under Śākyamuni Buddha, Śākyamuni Buddha realized the truth under Kāśyapa Buddha.*" It was written like this. Seeing it, Dōgen decisively believed in the succession of the Dharma from rightful successor to rightful successor. [The certificate] was Dharma that I had never seen before. It was a moment in which the Buddhist patriarchs mystically respond to and protect their descendants. The feeling of gratitude was beyond endurance.[52]

This passage thus communicates Dōgen's awe and reverence for the scroll itself, for it teaches him the continuous enlightenment of buddhas to buddhas from aeon to aeon. This particular trace of dharma transmission posits that the last of the seven buddhas of the past named Kāśyapa enlightened the historical Śākyamuni Buddha, and that Śākyamuni Buddha then enlightened his disciple Mahākaśyapa in one unbroken meeting of the minds. Dōgen thereby learns that Śākyamuni Buddha's awakening did not occur spontaneously for the first time *sui generis,* but rather that it was but the latest succession in a series of ageless and mutually validating awakenings throughout seven (that is, a symbolic perfect number of) world ages.[53] He therefore states in the *Shisho* fascicle that he has come to understand the Zen teaching that there were forty patriarchs from the seven buddhas of the past to the thirty-third patriarch Hui-neng, and more interestingly, vice versa as well. In this way, he comes to understand that "the so-called Seven Buddhas of the Past appeared in the infinite past *and yet they appear at the present.* Therefore, what permeates the face-to-face transmission throughout the forty patriarchs is the way of the buddhas and the succession of the buddhas."[54] This confirmation of buddhas mutually meeting eye to eye "alone together with buddhas" was revelatory for Dōgen, and for this reason, he is understandably awed and grateful for this new manifestation of the dharma. The format of the scroll itself reveals the timeless ranging of the dharma transmission forward and backward from master to disciple and back again, so Dōgen is overcome with gratitude for being able to see (i.e., meet and participate in) their timeless mind-to-mind transmission. In a sentiment of pseudosynchronicity, he remarks that it is almost as if the patriarchs knew and mystically answered his wish to "see" them. They consequently revealed the truth of their realization to him in this scroll.

Thus, for Dōgen, the scroll itself embodies and materializes enlightenment directly and exemplifies how insentient objects can preach the dharma.

This is a doctrinal formula known as *mujō seppō* that will be discussed further in chapter 4. The scroll itself may be a fixed, spatial object, but it was material evidence that disclosed the true nature of realization in and through time. For him, the *shisho* reconciled the tensions between original and acquired enlightenment, universal and individual enlightenment, eternal and momentary awakening, realization and practice. It showed all the patriarchs who had practiced and automatically realized their innate potential across the aeons, and as such it was to be revered.

This was especially the case as Dōgen strove to widen the circle of understanding and extend the lineage to his own dharma successors in Japan. For this reason, as his fatal illness markedly worsens in the seventh month of 1253, Dōgen knowingly instructs his pupil Gikai (1219–1309) to dedicate the merit of seeing the *shisho* to his fellow monk Ekan, a former Daruma-shū adept who had joined Dōgen in 1241 and died c. 1251. Dōgen did this just a week before he officially bestows his robe to his dharma heir Ejō (1198–1280).⁵⁵ These final acts of a dying Zen master indicate the important status that these visual and material markers of enlightenment held for him.

Like Kūkai, who later acknowledged the temporal dimension after he established Mikkyō on the ground, Dōgen does specifically discuss space after establishing the Sōtō Zen lineage in Japanese history. After sixteen years of gathering students in Kyoto and Fukakusa, he moves to Echizen province, establishes Eiheiji Temple in 1243, and writes a fascicle on *Space* (*Kokū*) in 1245. Yet even in this fascicle, Dōgen relativizes the importance of space and recognizes the interdependence of space and time together. Dōgen opens the fascicle by citing Ch'an master Huang-po's question to Emperor Xuan:

> Provoked by the question "what is right here?" the way is actualized and Buddha ancestors emerge. The actualization of the Buddha ancestors' way has been handed down heir by heir. Thus the whole body of skin, flesh, bones and marrow hangs in empty space.⁵⁶

Put simply, because there is space, there is time and vice versa. That is, Huang-po's very act of asking a spatially locative question occasions the unobstructed manifestation of all buddhas and ancestors who transmit the way in and throughout ranging time. Conversely, because buddhas and patriarchs transmit from rightful successor to rightful successor in time, the whole body of enlightenment (i.e., the *dharmakāya* metonymically represented by various constituent body parts) itself abides in space, as if it were hanging in emptiness.

Yet even Dōgen's last sentiment of "the whole body hanging in space" connotes his typical temporalization of space, for it alludes to a special poetic reference involving nondirectionality, formlessness, and the eternal wisdom of buddhas and patriarchs. In his *Makahannyaharamita* fascicle, a commentary on the eponymous *Perfection of Wisdom Sūtra*, Dōgen quotes an ode to a windbell by his teacher Nyojō and then comments on it. Nyojō's original poem reads: "The whole body like a mouth, hanging in emptiness, does not question whether the wind is north, south, east or west, but simply rings out *prajñā* to all others equally, with the [tinkling chattering chime] *teichin tōro teichin tō*"[57] Dōgen comments on this onomatopoeia, saying, "This is the chattering of *prajñā* [transmitted] by Buddhist patriarchs from rightful successor to rightful successor."[58] By sampling Nyojō's imagery in his *Kokū* and other fascicles, Dōgen therefore problematizes spatial location, empties out the substance of the whole body of the bell, and seizes upon yet another opportunity to emphasize the transmission of buddhas and patriarchs from generation to generation throughout unobstructed time.

Experiencing the Spatial and Temporal Form of Emptiness

Now that we have established Kegon as the common ground for comparing Kūkai's and Dōgen's thought and looked more closely at Mikkyō's Two World mandalas and Sōtō's transmission certificates, let us examine how these spatial and temporal conceptualizations impact the way Kūkai and Dōgen each envision the enlightenment experience. Let us see where and when they locate the realization of emptiness.

As the modern Japanese philosopher Yuasa Yasuo states in his essay on "Space-Time and Body-Mind Integration," "The activity of the mind is an experience of time, while the activity of the body is an experience of space."[59] Because space-time integration consequently and necessarily implies body-mind integration and vice versa, the manner in which one cognizes or emphasizes space or time will necessarily impact the way one realizes or understands the enlightenment experience. Kūkai's notion of awakening in this very spatial body (*sokushin jōbutsu*) through temporally-accelerated esoteric techniques reveals his preoccupation with spatialized temporality. Inversely, Dōgen's preoccupation with the time of mind-to-mind transmission in and through the body's seated zazen position and practice reveals Zen's temporalized spatiality.

In this regard, it is important to see where both patriarchs locate the energy source fueling their enlightenment in relation to the practitioner's body. One can recall that Nāgārjuna ascended the iron tower in southern India to obtain the esoteric teachings, and that Kūkai mentioned ascending the five ranks of bodhisattvahood. Likewise, one can recall Nāgārjuna's heroic journey to the dragon king's palace at the bottom of the sea and Dōgen's advice to drop off body and mind. These directional metaphors indicate that Kūkai locates Dainichi's cosmic, mysterious power externally, and that one must rise up to merge with it (that is, until one gets enlightened and realizes nonduality between inside and outside, upward and downward). Dōgen, by contrast, locates the energy source internally, so that one must journey deep down within oneself to realize it (again, until one gets enlightened and realizes nonduality).

To use the analogy of electricity, in the Mikkyō context, one first "plugs into" Dainichi's self-illuminating power by the three ritual prongs of body, speech, and mind. Figure 2.15, for example, illustrates an esoteric visualization for circulating mantras in order to achieve *kaji* mutual empowerment between self and Buddha. By connecting one's own speech and by extension body and mind to Dainichi's, a mutual exchange of energy (*kaji*) occurs

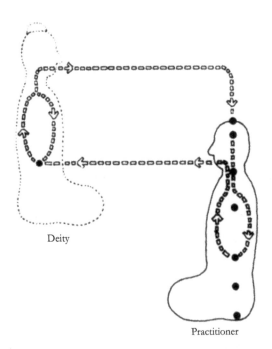

Deity

Practitioner

Figure 2.15. Shingon visualization for circulating mantras in order to achieve *kaji* mutual empowerment between self and Buddha. From *Shingon,* by Taiko Yamasaki, © 1988 by Taiko Yamasaki and David Kidd. Reprinted by arrangement with Shambhala Publications Inc., Boston, MA. www.shambhala.com.

between two beings in holographic space. As the *Jūhachidō* eighteen-step ritual manual instructs,

> Contemplate as follows: the principal deity (*honzon*) sits on a mandala. I sit on a mandala. The principle deity enters my body and my body enters the body of the principal deity. It is like many luminous mirrors facing each other, their images interpenetrating each other.[60]

Thus, the individual self and universal emptiness as personified by Dainichi unify to embody Kegon's message of one is all, all is one. This sentiment of reflexivity and mutual empowerment characterizes the unitive experience of *kaji* in which "Buddha enters me, I enter Buddha" (*nyūga ganyū*).

This sentiment of union also reflects and reinforces Kūkai's general understanding of form and emptiness as expressed by the *Heart Sūtra's* pithy axiom "form is emptiness, emptiness is form." In keeping with his primarily spatial approach to reality, Kūkai understands the epithet as a nondual equation or reflexive statement of the two terms. Like a room and its walls, one needs both empty space and concrete contours, nonstructure and structure to make a room such as it is. According to Mikkyō doctrine, this reflexivity is everywhere: forms self-dissolve into luminous emptiness and concomitantly, immediately, and reciprocally, shining emptiness self-manifests as forms, oneself included. As Kūkai states in his dharma lecture at Tōdaiji in 813:

> Bodies dissolve and harmonize with
> The Buddha's sunlight and moonlight,
> [And conversely]
> The Golden Body and the Diamond Body
> Provisionally manifest to save all.[61]

This citation describes neither a strict monism nor a divine or neoplatonic emanation theory. Rather, it simply indicates two ways of seeing the coterminous interplay of form and emptiness in the world. Alternately schematized below, it indicates two ways of seeing what is actually the singular function of Dainichi, the personification of emptiness. From the unenlightened perspective (from the bottom up), Dainichi appears above the practitioner on a higher plane. At this stage, form dissolves into emptiness, self enfolds into Dainichi, I enter Buddha. However, from the enlightened perspective (i.e., from the top down), one realizes that the self and everything else are nothing other than Dainichi already. One understands how emptiness manifests as form, Dainichi unfolds into self, and Buddha enters me. In the Shingon Mikkyō system, these two views of reality are nondual. They are graphically schematized in the colorful Womb and Diamond World mandalas, whose iconographic interresonances reveal the nonduality of Daincihi's phenomenal and noumenal realms of potential and perfected enlightenment. Again, in order to realize the reciprocal nonduality of self and Buddha, form and emptiness, as well as Womb and Diamond World mandalas, Kūkai must construct a special field or spatial system where such syntheses might occur. This exchange can be schematized as follows, noting the upward directionality inherent in Mikkyō's foundation legend (fig. 2.16).

It should be noted that Kūkai's notion of nondual union is not the same as oneness. Union presupposes that there are two entities that come together, whereas oneness refers to a single singularity or monism, which reduces all difference into sameness. Union, and particularly the nondual union of which Kūkai speaks, recognizes the continued existence of self and world as personified by Dainichi, but dissolves both self and world into emptiness so that the usual lines distinguishing the two become blurred. Again, this paradigm requires an open, unobstructed, Kegon-like space in which to occur.

In contradistinction to Kūkai's "plugging in" to the external source of his enlightenment, Dōgen relies on *jiriki* or self-power, which means that the body-mind complex contains its own battery pack so to speak (fig. 2.17).[62] One's "on" switch gets flipped when one practices zazen seated meditation, in particular. This is why Dōgen maintained that practice and realization are one and why he exhorted his students to "just sit" (*shikan taza*).

According to Dōgen's scheme, one begins naturally with an everyday sense of one's own body and mind, separate from other being-times. This is the first movement of asserting the self. In time, after long practice, however, one forgets one's everyday sense of self completely by "dropping off the body-mind of

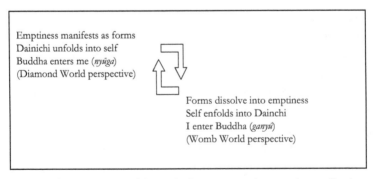

Figure 2.16. Kūkai's Unitive Model: nondual union in unobstructed space (*kaji*)

Figure 2.17. Zen Meditation. Adapted from *Shingon,* by Taiko Yamasaki, © 1988 by Taiko Yamasaki and David Kidd. Reprinted by arrangement with Shambhala Publications Inc., Boston, MA. www.shambhala.com.

self and other completely." This second movement of negation is the telltale moment of *shinjin datsuraku* in which all sense of self evaporates within the sphere of emptiness. In the third movement of reaffirmation, the forgotten self within Dōgen's special Kegon-inspired temporal matrix then gets reaffirmed as a contemporaneous being-time by all other being-times before, during, and after it. That is, when one negates one's self into emptiness, from within the sphere of emptiness all other forms rush back in to confirm one as but one of many *dharmas* in an interconnected whole, which Dōgen elsewhere describes as Total Dynamic Functioning (*Zenki*) or One Bright Pearl (*Ikka myōju*). One consequently recognizes one's interpenetrating and dynamic partici-pation in all *dharmas* at all times, always. Dōgen claims the True Dharma Eye of enlightened vision results when this threefold movement of assertion, negation, and reaffirmation of self and world is completed in and through unobstructed time. This purgative enlightenment paradigm is schematized in figure 2.18, noting the downward directionality of Zen's foundation legend.

Whereas Kūkai sets up and then synthesizes the dichotomous complex that we construct for ourselves and our world, Dōgen simply starts with all forms as a whole, everything. Then in a second movement, there is a radi-cal and complete dropping off, then a third and final movement when the

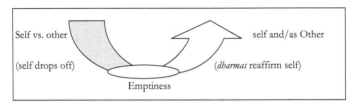

Figure 2.18. Dōgen's Purgative Model: assertion, negation (*shinjin datsuraku*), and reaffirmation in unobstructed time

self gets reconfirmed by virtue of all the world's myriad *dharmas*. The result is a shift from relative self-centeredness to other-centeredness and the recognition that the self exists only by virtue of everything else. This traceless enlightenment, Dōgen says, continues on and on endlessly within this special temporal matrix.

Dōgen's sequential threefold movement is not unique, however. Rather, it relies upon a standard trope in Buddhist dialectics. Dōgen's lineage master, Seigen, famously remarked that when he first began Zen practice, he saw mountains as mountains and rivers as rivers. As his practice gradually deepened, he said he no longer saw mountains as mountains or rivers as rivers, but that when he truly understood Zen, he once more saw mountains as mountains and rivers as rivers. This triple movement from form, to nonform, back to transformed form once more also appears in the *Diamond Sūtra*. Shigenori Nagatomo has identified this dynamic sequence as The Logic Of Not, formally articulated as "A is Not-A; Therefore it is A" (A,~A, ∴A), while Shohaku Okumura simply describes it with the pithy formula "Is, Is Not, Is."[63] Malcolm David Eckel has also noted the triple movement characterizing Bhāvaviveka's sixth-century Madhyamaka logic. He writes,

> Reduced to a single three-part formula, these are the three stages of Bhavaviveka's quest: There is an assumption of distinctions, followed by a denial of distinctions, and then by a reappropriation of distinctions that brings the quest to its conclusion and at the same time returns it to the point from which it began.[64]

Dōgen is thus following this standard trope when he famously remarks in the *Genjōkōan* fascicle

1. to study the self is
2. to forget the self. To forget the self is to be
3. confirmed by all *dharmas*.

[Inversely], to be confirmed by all *dharmas* is to effect the dropping off body-mind of self and other completely.[65]

Dōgen concludes, moreover, that this transformative process results in the enlightened perception of a Kegon-like, unobstructed temporal matrix of being-times. He concludes that "All traces of enlightenment [then] disappear, and this traceless enlightenment is continued on and on endlessly."[66] In other words, the third movement's rushing back in of all *dharmas* is radically and simultaneously collective. It permits of no single causal pathway, no one trace of sequence or consequence. It is instantaneous and total. It automatically implies Kegon's nonlinear awareness of the interpenetration and interdependence of all things, all at once, within the field of awareness. It is for this reason that those buddhas and patriarchs who have realized this total awareness of self and/as the world are arranged in the *shisho's* circular and nonlinear format.

Dōgen reiterates this threefold structure of the Zen experience elsewhere as well. In the *Seeing the Buddha (Kenbutsu)* fascicle, Dōgen quotes the *Diamond Sūtra* and reaffirms Śākyamuni's address to a great assembly: (1) "If we see the myriad forms (*shosō*), and (2) no forms (*hisō*), (3) we at once see the Tathāgata."[67] He also opens the entire *Genjōkōan* fascicle by outlining the structure of his experiential paradigm. In the first of four sentences, Dōgen initially asserts the world's dualities when seen from an everyday vantage point. From this starting point, one understands intellectually, but not yet experientially, that all *dharmas* are originally enlightened:

"When all *dharmas* are the Buddha-Dharma, there is illusion and enlightenment, practice, birth, death, Buddhas and sentient beings."

In the second movement expressing the standpoint of *shinjin datsuraku*, Dōgen rejects all such formal dualisms:

"When myriad *dharmas* are without self, there is no illusion or enlightenment, no Buddhas or sentient beings, no generation or extinction."

In the third movement, which transcends assertion and negation, Dōgen explains that the Buddha Way is beyond dualisms. He therefore reaffirms the distinctions of the world, but these are now seen in a transformed, enlightened light.

"The Buddha Way is originally beyond fullness and lack, and for this reason there is generation and extinction, illusion and enlightenment, sentient beings and Buddhas."

In a fourth and final wrap-up, Dōgen asserts his own individual sentiment in recollapsing the collapsed dualism and reassuming an everyday stance that has nonetheless been transformed by the rigorous process of asserting, negating, and reaffirming form. Enlightened vision has been acquired in the third movement, but that should not prevent one from engaging with the world in a compassionate and realistic manner.

"In spite of this, flowers fall always amid our grudging, and weeds flourish in our chagrin."[68]

As Heinrich Dumoulin explains "The first sentence asserts.... The second sentence is expressed in negative terms.... The third statement takes up from the first, but articulates the transcendental character of reality.... The fourth sentence turns to the impermanent world of becoming in which we live and in whose impermanence we participate."[69]

In this way, Dōgen interprets the *Heart Sūtra* maxim differently than Kūkai. In keeping with his primarily temporal approach to reality, Dōgen sees the phrase "form is emptiness, emptiness is form" not as a reflexive, ontological statement of the way things are, but rather as an epistemological hint as to the way things should be perceived properly. To borrow the terminology of Western European medieval mysticism, Kūkai interprets the phrase to reflect the *ordo essendi* or the order of existence, while Dōgen interprets it to mean the *ordo cognoscendi* or the order of experience that charts how one can come to know or cognize the way things are. It is in this more epistemological and ultimately soteriological sense that Dōgen consecutively shifts and alternates his focus from form to emptiness and then back to form again as one transformed.

Kūkai	Dōgen
Form = Emptiness	Form → Emptiness
Emptiness = Form	Emptiness → Form (transformed)
"I enter Buddha;	To study the self is to forget the self;
Buddha enters me"	to forget the self is to be confirmed by all dharmas."

This shift to highlighting the order of experience and not the spatialized order of being is what gives Dōgen's work its temporal spin. It is also what makes it so difficult for him to recognize fixed, unmoving graphic art as legitimate, unless it is an exceptional Zen icon such as the *shisho* certificate mentioned earlier. That is, Dōgen experiences awakening as a time-oriented, sequential assertion, negation, and then reaffirmation of the body-mind in unobstructed time. Because enlightenment for Dōgen is fundamentally a lived event of time and in time, icons can never represent the moment of enlightenment in the very literal sense of making it present again. One simply has to live it. As soon as one tries to freeze-frame that ineffable lived moment in a fixed graphic format, it's lost.

Thus Kūkai's and Dōgen's experience of emptiness by necessity is conditioned by their primarily spatial or temporal understandings of the world. Kūkai's unitive goal of nondual union or *kaji* requires an expansive, unobstructed space in which unification may take place, and Dōgen's purgative *shinjin datsuraku* experience of absolute cessation requires a special unobstructed time within which that moment of ineffability may occur. The Mikkyō enlightenment experience envisions a certain bidirectional energy exchange and eventual unification within the open space of meditation. The Zen enlightenment experience sequentially asserts, negates, and reaffirms the self in time.

Summary

To conclude, in this chapter we established Kegon cosmology as the common denominator for comparing Kūkai's and Dōgen's practical philosophies. It was argued that *relatively* speaking, Kūkai places emphasis on holographic space, whereas Dōgen emphasizes holochronic time. For Kūkai, the form of emptiness is the micro-macrocosmic space of Dainichi's body, speech, and mind. This means that enlightenment involves realizing the emptiness of every single mental and material thing in the universe.

For Dōgen, however, the form of emptiness is time. All beings are times, all things are temporary occurrences. For Dōgen, therefore, the form of emptiness is realizing the instant and eternal time of the buddhas and patriarchs. This means that enlightenment involves realizing the emptiness of every single action and event whenever it occurs.

Consequently, Kūkai tries to locate or visualize oneself as the *dharmadhātu* realm of enlightenment, which he says is "as vast as empty space." Dōgen, by contrast, attempts to live or actualize the total dynamic functioning (*zenki*) of the ever-moving *dharmadhātu*, which he observes, manifests as all the timeful being-times of bathing, cooking, cleaning, begging, praying, and naturally, sitting in Zen meditation.

After establishing this common Kegon inheritance, Kūkai's and Dōgen's spatial and temporal understandings were discussed vis-à-vis their practical experiences. Analogically speaking, the Mikkyō ritual practitioner "plugs" the self into an external energy source to effect a simultaneous exchange and unification with Dainichi's all-in-one spatiality. The Zen meditator by contrast, over the course and in sacred time, is able to switch on his own internal energy source by sequentially negating and reaffirming self and other. Mikkyō ritually locates the practitioner in holographic space to achieve communion with the cosmic Buddha-body-speech-mind. The Sōtō Zen practitioner by contrast drops off body-mind of self and other to participate in the holochronic time of the eternal present that facilitates the authentic transmission from Buddha to Buddha.

When Mikkyō and Zen thought is considered side by side in this manner, certain Buddhist truths begin to emerge. Taken together, we can consider that the form of emptiness is both here and now, everywhere and always. As Kūkai's Two World mandalas suggest, compassionate method *is* nondual with wisdom, just as undertaking zazen practice *is* tantamount to realization in Dōgen's scheme. Investigating the where and the when of the enlightenment experience in this way provides us with a helpful conceptual tool for analyzing Kūkai's and Dōgen's writings and art-related projects.

Kūkai values highly imagistic visualizations, hand mudras, and verbal mantras to bring about the mutual empowerment of *kaji* when "I enter Buddha, Buddha enters me." On the other hand, Dōgen insists on "just sitting" without any visual props or elaborate esoteric ritual, until that pivotal moment when one can cast off of body-mind completely and forget the self in order to be confirmed by all *dharmas*. These two paradigms, that is, the one that requires a spatial ground for the nondual union of *kaji* to take place, and the other that requires a temporal duration for the self-negation of *shinjin datsuraku* to occur, are distinct yet complementary modes for realizing innate Buddhahood.

Both of these two understandings of the nature and process of religious awakening are equally and undoubtedly Buddhist. Kūkai and Dōgen simply inherit different strains of Buddhist meditative techniques that tend to translate into two different modes of artistic expression. Distinguishing between these two kinds of unitive and purgative mysticisms in Kegon's unobstructed space and time may help to explain Kūkai's principally iconic and Dōgen's principally iconoclastic views. For Kūkai, seeing the mandalas in a single glance can automatically enlighten the viewer, but for Dōgen, the True Dharma Eye is only gained through experiencing emptiness directly in meditation. For Kūkai, the two mandalas are better than scriptures at directly conveying the dharma, but for Dōgen, fixed graphic art can never fully represent the lived experience of awakening, apart from a few exceptional cases. Chapters 3 and 4 in particular will analyze the specific religious images that Kūkai and Dōgen valued highly (and qualified each in their own ways) and will contextualize them both within their experiential systems.

3

Kūkai on the Art of the Ultimate

NOW THAT WE have established the comparability of Kūkai's and Dōgen's thought, the next two chapters will look into the ideas of each master in more detail. This chapter focuses on Kūkai's philosophy of form, which informs all of his esoteric arts, letters, and ritual science to be discussed at length below. It is necessary to begin in this way, so that one may gain a better appreciation for the ways in which Kūkai both constructed and deconstructed the importance of his esoteric imagery.

This chapter first analyzes Kūkai's considerable calligraphic talents in light of his unique theory that worldly forms constitute an alphabet of image-letters (*monji*) that spell out and preach the truth of the dharma. This is known as the Mikkyō doctrine of *hosshin seppō* or the *dharmakāya* itself expounding or demonstrating the dharrma. More specifically, Kūkai theorizes that all the sights, sounds, and even immaterial imaginings of the world are nothing other than the universal body, speech, and mind of the cosmic Dainichi Buddha. To borrow the phraseology of Mikkyō doctrine, the cosmic Dainichi Buddha incessantly reveals himself in physical, verbal, and mental modes of action to disclose the truth of suchness for his own enjoyment (*jiju hōraku*).[1]

By extension, therefore, this means that we too are nothing other than Dainichi. In keeping with standard Mahāyāna Buddhist philosophy, in Kūkai's estimation, enlightenment is originally never separate from the forms of the universe, ourselves included. However, according to the Mikkyō scheme, one needs especially powerful esoteric techniques, such as the *ajikan* visualization in order to actualize one's innate potential and become a Buddha in this very body.

In addition, Kūkai believes that one needs to be initiated into the secrets of the especially powerful Two World mandalas so that one's ritual practice can be empowered by Dainichi's enlightening and enlightened imperial presence. The Womb and Diamond World mandalas lay out two architectural floor plans for Daincihi's residential and official palaces of enlightenment. Within its painted assembly halls and courtyards, the solar emperor Dainich is pictured holding court with his royal retinue of deities to illuminate and rule over the entire *dharmadhātu* realm. Given Kūkai's theory that the mandalas directly manifest Dainichi's presence even better than other kinds of *monji*, the act of displaying these two paintings on a temple wall automatically creates a palatial environment of perfect enlightenment—a pure land on earth—that instantly empowers one's ritual practice within the temple hall. At Mikkyō sites, such as Tōji, Kōyasan, and the Shingon'in, Kūkai accordingly mobilized and manipulated the mandalas' recombinant reservoir of esoteric figures to empower a wide range of ritual protocols and purposes. He copied, sculpted, rearranged, and regrouped figures from the two mandalas in specific recombinations to protect the state, bring rain, avert misfortune, and cure illness. Thus, theoretically speaking, Mikkyō's "immanental theocratic"[2] model means that all the objects, ideas, images, and words of the world are coequal manifestations of Dainichi's enlightened sovereign realm. The mandalas are special, however. They succinctly and graphically map out the dharma better than words, and they are so powerful and profound, Kūkai claims, that they can automatically enlighten in a single glance.[3]

Mikkyō's absolute and automatic equation of signifier = signified will become an important point of comparison when we turn to Dōgen's shifting views in chapter 4. Dōgen consistently maintains the gap between signifiers vs. signified and believes that fixed imagery and conventional language can never fully represent transient objects/experiences in the sense of making them fully present again. At the same time, however, Dōgen does occasionally dissolve the distinction between representation vs. real world referents when discussing the exceptional nondual perception of the True Dharma Eye, which can embrace art and language not as mediations, but rather as direct manifestations of suchness. This comparison of views regarding text, image, and the real forms (or being-times) of the world will become the focus of the remainder of this investigation.

Thus, to recall our general comments from the Introduction, if early classical Indian Buddhism presented an iconography of absence and Mahāyāna Buddhism promoted an iconography of embodiment, then esoteric Buddhism advances an iconography of the ultimate. It systematically samples imperial imagery to explain the ultimate authority and efficacy of an extremely elaborate ritual, philosophical, and visual system. It not only views the forms of samsara as already being inherently enlightened, but it also extols and exalts their potential for being the fuel for the fastest vehicle for realizing enlightenment in this lifetime's embodiment. By shifting the emphasis away from metaphysical philosophizing to soteriological-ritual methods for actualizing enlightenment through the three secrets of body, speech, and mind, Mikkyō places unprecedented value upon the material forms of the universe. Furthermore, as argued in chapter 2, it does so by emphasizing the spatial dimension of these forms. This chapter will specifically examine Kūkai's textual and visual projects that reveal his systematic and spatialized approach to perceiving and achieving enlightenment in, with, and as the forms of the world

Representation and Perception

Visuality was already an important element in the early writings of Kūkai. In *The Indications of the Goals of the Three Teachings* (*Sangō shiiki*), written in 797 at the age of twenty-four, Kūkai uses numerous visual metaphors to establish the superiority of Buddhism over Confucianism and Taoism. Kūkai invents a fictitious Buddhist character named Kamei-Kotsuji (Mendicant X) and has him directly address his Confucian and Taoist counterparts. His Buddhist character first distinguishes between the wise man who can see things clearly and the fool who cannot. He then critiques his interlocutors' limited views and suggests that their foolish arguments are as provisional as sculpting ice, as futile as trying to write or paint on water, as partial as a blind man touching and describing only one feature of an elephant, and as cowardly as Yeh Kung who liked to paint dragons but then fled when he encountered a real one. He finally urges them to look into the legendary mirror of truth owned by Emperor Shih Huang of Chih, where they can see the error of their ways and directly confront reality with courage.[4]

In addition to showing off Kūkai's command of Chinese classical literature and lore, this early text engages the themes of representation and perception to tackle the problem of unenlightened vs. enlightened understanding. It draws upon the long-standing Buddhist analogies of blindness equaling ignorance and self-reflective insight mirroring truth. Any other means of representing reality that does not mirror the totality of the whole fully and directly is inadequate for Kūkai. Discerning but a fraction of a form (such as an elephant) is no better than being overwhelmed by its entirety (such as a dragon) and trying to describe the totality using insufficient means (such as ice sculpture or water painting) is equally inadequate.

Thus, in this early text, Kūkai proposes a clear difference between authentic and inauthentic representation and perception. He argues that only Buddhist vision can directly and authentically reflect the vital power of all reality in an unmediated fashion. Like a mirror, the Buddhist mind is able to take in and truly replicate all the forms of the universe without any distortions, judgments, expectations, or other colorings. Confucianism and Taoism, by contrast, feebly attempt to symbolize aspects of reality in partial, provisional, and ultimately futile, metonymy. He believes that only the enlightened perception gained by the Buddhists can intuitively and courageously grasp the entirety of the whole. The false perception of Confucians and Taoists, conversely, mistakes the map for the territory and prefers the second-generation loss of weak description over the direct experience of reality itself.

Kūkai extends these same visual motifs and metaphors in three texts written in 817 or 818 at the age of forty-four or forty-five. In *Becoming a Buddha in This Very Body* (*Sokushin jōbutsugi*), Kūkai explains that buddhas are able to become enlightened precisely because their round bright mind-mirrors are able to take in and reflect all forms (*shikizō*) fully and without distortion.[5] In addition, in *The Meaning of the Word Hūṃ* (*Unjigi*), Kūkai employs the metaphor of the painter to describe how one's mind can construct and completely color one's experience of reality. He says that the unenlightened foolishly paint self-deluding appearances; they are like ignorant painters who paint dreadful demons in colorful detail but then faint out of fear. By contrast, the enlightened paint truth in wise and compassionate ways, for they are like "painters of the Buddha's wisdom who manifest his mandala of Great Compassion freely and without restriction."[6] Finally, Kūkai exhibits some of his most mature thought on Buddhist views of imagery and perception in *Sound-Letter-Reality* (*Shōji jissōgi*). He launches an extensive analysis of the six objects of sense (i.e., sights, sounds, smells, tastes, touches, and thoughts) but only discusses the objects of sight, implying the others in keeping with Indian rhetorical convention.[7] He first points out that sentient and insentient objects of sight (i.e., anything with color, form, and/or movement) can be seen in two ways. From a conventional, unenlightened viewpoint, the act of seeing (*nōen*) and the objects of sight (*shoen*) are differentiated and can cause attachment and delusion.[8] From the ultimate Mikkyō perspective that sees forms as fuel for enlightenment, however, objects of sight do not cause attachment or suffering, but rather the opposite. Kūkai concludes *Sound-Letter-Reality* by saying that the various objects of sight are "harmful like poison to the foolish, but beneficial like medicine to the man of wisdom... [they have] the ability to delude or to enlighten" (*nōyuiyaku nōgō*) depending upon one's perspective.[9] From the wise man's ultimate perspective, therefore, the distinction between perception and the perceived is collapsed in the open, empty space of codependent arising. As Kūkai writes in *Becoming a Buddha in This Very Body,*

> Differences exist between matter and mind, but in their essential nature they remain the same. Matter is no other than mind; mind, no other than matter. Without any obstruction, they are interrelated. The subject is the object; the object, the subject. The seeing is the seen and the seen is the seeing. Nothing differentiates them. Although we speak of the creating and the created, there is in reality neither the creating nor the created.[10]

Kūkai reiterates all of these visual themes toward the end of his life in two monumental works known as *The Ten Stages of Mind* (*Jūjūshinron*), later summarized as *The Precious Key to the Secret Treasury* (*Hizō hōyaku*). Written in 830 at the age of fifty-seven, these texts systematically rank Buddhist doctrines in typical *kyōhan*[11] fashion and conclude with Shingon occupying pride of place as the tenth and ultimate doctrine. He opens his treatise with a poem lamenting the fact that blind men in samsara cannot see their own blindness, just as madmen are oblivious to their own madness. Thankfully, however, he explains that Buddha has compassionately provided a range of teachings to address each and every one of our blind spots. In the fourth stage of mind, after discussing non-Buddhist doctrines, Kūkai credits Tripitaka masters with at least providing men with a Buddhist path to clear their vision, open their eye of wisdom, and attain nirvana. In the fifth stage of mind Kūkai warns against the cessation of body and mind discussed previously. In the sixth stage, he applauds the Yogācāra sect for severing attachments to real and imagined sense objects[12] and in the seventh Madhyamaka stage, he continues to analyze the inseparable relationship between form and emptiness.

In the eighth stage of mind, when discussing the Tendai sect, Kūkai says that the mind of enlightenment is identical to empty space and reflects all images fully and clearly just like still water or a golden mirror. This enlightened state permits no gap between the reflecting mind and the reflected image. It is "signless" and "without aspect" (*musō*).[13] This state of mind is like empty space because it transcends all characteristics (e.g., all colors, dimensions, and gender), all locations in the Buddhist cosmology (specifically in the realms of desire, form, or formlessness), all perceptions, and even the categories of being and nonbeing. It negates all distinctions and dualities, but Kūkai nevertheless maintains that this One Mind of Tendai is still only preliminary from the esoteric point of view. He fundamentally reiterates this message in the ninth stage of mind addressing Kegon view, so it is only in the final and tenth Shingon stage that Kūkai's ultimate last word on form and imagery appears.

In the tenth *Secret Magnificent Stage of Mind* (*Himitsu shogon shin*),[14] Kūkai claims that Mikkyō alone removes stains from the mind's eye to gradually discern the magnificence of the mandala realm. He does not deny the insubstantiality, emptiness, and interpenetration of forms that is articulated in Tendai and Kegon doctines, but he claims to transcend their abstract doctrines and theoretical speculations about emptiness. He instead extols all the forms of the universe such as they are, and embraces their unique capacity to elicit enlightenment. To provide an example and a method for doing so, he outlines the *ajikan* visualization to be discussed in detail below. This meditative practice exploits the full capacity of one's entire being; one's eyes, mantric invocations, and mental images of enlightenment are fully mobilized to mirror and mimic the projected idea of Dainichi's enlightened body, speech, and mind. By practicing this esoteric path that locates Dainichi within one's very being, one comes to realize speedily that one can indeed become a Buddha in this very embodiment.

One can tentatively conclude here that out of Tendai's emptying negation of nondualism and out of Kegon's theoretical interlace of cosmic existence, Kūkai concretely extols all the physical, verbal, and mental forms of originally enlightened existence. This dynamic interaction of all three secrets of object, idiom, and image-idea brings us to a discussion of Kūkai's theory of *monji* and the unmediated expression of truth in and as the word-images of the world.

Monji: Word-Images, Visual Texts

Any discussion of Kūkai's view of imagery must also take account of the emphasis he placed on the power of language.[15] For Kūkai, the language of art and the art of language were two sides of the same coin. According to Mikkyō doctrine, the middle term of speech in the three secrets of body, speech, and mind is the middle factor that links matter and mind. This means that words, and especially mantras, are tantamount to Dainichi's tangible and intangible shapes, real and imagined forms, his visible realm of perceived objects and his invisible realm of mental images.

For Kūkai, therefore, texts and images are mutually reinforcing, not mutually exclusive modes of manifesting truth. Drawing and writing for him were both products of the brush, and physical, verbal, and mental objects were equal partners in revealing the realm of enlightenment. By necessity, therefore, this analysis will include language in the analysis of Kūkai's views of imagery, and will consider the word-art of Kūkai's calligraphy, as well as the visual texts of the two-world mandalas.

Most textual scholars trained in religious studies tend to focus on purely linguistic issues in Kūkai's newly imported *mantrayāna*. Scholars such as Kasulis (1988), Ingram (1990), Rambelli (1994), and Abé (1999) have explored in depth Kūkai's linguistic theory and his systematic justifications for the power of mantra invocation. Yet as Rambelli has demonstrated, texts also functioned as material and performative bodies. Sutras were treated as liturgical performance objects, fanned out accordion style, and symbolically "read" with dramatic flourish as part of Buddhist ritual theater.[16] Conversely, material and performative bodies also functioned as texts. More specifically for Kūkai, everyday objects and events were considered to be sacred texts. They were considered to be but shape-shifting aspects of the *dharmakāya's* universally enlightened world-body. It is therefore important to remember that for every reference that Kūkai makes to the power of speech and mantra, there are an equal number of references to images and forms.

Kūkai views the entire cosmos as a massive visual text whose alphabet of empty forms spell out suchness, the truth of the way things are. The recombinant components of this vast visual alphabet are called *monji* (lit. pattern-letters). These are the idea-graphic shapes that compose reality writ large. They are the created and creating factors of existence, empty of any fixed essence and therefore free to change and compose new *monji*. Such image-letters emerge as an infinite netscape of mutually implicit composite forms that spell out reality in a never-ending narrative of linked verse. *Monji* are the formed and formative factors of existence that convey the truth of things in linguistic-imagistic name-form permutations. The problem of names and real or imagined forms (*nama-rūpa*) in samsara as opposed to nirvana had plagued early classical Buddhism, but Kūkai's fully developed theory of *monji* links sights with sounds, forms with names, and objects of vision with objects of thought to disclose Dainichi's enlightened realm in and as the world. *Monji* are thus the basic building blocks for Kūkai's entire cosmological and soterio-logical system, as they directly constitute and reveal the unobstructed realm of enlightenment. This unobstructed, enlightened realm is accessible to all provided that one refine one's visual literacy and learn how to perceive and participate in it properly through esoteric training. To read Dainichi's cosmic code of intertextual, intericonic signs correctly is to be enlightened.[17]

More specifically, in essays such as *Sound-Letter-Reality* and *The Meaning of the Word Hūṃ*, Kūkai explains that everything in the world, every physi-cal, verbal, and mental object, appears as a particular pattern (*mon*). These patterns make up Dainchi's world-body in all of its changing colors, forms, and movements. These patterns also exist as letters (*ji*) in the dimension of Dainichi's ever-unfolding enlightened speech, so that reality = language, things = words, and forms = names. As a result, Kūkai states that each differ-ent pattern composes a specific sign or character (*ji*) of its own suchness. Each *monji* is therefore a sign or letter unto itself that is wholly unique or distinct from all other image-words in Dainichi's universal palace. As Kūkai asserts in the *Ten Stages of Mind*, "All things of the world, manifesting themselves in all sorts of color, shape and modes... are letters, which show their distinctive forms as the very emptiness free of forms. These are the letters that constitute the cosmic body of the *dharmakāya*, which is his mandala."[18] As the summary in the *Shōji jissōgi* further explains:

> The five elements [of earth, water, fire, air and space] have sounds
> The ten realms [i.e., the six realms of samsara and the four Buddha realms] have words
> The six worldly objects [of sense] are *monji*
> The *dharmakāya* is their true reality.[19]

In this passage Kūkai equates all the elements, existential realms, and sense objects contained within Dainichi's universal body with his enlightened speech. Kūkai further stresses that these *monji* are not signifiers, but rather nothing other than signs, manifestations or the "true reality" of the *dharmakāya* itself. The basic elements constituting sentient and insentient forms in all ten dimensions, as well as the six objects of sense (i.e., all the sights, sounds, smells, tastes, textures, and thoughts in the world) are nothing other than Dainchi's world-body of emptiness. Their very lack of fixed essence allows them to appear temporarily in the world such as they are. The enlightened person is one who can "read" the *monji* of the world; he or she can hear, see, taste, touch, and smell them all as empty and as therefore constituting the world-body of enlighten-ment. Although personified as Dainichi, this world-body of Buddhahood is not to be envisioned as any separate, transcendent deity, but rather as merely the personification of the true empty nature of the thing-words themselves. One can thus understand that *monji* are not merely man-made letters that mediate reality through arbitrary human language. They are not just symbols, referents, or signifiers to some displaced transcendent signified. Rather, for Kūkai, each and every thing is a sign of enlightenment, onself included.

In the *Catalogue,* Kūkai further elucidates that "The dharma is beyond speech but without speech it cannot be revealed. Suchness transcends forms, but without depending on forms it cannot be realized."[20] This double consideration of language and image on the ultimate and conventional levels not only reflects Kūkai's theory of *monji,* but it also informs his doctrine of *hōsshin seppō* or Dainchi incessantly preaching the dharma in and as the physical, verbal, and mental forms of the world.

Hōsshin seppō

Kūkai's unequivocal declaration that the dharma is both within and without linguistic form or visual format challenged the long-held beliefs of the Nara Buddhist establishment. This establishment adhered to a traditional scholastic view that the *dharmakāya* or Dainchi Buddha, as the cosmic embodiment of emptiness, was utterly beyond verbalization or conceptualization. For them, only the *nirmaṇakāya* or historical transformation body of Śākyamuni Buddha actively preached the dharma using the expedient means of words and forms, such as his famous flower sermon that silently enlightened the disciple Mahākāśyapa. In contrast to the exoteric Nara establishment that held that the *dharmakāya* is beyond form and words, however, Kūkai proposed that the *dharmakāya* itself transcends the distinction between words vs. silence, appearance vs. disappearance. Rather, "like a gem hidden in the ground" as the *Catalogue* versifies, the level of an individual's awareness determines whether it is seen or unseen.[21] For one who has gained this enlightened insight, one sees that Dainichi incessantly preaches the dharma through the empty forms and images of the world. In this vision of the universe, as mentioned in chapter 2, emptiness self-manifests as forms and forms self-dissolve into emptiness. Even plants, trees, and insentient entities disclose the dharma for Kūkai, a theme that Dōgen will later take up and formally call *mujō seppō* or the insentient preaching of the dharma.

In his own historical context, however, Kūkai's worldview was radical. He first addresses the topic by rhetorically positing a mock debate between exoteric and esoteric figures in *The Difference Between Exoteric and Esoteric Buddhism* (*Benkenmitsu nikkyōron*), written in 814 at the age of forty-one.[22] Kūkai argues that the *dharmakāya* embodies emptiness yet always and everywhere discloses itself as nothing other than physical, verbal, and mental forms. One's level of awakening merely determines whether one sees this or not. Kūkai claims that evidence for his argument already exists in exoteric sutras, but that scholastic clerics either ignore or misinterpret these scriptures to fit their own sectarian doctrines. To support his esoteric argument, he cites scriptural passages, such as "the *dharmakāya* Buddha preaches" from the *Laṅkāvatāra sūtra*[23] (Ch. *Leng-ch'ieh ching,* Jp. *Nyūryōgakyō*) or "the *dharmakāya* possesses exquisite form" from the *Mahāprajñāpāramitopadeśa* (Ch. *Ta-chih-tu lun,* Jp. *Daichidoron*).[24] He reiterates his message in the *Unjigi* three years later when he refutes the opinion that *dharmakāya* is without color, form, or voice. He clarifies that Dainichi's seed-syllable *A* indicates the unborn, but that it does not imply the complete negation of formal qualities. Rather, Dainichi's root mantra *A* embraces all forms as emptiness. "*A* is the mother of all sounds"[25] he writes, which by extension includes all letters and all forms of reality.

Kūkai also poetically articulates his notion of *hosshin seppō* in the *Collection of Verses Expounding Spiritual Essences* (*Henjō hakki seireishū*), also simply known as the *Seireishū*. These verses describe how the world explains and unfolds itself as a visual text of forms for its own reading and viewing pleasure. To borrow Mikkyō parlance, the *dharmakāya* is always and everywhere revealing itself as itself for its own enjoyment.

> Mountain-brushes and ocean-ink [write]
> Heaven and earth which contain the scriptures,
> Every point [in these character-things] contains the ten thousand forms,
> And even desires born from the six types of defilement are written texts.
> [Dainichi's] comings and goings echo like a bell in a valley
> A conversation so sharp it bends the tip of a blade.[26]

In this passage, mountains are likened to brushes that write out reality (i.e., heaven and earth) with the ink of oceans. These mountain-brushes and ink-oceans simultaneously write the world and are the world; they are self-inscribing agents and referents of the world-text. Heaven and earth, consequently, contain the sacred and secular texts of life (lit. sutras and registers [*keiseki*]). Kūkai here emphasizes that all the word-forms of the world coauthor one another's suchness in an essentially tautological process, since all the world (mountains and oceans) draws the entire world (heaven and earth) into being and writes all its own self-contained, self-referential truth (world-as-scripture). Furthermore, in keeping with Kegon's unobstructed worldview, every miniscule dot or point in every stroke-element of every one of these character-things contains all the other *monji* in the world. In this way Kūkai stresses that all forms are enfolded in, and can unfold from, language.[27]

As he reiterates in the *Precious Key to the Secret Treasury*, "Each mantra contains the ten thousand images of the universe."[28]

Kūkai's all-embracing vision in the *Seireishū* verse includes even one's deluded desires born from the six objects of sense (i.e., sight, hearing, smell, taste, touch, and thought). In true Mikkyō fashion, even deluded states and sensory desires can originally spell out emptiness to an awakened mind. As stated in the *Rishukyō* (Skt. *Adhyartha Śatrikā-prajñāpāramitā sūtra*), lust, desire, touch, sight, ecstasy, pride, solemnity, bright lights, bodily pleasure, voice, smell, taste, and all *dharmas* are originally pure (*seisei, shōjō*).

In the last lines of the *Seireishū* poem, Dainichi's cosmic movements resonate throughout the world like a bell in a valley, announcing his own suchness in a dynamic, self-echoing conversation that cuts through delusion like a knife. This book of life, therefore, is not only written but also proclaimed aloud with resounding truth. In this way, Kūkai reiterates the refrain that all things constantly express their innate enlightenment in and as Dainichi's empty body of interfusing, interresonating *monji*.

Finally, this same confluence of self-expressive sights and sounds is taken one step further in Kūkai's fascicle on *The Secret Treasury* (*Hizōki*). Here he sets up a triad between the sights and sounds of reality, their direct re-presentation as the myriad deities of the mandala, and their direct re-presentation in the mirror of the perceiving mind. Ultimately, all three versions of these seen and heard *monji* are coequal in the unobstructed space of emptiness. He writes:

> Practitioners must therefore understand that all the objects of their sight are the all-permeating body [of the Dharmakāya]. All the sounds they hear are dhāraṇīs, the voices of the [Dharmakāya] Buddha's preaching of Dharma.... The practitioner's mind that understands this principle underlying the sights and sounds of the world is the reality that is the divinities of the maṇḍala. The reality is the divinities; the divinities, the practitioners' own minds.[29]

Thus, for Kūkai, Buddhist truth incessantly reveals itself either as material or immaterial form, but it is never without form. Dainichi, the Great Sun Buddha who personifies the universal illumination of the *dharmakāya*, in a sense represents the overarching principle of forms' original enlightenment, but it is never separate from forms themselves—ourselves included. When abstracted from concrete beings, it is too big to depict even with "the earth as ink and Mount Sumeru as brush" as he versifies in the *Unjigi*.[30]

However, this stance does not negate the fact that emptiness as personified by Dainichi actively and continually constructs a universal palace of suchness by disclosing itself as *monji* in a blissful, never-ending monologue of self-expression.

Calligraphy as Monji

Kūkai's overarching concern for phonetic, semantic, and ontic relationships amongst forms is fully explored in his *Shōji jissōgi* essay on the sounds (*shō*) of pattern-letters (*ji*) and their real world referents (*jissō*). However, if one departs from such doctrinal tracts and instead looks to Kūkai's calligraphic works, one begins to appreciate the expressive value of his *monji* word-imagery. One begins to see that Kūkai considers the shape of the character itself to be but another unobstructed form of the *dharmakāya's* body, and its pronunciation but another unobstructed expression of Dainichi's speech. In this way, marrying the doctrinal insights from religious studies with the expertise of art history and literary studies may further amplify our previous understanding of Kūkai's view of imagery. For him, words *are* pictorial forms; objects of vision *are* texts, and texts are equally objects of vision.

It should be noted at the outset that Kūkai's roles as linguist, calligrapher, court poet, and literary ambassador were unparalleled in an age when such accomplishments were the hallmark of erudition and style. When Emperor Saga (786–842) appointed Kūkai to the Ministry of Secretarial Affairs (*Nakatsukasa shō*) in 819, Kūkai compiled a treatise on the rules and conventions of classical Chinese poetry called *The Secret City of the Mirror of Writing* (*Bunkyō hifuron*). This was later condensed into *The Essentials of Poetry and Prose* (*Bumpitsu ganshinshō*). In terms of poetry's related calligraphic arts, Kūkai is also esteemed as one of the three great brushes of the Heian period along with Emperor Saga and Tachibana Hayanari (782–844). Kūkai has been mistakenly credited with formulating the cursive *hiragana* syllabary, which probably traces its origins to the seventh-century Asuka period, but he is responsible for writing one of the first dictionaries in Japan. He compiled and edited the *Dictionary of Ten- and Rei-Style Letters* (*Tenrei banshō myōgi;* alt. *meigi*) in his fifties, providing both ways of writing seal-style and square-style characters, as well as furnishing the pronunciations and meanings of each term.[31] Kūkai also resuscitated in Japan one particularly decorative style of Chinese calligraphy that based its fanciful designs on the standardized *ten* and *rei* ways of rendering ideographs. This *zattai-sho* style of calligraphy was a form of writing that was extremely popular at the T'ang dynasty court that adds cursive flourishes and finials to each stroke. Figure 3.1, for example, is a tenth-century copy of Kūkai's 825 preface and inscription commemorating the completion of Lake Masuda in Yamato Province (*Yamatokuni masudaike himei narabinijo*). These title characters appear to the extreme right of the scroll, embellished with Kūkai's *zattai* variations. The rest of the text commemorates the gifts of water to all sentient beings who benefit from it:

> Mandarin ducks and snipe sport on the waters, singing. The long-lived black crane and the snow goose vie with each other in dancing playfully at the water's edge.... When one man has joy, the myriad people put their faith in him. They dance and skip, slap their bellies, and, clapping their hands and stamping their feet, shout "Long live" and so forget their labors.[32]

Instead of writing in standard scripts, such as the *ten* and *rei* seal and square styles, however, or in the semicursive *gyōsho* or cursive grass *sōsho* styles, most of the characters in this poetic document exhibit the combined *zattai* style, though the document does also exhibit some characters written in the contemporary T'ang dynasty style of *sokuten* calligraphy.[33] All of these styles indicate that for Kūkai, the visuality of language and the meaning of images are inseparable.

Early examples of *zattai-sho* had already entered into the Nara court in Japan earlier in the eighth century along with many other kinds of script, but Kūkai helped to update and popularize it at the Heian court. The Shōsōin

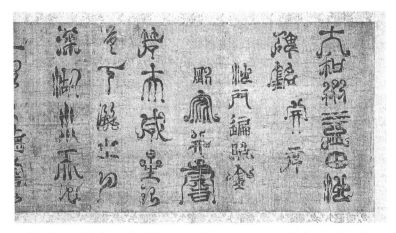

Figure 3.1. *Yamatokuni masudaike himei narabinijo* with *zattai-sho* decorative calligraphy, Kōyasan Reihōkan. Used with permission.

collection of Emperor Shōmu (r. 724–749) for example, housed his wife Empress Kōmyō's (701–760) collection of one hundred folding screens of Chinese aphorisms rendered in *zattai-sho* variations above standard characters. Extraordinarily, on three of these screens, the characters are covered with the feathers of the Japanese copper pheasant.[34] This aviary reference calls to mind another calligraphic form called the *hihaku* flying white script. Also called the *hake* brush-style script, the finial strokes of *hihaku* characters wave like banners in the wind as if flying off the white paper or silk. Examples of the *hihaku* style can be seen on the portraits of the seven esoteric patriarchs at Tōji, Kyoto. The images of five Mikkyō patriarchs (Śubhākarsiṃha, Amoghavajra, Vajrabodhi, I-hsing, and Hui-kuo) were painted and inscribed with the flying white script in China in 805 and imported to Japan by Kūkai in 806. The matching inscribed portraits of Nāgārjuna and Nāgabodhi are ascribed to Kūkai c. 821. Figure 3.2 depicts the patriarch Nāgabodhi. The pairing of text and image in this picture demonstrates yet again that writing portraits and imaging inscriptions are symbiotic operations for Kūkai. One may read the iconography of each patriarch's pose, their mudras, their robes, and their water pitchers signifying the direct transmission of esoteric teachings from one vessel to another,

Figure 3.2. Nāgabodhi Portrait and Inscription by Kūkai, Tōji Temple, Kyoto c. 821. Courtesy Benrido.

just as one may aesthetically appreciate the calligraphic qualities of the *hihaku* rendering of the Siddham letters surrounding each image.

One final example of *monji* word-art in whimsical *hihaku* script is depicted in figures 3.3a-c. These show three extant examples of an original series of *Ten Factors of Existence*, also known as the *Ten Examples of Suchness* (*jūnyoze*).[35] This tenfold list first appears in the *Lotus Sūtra,* and characterizes the world in terms of form, nature, substance, power, activities, primary causes, environmental causes, effects, rewards and retributions, and the totality of the above nine factors.[36] The three surviving images artfully render the Chinese characters for forms, activities, and substance. These three calligraphic images are undated and unsigned, though scholars attribute them to Kūkai due to their mastery and provenance. They continued to exist into the modern period at Jingoji, Kūkai's first temple on Mount Takao in Kyoto, but exist today only as photographs. In the late nineteenth century, Emperor Meiji and the Minister of Education Machida Hisanari (1838–1897) saw them in 1872, remarking how rare and "unique" (*mezurashii*) they were. After being photographed and returned to Jingōji, however, they were soon reported stolen. This caused great public outcry, which allegedly prompted the nervous thieves to then destroy the images by fire.[37] Despite their uncertain attribution, they are noteworthy for their explicit illustration of Kūkai's views regarding the intimate relationship amongst sound, written letter, and the image of reality. They are therefore included here for consideration.

(a)   (b)   (c)

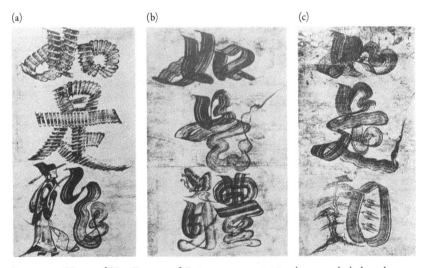

Figure 3.3. Three of Ten Factors of Existence. a. activities (nyoze-saku), b. substance (nyoze-tai), and c. form (nyoze-sō) Undated, whereabouts unknown. (*Kōbōdaishi ten*, unpaginated).

The images themselves are brushed with *hinoki* cypress bark instead of the more common animal hair brushes, and they fully exploit the expressive qualities of the medium. The first two characters for *nyoze* or suchness, for example, are rendered with staccato, punctuated rhythms or flowing, liquid lines. They visually convey the reverberation and phonic power of the word for thusness itself; as if the mantric energy of the sound of suchness is chanted aloud here in graphic form.[38] Furthermore, the calligrapher artfully writes the first two characters for suchness (*nyoze*), but alters the radical of the third character significantly to show the factor of existence such as it actually is. In 3.3a, the character for the verb "to make" or "to do" (*saku* 作) indicates the fifth factor of existence "activities," but the calligrapher does not write the standard stylized radical for person. Rather, he draws an actual cap-wearing, baton-wielding Confucian gentleman in the left-hand radical, then completes the character with the swirling flights of the *hihaku* flying white script. In figure 3.3b, the ancient character for "body" (*tai* 體) indicates the third factor of existence "substance," but the presence of an actual butterfly in the character visually communicates the impermanence of such substances, just as a butterfly's body is but the result of the chrysalis' transformation. In figure 3.3c, the word for "mark" or "aspect" (*sō* 相) indicates the first factor of existence "form," but it is not written with the standard radical for tree. Rather, the calligrapher draws an actual tree, then populates it with birds by using imaginative strokes instead of straight lines in the right-hand element of the character. The representational figures in these examples, like the staggered setting down of the bark-brush in the *nyoze-saku* example, show a more intimate and direct correspondence between sound, written letter, and the actual forms of reality that they embody. As a result, the viewer comes to understand that this calligraphy does not merely symbolize, but rather procreates a new form of reality, based on reality. It is a meditation on *monji* (images, reality, words, sounds) made with *monji* (cypress bark, paper, ideas, hands) that makes new *monji* (calligraphic illustrations, new thusnesses, new scripts). This reciprocity of text and image, and the transformation of infinitely recycling, inspiring, feedback-looping *monji* reinforces the notion of Dainichi's continuous preaching of the dharma.

Some Monji Are More Dainichi Than Others: *Ajikan and the Two-World Mandalas*

Kūkai's calligraphic works thus can be seen as directly expressing the eternal and ever-present dharma in both form and content, just like all other *monji* in the world. To paraphrase George Orwell, however, some *monji* are more equal than others. For Kūkai, everything is Dainichi, but some esoteric things are more Dainichi than others.

This kind of logic is not at all surprising when considered in light of Kūkai's early mountaineering practices. Theoretically speaking, idealized constructions of Japan's indigenous worldview considers all of nature to be sacred, yet historically and in actual practice only individual mountains, specific trees, or selected rock formations are singled out and revered as *kami*. They are specifically identified as somehow being uniquely endowed with more sacred presence than others. This provides the rationale for activities such as purification, pilgrimage, mountain climbing, and other austerities, for one automatically participates in the divine nature of *kami* when in proximity to their sacred sites. Likewise, in Kūkai's esoteric Buddhism, in principle all *monji* including oneself have the same enlightened nature, yet they differ according to the potency, intensity, and level of realization of that innate potential. When in proximity to the *monji* of the Two World mandalas or other esoteric objects, likewise, one automatically gets reconnected with and empowered by Dainichi's nature, which is one's own nature, only perfected. When speaking of everyday *monji* vis-à-vis esoteric artforms, therefore, it is not a question of kind, but of degree.

The *Ajikan* visualization is a case in point. The sacred Sanskrit syllable *A* illustrated in figure 3.4 immediately abbreviates, invokes, condenses, and

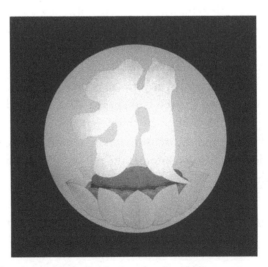

Figure 3.4. Ajikan disk. Sankrit syllable *A* rendered in Siddham script on a lotus base and moon disk. Photograph by the author.

conveys the concept of *anutpāda*, the unborn, which as mentioned previously is the definitive moniker for the *dharmakāya*. Kūkai advocates visualizing the letter *A* in order to train the adept to see one's self and one's world as enfolded in and unfolding from the calligraphic image-letter of Dainichi's suchness itself. Kūkai explains in *The Meaning of the Word Hūṃ* that this special esoteric *monji* symbolizes Dainichi as the source of all things, the first letter of the world's alphabet of forms, and the mantra which, like a lotus bud unfurling its petals, both contains and reveals all the other *monji* of the universe. Conversely and simultaneously, however, this *bīja* seed syllable can also function as a negative prefix. Like a full moon disk that is wholly illumined but empty of content, *A* can also indicate the mind that grasps the ultimate emptiness of oneself and one's world.[39] Taken together, therefore, the letter *A* indicates the middle path of unborn, uncreated nonorigination, that is, "the absence of the two extremes [of] being and non-being."[40]

In this visualization, Dainichi's calligraphic Siddham seed syllable *A* lies within a white moon disk rising up from a lotus base. In its most developed form dating to the Kamakura period, the *A* is first imagined in the practitioner's heart, before the eyes, and ultimately expanding throughout the entire *dharmadhātu*. At the peak of the meditation, the practitioner imagines and ideally experiences a state of *kaji* in which the self and world unite in the nondual, unobstructed, and open space of emptiness. The meditation ends with constricting the image-letter back down to its original size, and imagining the Buddha returning to his Pure Land and to his palace within the practitioner's own heart.[41] Kūkai partially explains and comments on this process in the tenth and final stage of mind of *The Precious Key to the Secret Treasury*:

> Visualize: a white lotus flower with eight petals,
> [above which is a fullmoon disk] the size of a forearm in diameter,
> [in which is] a radiant silvery letter *A*.
> Unite your *dhyāna* with *prajñā* in an adamantine binding;[42]
> Draw the quiescent *Prajñā* of the Tathagata in [your mind].
> If (Shingon adepts) gradually increase their competence in this meditation, they will finally be able to magnify it [the moon disk] until its circumference encompasses the entire universe and its magnitude becomes as inclusive as space. Being able to freely magnify or reduce it, they will surely come to be in possession of all-inclusive wisdom.... Indeed, the ordinary man's mind is like a lotus flower yet to open and the Enlightened One's Mind, like the full moon.[43]

The calligraphic word-art of the Siddham letter *A,* therefore, is not an everyday *monji.* Technically all *monji* are ontological self-expressions of Dainichi's emptiness/suchness with the capacity to enlighten. However, embodying, chanting, and visualizing this calligraphic condensation of Dainichi's body, speech, and mind is a particularly powerful soteriological agent that can effectively transform the initiate to possess "all-inclusive wisdom" or enlightenment. Elsewhere in the *Precious Key to the Secret Treasury,* Kūkai actually lays out the enlightenment process in terms of differing stages of *A*:

1. *A* stands for the enlightened mind (*bodhicitta*);
2. *Ā,* for practice to bring out enlightenment;
3. *Aṃ,* for realization of enlightenment;
4. *Aḥ,* for Nirvana;
5. *Āḥ,* for wisdom perfectly provided with skillful means.[44]

The word-art of the Siddham script, however, is not the only visible means to Shingon's enlightened end. Rather, the lotus and moon disk imagery in the *Ajikan* visualization borrows from the paradigmatic Two World mandalas, which likewise are considered to be especially empowering agents of enlightenment. Specifically, the lotus symbolizes potential enlightenment most fully expressed by the central Lotus Court in the Womb World mandala, and the moon disk symbolizes perfected enlightenment most fully expressed in the Diamond World mandala's many courts.

Everyday *monji,* therefore, are the primary carriers and constituents of the Buddha's enlightened and enlightening power, but this power can also be condensed and compacted into powerful corporal, scriptural, or pictorial formats. For example, relics were believed to possess supernatural capacities,[45] and some esoteric scriptures were held up as being super-concentrated forms of Dainichi's power.[46] However, Kūkai occasionally subordinates the importance of texts to the primacy of image. For example, Kūkai's 806 *Catalogue of Imported Items* states that the Two World mandalas are the best forms for condensing and presenting the deepest meaning of all the esoteric teachings. According to this text, Kūkai's master Hui-kuo initiated Kūkai into both the Womb and Diamond World mandalas before his death in 806, affirming that "the sutras and commentaries of the secret treasury of Shingon are so mysterious that they can only be transmitted through images (*zuga*)."[47] Earlier in the same text, Kūkai also clearly asserts that:

The Esoteric teachings are so profound and mysterious that they are difficult to record with quill and ink [that is, in writing]. Thus we resort to the expedient of diagrams and paintings to reveal them to the unenlightened. The various postures and mudrā [depicted in the mandalas] emerge from [the Buddha's] great compassion; with a single glance [at them] one becomes a Buddha.[48] The secrets of the sutras and commentaries are recorded in a general way in diagrams and images, and the essentials of the Esoteric teachings are actually set forth therein. Should these be discarded there will be difficulty in transmitting and receiving the dharma, for they are none other than the foundation of the ocean-like assembly [of enlightened ones].[49]

In this oft-quoted passage, there is a presupposition that these two pictures are worth a thousand words. They directly reveal Dainichi's assemblies of aspect-deities in all their relationality, functionality, and enlightening ability instead of describing them, their attributes, and their significances in words. This is not merely a question of didactic art making rarefied doctrines accessible to illiterate, unenlightened masses, though it certainly did help to do this. Rather, on a more profound level, Kūkai genuinely argues here that the depth of Mikkyō doctrines cannot be expressed fully in writing, but that their mysterious secret *power* is best conveyed through diagrams and images. These mandalas are so powerful, he claims, that one glance at them can enlighten one immediately. They are so indispensable, by extension, that he claims that the true dharma would be lost if the images were lost. Consequently, in this case, Kūkai actually privileges the supremacy of vision over language and argues that images can signify and lead to enlightenment even better than scriptures can. He believes that the Two World mandalas are better than texts at mirroring and condensing the entirety, truth, and power of the *dharmakāya* as personified by Dainichi Buddha in all his aspects. For this reason, after he provides a typically nondual expression of the dharma's visible and invisible nature, he concludes the *Catalogue* with a prayer that squarely reveals his belief in the efficacy of the visible mandalas:

> The Dharma knows neither appearing nor concealing;
> Depending on the individual it becomes manifest or hidden
> Like a gem hidden in the ground difficult to obtain.
> If a man attains it he will open his spiritual eyes.
> … May each and all be freed from their anxieties
> By listening to the teaching and by seeing the mandalas.[50]

The *Catalogue* represents Kūkai's early and clearly self-interested claims for the power and efficacy of his newly imported mandalas, but Kūkai did also earnestly continue to stress the primacy of image over text throughout his life. In particular, he emphasizes their indispensable role in ritual practice. In late 834, only a few months before his death in the spring of 835, Kūkai requested imperial permission to inaugurate a new Buddhist state-protecting ritual at the start of the New Year. He proposed a Latter Seven-Day Rite (*Goshichinichi mishuhō*), known simply as the Mishuhō, that would provide a Buddhist complement to other ceremonies and celebrations that were held during the first week of the year. For this new esoteric Buddhist ceremony, Kūkai insisted on the necessity of proper imagery. In his letter to Emperor Ninmei (833–850), Kūkai reasoned that the old Nara establishment's state-protecting *Golden Light Sūtra*[51] had long been chanted ritually and explained during the annual Misae sermon, but that

> it is [merely] read and its meaning is emptily discussed. Images are not drawn, and an [esoteric] altar is not established nor is a ritual conducted. Although lectures on the nectar [of practice] are heard, its sublime taste is probably not acquired.[52]

In this passage, Kūkai implies that the Misae's scriptural chanting and analytical lectures insufficiently describe the sweet taste of the dharma, but that the Mishuhō's full enactment of the ritual with painted images and proper esoteric altar arrangements allow one to actually taste and be nourished by the nectar of the sutra's content. He explains earlier in the same letter by means of medical analogy that extracting the sutra's essence and explaining it to the ill does not cure them of their disease-delusions. Only properly combining medicines (i.e., arranging specific combinations of image-ingredients appropriate to the delusion) and actually ingesting the cure (i.e., viewing and performing rituals before these visual medicines) will actually eliminate the problem and preserve life, or in this context, protect the state.[53] Consequently, in this case, images assume not only a theoretical, but also a ritual-functional priority over words. For Kūkai, the state-protecting powers suggested in the sutra can only be fully mobilized in image-filled ritual; for him only visible images and ritual performance can immediately make present the potency and protection of esoteric forces. Specifically, the Mishuhō rites in the newly built Shingon'in sanctuary would telescope the macrocosmic structures and powers of Dainichi's universal palace into increasingly condensed, microcosmic spaces. Dainichi's universal palace would first be replicated by the Heian Imperial Palace, which, like a Russian doll, would contain the ritual Shingon'in hall protected by wrathful deities, the Two World mandala-palace paintings, two

Figure 3.5. Mandala installation and altar arrangements for the Mishuhō, Shingon'in chapel of the Heian Imperial Palace. Detail of Sumiyoshi Jokei's seventeenth-century copy of Tokiwa Mitsunaga's late twelfth-century *Handscroll of Annual Ceremonies* (*Nenjū gyōgi emaki*). Private collection, used with permission.

ritual altars featuring Dainichi's symbolic *gorintō* reliquary, and within this, the Buddha's relics themselves. This ultracondensed and empowered esoteric mini-universe would replicate the *dharmadhātu* on earth and manipulate Dainichi Buddha's enlightened powers for the protection of the state as a whole. As a result, in response to Kūkai's request, Emperor Ninmei sponsors the ritual and in 835 constructs the Shingon'in chapel for the Latter Seven-Day Rite within the Imperial Palace grounds. It is only the third Buddhist temple allowed in the new capital after Tōji and Saiji.

One cannot be certain of Kūkai's original iconographic arrangement for the Mishuhō rite, but an undated anonymous diary describing the ritual in 921, another anonymous diary dated 1142, and a copy of a late twelfth-century hand scroll illustration of the Shingon'in provide the earliest clues.[54] According to these sources, the Two World mandalas are suspended flush against the side walls of the Shingon'in with the Womb World mandala on the viewer's right confronting the Diamond World mandala directly across the hall to the left (fig. 3.5). Two altar platforms are placed on the floor directly below each mandala painting; each altar accommodates the mandalic arrangement of vajras, bells, offertory cups, vases, and other ritual paraphernalia.[55] The focus of the Mishuhō state-protecting rites shifts between these two altars every year, as a miniature five-element stupa (*gorintō*) containing precious relics alternates between the two mandalic altars each year. This stupa represents the samaya or symbolic form of Dainichi and contains the relics that Kūkai supposedly inherited from his master Hui-kuo, though they miraculously self-multiplied and were distributed to important power brokers every year to help cement church-state relations throughout the medieval period.[56] Moreover, for the Mishuhō rite, five distinctive paintings of the wrathful five wisdom kings (Jp. *godaimyōō*, Skt. *vidyarājā*) are arranged along the far back wall of the Shingon'in with small offertory stands before each one. Their function is similar to that of the four deva kings mentioned in the *Golden Light Sūtra,* who vow to protect the four corners of the land and its center. Surrounding this is an outer peripheral enclosure dedicated to ensuring the proper functioning of the Shingon-in's symbolic world. Rites for the purification, prosperity, and fertility of the land are performed in this outer corridor before two goma fire altars and altars to Shintō *kami* and the fertility god Kanjiten (Skt. Gaṇapati, also associated with Ganesha). In addition, paintings of the twelve generals of the zodiac hang along the right-hand wall of the hall's outer enclosure. These personifications of the twelve months figure in the *Golden Light Sūtra* to regulate the seasons and hence agricultural prosperity of the land. In a sense, therefore, the twelve generals represent another expression of spatialized time as theorized in chapter 2. Similar to the one thousand buddhas of past, present, and future who wrap around the central hall of the Diamond World mandala (chap. 2, fig. 2.5), these twelve generals appear around the idealized mini-cosmos of the Shingon'in inner sanctuary. Their peripheral position thus indicates that their militant command of time is subordinate to but nevertheless a part of Emperor Dainichi's smooth government of the world-palace.[57]

The Form of Emptiness: Imperial Palace-Cities and the Metaphor of the Mandala

As suggested above, the Two World mandalas are two-dimensional blueprints for three-dimensional palaces and other perfect religio-political spaces. The architectural floorplans of the mandalas visually invoke real and ideal models for Chinese imperial palaces and cities, as well as the state, the world, and the universe in general. This "superscription of symbols"[58] likewise associates Dainichi Buddha with real and ideal emperors who reside in and govern over these micro-macrocosmic spaces. It is therefore significant that Kūkai employed the Two World mandalas in designing an imperially sponsored, state-protecting ritual like the Mishuhō, for the motif of the mandala-palace symbolizes the perfect state and the emperor's sovereign rule over it. Manipulating Dainichi's supercondensed body forms, speech forms, and art forms on the microcosmic level necessarily meant manipulating them on the macrocosmic level as well. It is for these protective associations that Kūkai claimed in the *Catalogue* that the Two World mandala paintings were "as useful to the nation as walls are to a city."[59]

The mandalas themselves are based on two key sutras, though their visual content exceeds the scriptural descriptions found in the Diamond World's *Kongōchōkyō* and the Womb World's *Dainichikyō*.[60] Moreover, the original designer of the mandalas is unknown, although some credit Hui-kuo with visually mapping out and illustrating their two source sutras since he was initiated into both lineages. Where might the original graphic artist derive his architectural inspiration from?

Art historian Elizabeth ten Grotenhuis has argued that both mandalas reflect ideal Chinese notions of sacred and imperial space. The nine mini-mandalas of the Diamond World mandala, for example, mimic the 3 x 3 grid of the ideal centralized Emperor's City (*Wang cheng*) as described in *The Rites of Zhou* (Ch. *Zhou li*). However, it also reflects the real historical changes in Chang'an's palace city that shifted its location to the north of center during the T'ang dynasty. The result is that the Diamond World mandala's doctrinal focus may theoretically lie in the central Perfected Body Hall of the tick-tac-toe grid, but its visual focus undoubtedly rises to the top center square, where the imperially clad Dainichi sits regally in a single white moon disk.[61] Moreover, as I have discussed elsewhere, the Womb World evokes the capital-I-shaped *gong* plans of early Chinese ancestral halls, as well as the architectural elements of typical *ssu-he yüan* courtyard dwellings.[62] They both exhibit five entrance gates and an entrance hall associated with the family's ancestral progenitrix, akin to the Womb World's Buddha-mother. The courtyard dwelling also exhibits children's quarters on either side of the main courtyard, much like the Vajra and Lotus bodhisattvas on either side of the Lotus Court, and it locates the men's quarters in the back, much like where the mandala's wrathful wisdom kings reside. In addition, Northern Wei-style flaming triangle rooftop finials and even Chinese botanical features can be discerned when the mandala is analyzed in terms of architectural components. Consequently, I suggest that the anonymous designer of the Two World mandalas may have borrowed familiar Chinese tropes for perfect official and domestic spaces in order to situate and amplify the scriptural descriptions of deities.

These discussions center around the original design of the mandalas in China, but their explicit architectural associations were also further extended when Kūkai brought them back to Japan. To date, no conclusive evidence suggests that the pair of paintings were ever displayed together in China, but they were displayed together in Japan for the Mishuhō state-protecting

rites at least from the tenth-century onward. This double-display strategy, which is the hallmark of Japanese Mikkyō, visually and conceptually
mirrors the double-palace-cities of early eighth-century Japanese capitals.
Archaeological excavations of matching palaces at Heijō (or Nara 710–784),
Nagaoka (784–794), and Heian (794–1192) reveal that the Japanese faith-
fully replicated China's ideal bicameral symmetry to the letter, even though
the original continental palaces of Han and T'ang dynasty Ch'ang-an themselves deviated significantly from their own ideal plans.[63] Displaying the Two
World mandalas together in a Japanese ritual hall therefore microcosmically
replicated the Chinese ideal imperial city compound as it was understood
and actually built in Japan. However, unlike these Sino-Japanese capital cities
where the palaces are oriented to the south, the Womb and Diamond World
mandala-palaces are oriented to the east and west, respectively, to indicate the
solar associations of Dainichi's illuminating and illuminated light. Displaying
them together stresses the nonduality of these two light-filled mansions of
Dainichi's universal palace.

The architectural metaphor of the world-as-palace, and the imperial associations that this palatial universe is ruled by a sun king Dainichi who illu-
mines all equally, are made explicit in texts such as the *Kongōchōkyō* and the
Ninnōkyō.[64] However, Kūkai further amplifies the architectural metaphor
of Dainichi's universal palace in texts such as the *Abhiṣeka of the Abdicated
Emperor Heizei (Heizei tennō kanjōmon)*.[65] In this text, written for Emperor
Heizei's (r. 806–809) esoteric initiation in 822, Kūkai explains that Dainichi
and his retinue of buddhas and bodhisattvas eternally preach the secret treasury of *mantrayāna* while residing in two palaces. Dainichi either preaches
from his universal palace (*hokkaigū*) or from the palace of Samantabhadra's
mind (*fugen shinden*).[66] Dainichi's universal palace is primarily to be understood as the Diamond World (Ch. *Chin-kang fa-chieh-kung*, Jp. *kongō
hokkaigū*), and Samantabhadra's mind-palace is to be seen as the Womb
World, since Samantabhadra is associated with practice and is "symbolic of
the intrinsic potential for enlightenment all beings possess."[67] In Kūkai's writings, however, Samantabhadra's second edifice of enlightened mind is only
rarely mentioned. Why mention it here?

It is possible that Kūkai tailored his sermon to suit his imperial audience
and that he likened Dainichi's palatial movements to the retired emperor
Heizei, who also built and changed residences as befitting any virtuous world
ruler (*cakravartin*). In addition, however, a closer look at Kūkai's word choice
reveals an even deeper consonance between Heizei's real and Dainichi's ideal
imperial structures. Dainichi's *hokkaigū* indicates Chinese palace architecture

of substantial scale, whereas Samantabhadra's *shinden* (心殿) mind-palace is a homonym for *shinden* (寝殿), a Japanese type of royal or aristocratic mansion that is less opulent but characterized by a pleasing single-storied bilateral symmetry. During Heizei's rule from 806–809, Heian was still a relatively new capital, having been established only twelve years earlier in 794. The Imperial Palace was therefore still under construction during Heizei's reign, but by 805 it had completed both a Chinese style Daigokuden Great Audience Hall, as well as several more intimate *shinden* style buildings in the Dairi Inner Palace compound where the emperor actually resided. Kūkai therefore, seems to have deliberately referenced existing palace buildings familiar to Heizei when he attempts to spatialize Dainichi's enlightened world-rule.

On another level, the verbal delivery of this speech for Heizei's initiation could also have allowed for another double entendre of homonyms. Samantabhadra's mind-palace (*shinden* 心殿) could also be understood to mean his new-palace (*shinden* 新殿). This interpretation would simultaneously reference not only the two new kinds of residential and official architectures in Heizei's capital, but also refer to the two new copies of the mandalas that Kūkai likely used for Heizei's initiation in 822. Just two years previously in 820, Kūkai had twenty-six of his imported paintings copied at Takaosanji because, as he explained in his petition to Emperor Saga (809–823), "the images were [already] about to disappear" from the torn, stained silk after only fourteen years of use, mostly because of initiation ceremonies like Heizei's.[68]

These multivalent architectural associations, therefore, could conceivably conflate Dainichi's universal palace and Samantabhadra's mind-palace with Emperor Heizei's newly constructed official and residential palaces in the capital and Kūkai's newly copied Diamond World and Womb World mandalas in the initiation hall. This would automatically suggest to Heizei that although he was retired, he still resembled Dainichi as an ever-present, powerful ruler who resides in newly constructed double-palace compounds in both real and ideal space. The actual coronation sequence that is performed during the ceremony would merely cement those associations through ritual enactment.

Intericonicity

Mikkyō's figural code of deities, each with its own identifying mudra, attribute, and adornment, constitutes an alphabet of forms or a musical scale of notes, which can be rearranged in infinite permutations to compose different iconographic expressions of enlightenment. Just as the world of *monji* spell out constantly changing realities through infinitely recombinant pattern-letters, so too do the components of the Two World mandalas spell out new expressions of enlightenment through infinitely recombinant icono-graphies. Although all the painted figures in the mandala are fixed, individual figures can be borrowed and combined with others in new ways for doctrinal and ritual effect. I call this visual vocabulary of forms and its ability to regroup and imply other esoteric figures or ideas "intericonicity." It is indebted to the postmodern, literary-critical discourse of intertextuality, which argues that coauthored, linked narratives mutually transform one another.[69] It will be contrasted with Dōgen's sense of "intertemporality" in the next chapter.

Briefly defined, intericonicity should be understood to mean the citation of iconic elements within another iconic context to produce a metonymic effect of layered interresonance. This phenomenon of visual intertextuality has already been observed between and within the two mandalas themselves: the five wisdom buddhas in each of the Two World mandalas correspond to one another (chap. 2, fig. 2.11), and the first six halls of the Diamond World itself reiterate and condense the content of the central *jōjinne* Perfected Body Assembly Hall in varying symbolic and metynomic arrangements (Chap. 2, fig. 2.9). This section will examine the visual culture of two main Shingon temples that directly cite the Two World mandalas in innovative, intericonic ways.

The ninth-century sculpted mandala of Tōji temple in Kyoto provides a case in point. Kūkai became head of Tōji in 823, and obtained permission to build a Kōdō lecture hall there in 825. In this novel arrangement, Kūkai composes a unique combination of Diamond and Womb World figures. Bogel 2009 convincingly argues that from at least 922 it was understood as a Ninnōkyō mandala, but the primary statues at Tōji, with the exception of Gundari, are taken from the reservoir alphabet of figures in the Diamond and Womb World mandalas.[70] It is an example of esoteric intericonicity since its overall layout imparts the Buddhist message of nondualism by mixing and matching individual figures from the Two World mandalas. In so doing, it communicates the interchangeability and mutual implication of Dainichi's unobstructed aspects.

Figure 3.6 demonstrates that the usual associations and locations of Diamond and Womb World deities are switched at Tōji. Specifically, in most Shingon temples, the Diamond World mandala usually is hung to the viewer's left, but here at Tōji, sculpted versions of the Diamond World's five great bodhisattvas appear to the viewer's right.[71] Conversely, the Womb World

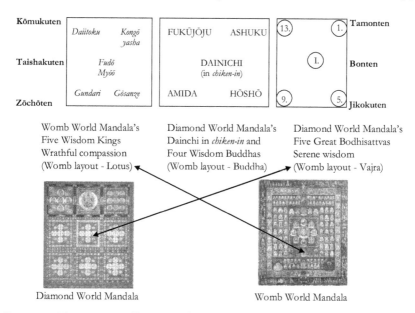

Figure 3.6. Tōji Lecture Hall Iconographic Program c. 825.

mandala is usually hung to the viewer's right, but at Tōji sculpted versions of the Womb World's five wisdom kings appear to the viewer's left.[72] Moreover, the Diamond World is usually associated with strong, vajra-wielding deities, but at Tōji the five great bodhisattvas exhibit only the serenest forms of Dainichi's adamantine wisdom. The Womb World, likewise, is often associated with soft, beneficent forms of Dainichi's compassionate method, but here the five wisdom kings exhibit only the most wrathful aspects of this compassion.

Finally, on a more general level of analysis, Tōji's central Dainichi group of Buddha sculptures clearly replicate Diamond World iconography.[73] However, the flanking sculptural groups of bodhisattvas representing compassion on the left and wisdom on the right clearly invoke the Womb World's layout for Lotus and Vajra families. As a result, even as the viewer regards the central Dainichi group of Diamond World Buddhas, the Womb World mandala's central Buddha section is invoked. To one attuned to the usual iconographic cues of the paradigmatic mandalas, reading the reconfigurations of sculpted deities at Tōji means seeing the metonymy at work and sensing the interresonance of all of Dainichi's aspects. In this way, the esoteric message of the nondualism of *richi funi* is conveyed in and as the sacred space of the lecture hall.

Another example of this interchangeable, intericonic symbol system outlined in the mandalas can be found today at Kongōbuji, Shingon's main mountain monastery at Kōyasan in Wakayama prefecture (figs. 3.7a-d). The eastern precinct of the present-day *garan* temple complex is dominated by a distinctive *tahōtō* "many-jeweled-pagoda" that is commonly referred to as the fundamental great pagoda or *konpon daitō* (fig. 3.7b). It represents the samaya or symbolic form of Dainichi, whose distinctive *gorintō* construction symbolically indicates the five elements. It combines a square earth base with a circular water dome, triangular fire roof, nine air rings, and a cintamani jewel radiating through space. It was first built in 837, burned in 994, and was succeeded by four more pagoda reconstructions until the present rebuild dating from 1937. It is unclear when exactly the interior iconography of this stupa began to combine Womb and Diamond elements, but a fascinating intericonic regrouping is evident here in the present day (fig. 3.7d).

Originally, Kūkai envisioned the eastern pagoda to be one of a pair of stupas that would separately enshrine Womb and Diamond World Dainichis to the east and west of the temple complex, respectively (figs. 3.7 a, b). As Kūkai wrote in a fundraising letter dated 823, he wished to "establish at

Figure 3.7. (a) Kongōbuji West Pagoda circa 1835, 27 meters high, 9 meters wide on each side (Courtesy Kongōbūji, Kōyasan); (b) Kongōbuji East *konpon daitō* circa 1937, 48.5 meters high, 23.5 meters wide on each side (Photograph by the author). (*Continued*)

(c)

(d)

Figure 3.7. (c) Kongōbuji West Pagoda: Interior Diamond Dainichi circa 887, surrounded by wisdom buddhas circa nineteenth century (Courtesy Reihōkan, Kōyasan. Used with permission); (d) Kongōbuji East *konpon daitō*: Interior Womb Dainichi surrounded by Diamond World buddhas, bodhisattvas circa 1942 (Courtesy Kongōbūji, Kōyasan).

Kongōbuji two stūpas that represent Vairocana as the Essential Nature of the Dharmadhātu [i.e., as depicted in] the two mandalas of the Womb and Vajra realms."[74] He had started building the eastern pagoda during his lifetime, harvesting the timber for the central pillar in 819, but Kūkai's double vision was only actualized posthumously in 887 when Emperor Kōkō (884–887) ordered Kūkai's disciple Shinzen Daitoku (804–891) to build the western pagoda according to his master's plans.[75] This second western pagoda for a Diamond World Dainichi was reconstructed in 1127, repaired in 1240, and destroyed by fire in 1377 (fig. 3.7a).[76] It appears in the bottom register of a Kūkai portrait dated to the fourteenth century,[77] but does not appear again in any maps or drawings of the *garan* owned by Kongōbuji until the late Edo period. After the fire of 1377, therefore, the western pagoda seems to have languished for centuries until the present rebuild dated 1835. Its central *chiken-in* Dainichi accordingly dates from c. 887, but its four surrounding wisdom buddhas date from the nineteenth century (fig. 3.7c).[78]

Consequently, sometime between the late fourteenth and early nineteenth centuries, the one eastern stupa began to take over the function of both. Shingon clerics promoted a familiar Mikkyō discourse to explicate the exterior symbolism of the single-stupa *garan*, while the interior symbolism of the eastern tower iconographically collapsed both mandalas into its one sacred space (figs. 3.7d, 3.8).

Specifically, according to Mikkyō rhetoric, the exterior symbolism of Kōyasan's location replicates a jewel in the lotus, or the presence of Diamond mind in the Womblike matrix of the material realm. Specifically, a single *tahōtō* many-jeweled pagoda rises up within a ring of eight petal-like

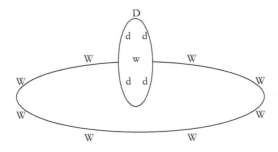

D= (exterior) Eastern Konpon Daitō pagoda
W=(exterior) 8 surrounding mountain peaks resembling 8 petals of the Womb World mandala
w= (interior) Central Womb World Dainichi statue in jō-in mudra
d= (interior) 4 surrounding Diamond Buddha statues (+16 Diamond World bodhisattvas painted on pillars)

Figure 3.8. Kōyasan Pagoda Exterior and Interior Symbolisms.

mountain peaks that are said to surround the temple complex. Converse to the exterior jewel-within-lotus symbolism, the interior of the great pagoda exhibits lotus-within-jewel symbolism. The interior iconographic program represents the seed of potential Buddhahood that lies at the heart of perfected wisdom in all its sculpted and painted aspects. Specifically, its interior iconography as it appears today symbolically surrounds a central sculpture of a Womb World Dainichi in *jō-in* with statues of the four Diamond World wisdom buddhas and paintings of the Diamond World's sixteen great bodhisattvas on supporting pillars (fig. 3.6d).[79] These present-day paintings were completed in 1942 by the famed Mikkyō-trained iconographer turned avant-garde artist Dōmoto Inshō (1891–1975) who records that he "reverently copied (*haisha*) every single figure on these pillar paintings with strong, brilliant colors, and determined their magnificent adornments (*shōgon*)" according to textual sources.[80] Thus, seen from the outside and the inside, the mixing and matching of Womb and Diamond World deities convey the esoteric message of nondualism.

At Kōyasan, therefore, the Diamond and Womb World imagery of jewel/vajra and lotus is thus manipulated in both directions. Kōyasan telescopes the external lotuslike ring of mountains into the one internal Womb World figure of Dainichi in *jō-in*, and it refracts the single exterior jewel-like *tahōtō* tower into Dainichi's interior four wisdom buddhas and sixteen great bodhisattvas. Condensing multiplicity down into metonymy and/or blowing apart singularity into refracted plurality is the hallmark of intericonicity. In the Kegon-influenced Shingon view, everything mutually implies everything else in the unobstructed space of the infinite *dharmakāya*. The same can be said of Dōgen's view of intertemporality, as singular *nikon* just-now moments and plural *kyōryaku* rangings are infinitely interchangeable. More of this will be said in the next chapter.

Nuancing Kūkai's Views: Deconstructing the Mandala

Kegon's infinitely iterating cosmology may make room for the explosion and manipulation of images in Shingon, but it should be recalled that such iconographic reconfigurations are empty of fixed essence. Lest one cling too closely to the intricacies of the mandalas' iconography or attach too much importance to deciphering the visual code of esoteric altar arrangements, Kūkai repeatedly reminds his readers to empty them of substance. In so doing, Kūkai consistently compels the Shingon adept to see the space between, within, and without the walls of the world. In this way, "Kūkai's deconstructive strategy is a path by which he constructs and reconstructs a concrete model of the cosmos."[81]

This results in a series of apparent contradictions within Kūkai's writings, though such contradictions usually resolve themselves when they are read with either a conventional or ultimate perspective in mind.[82] That is, from a conventional standpoint that focuses on the dependent-arising of forms in the world, Kūkai embraces esoteric imagery as the visible embodiment of the *dharmakāya* and argues for its unparalleled power to enlighten. From the ultimate perspective, however, Kūkai shifts his emphasis from soteriology to ontology as he focuses on the empty nature of these real, tangible forms of the *dharmakāya*. As he explains in the *Shōji jissōgi*, all objects of sight can be seen in either their conditioned or unconditioned aspects,[83] and as he explains in the *Catalogue*, suchness ultimately transcends forms but it cannot be realized without them. Only one's level of enlightenment determines whether this is discerned or not. This section will examine three representative examples that demonstrate Kūkai's facility in navigating between these two conventional and ultimate discourses when addressing the power of images.

First, Kūkai occasionally samples the anti-imagistic rhetoric of early Buddhism to remind adherents that esoteric images are ultimately essenceless. For example, he cautions his audience not to fixate or reify esoteric images too much:

> Full of strange things is the world of yoga in which manifold images appear.
> There is a moment when we are drawn into a luminous world of reality.
> Do not be proud of or deceived by it;
> Such a vision is yet provisional.
> Away with all images;
> The great samadhi of void is to be our companion.[84]

In his *Catalogue*, Kūkai claimed that the mandalas could enlighten in a single glance, yet here he considers the moment of perceiving Mikkyō's many luminous images to be only "provisional." Also in the *Catalogue*, Kūkai claimed that the entire dharma would vanish if the Two World mandalas were lost, yet here he urges that we do "away with all images." Certainly the promotional context of the *Catalogue* and his competition with Saichō color Kūkai's claims for the mandalas' efficacy. Beyond this, however, it is also important to acknowledge that Kūkai occasionally employs anti-imagistic rhetorical devices to exhibit the flexibility of mind required to embrace all dualities in true Mahāyāna fashion, both form and emptiness, speech and silence, seeing and seen, Diamond and Womb worlds.

Second, Kūkai's intermittent deconstructionist reminders are particularly salient given his tendency to spatialize the realm of enlightenment and use architectural metaphors in both his writings and in his practice. As argued at length above, both Kūkai's doctrinal treatises and his mandalic mise-en-scène for ritual activity reiterate the metaphor and replicate the model of Mahāvairocana's universal palace of suchness. However, in his more poetic moments, Kūkai does also occasionally deconstruct these architectures of enlightenment. In *Poems That Contemplate the Ten Images of Illusion* (*Jūyukan*) written in 827 at the age of fifty-four, Kūkai considers the insubstantiality of ten analogies for emptiness first mentioned in the *Dainichikyō*.[85] These are namely phantoms, heat waves, dreams, shadows in a mirror, Gandharva Castle, echoes, images of water moons, foam, flowers in the sky, and a whirling ring of fire.[86] Of particular note to the present discussion is his poem inspired by the image of Gandharva Castle, where the god Gandharva plays exquisite music to entertain the divine Indra in his heavenly palace. This poem serves to remind the reader to empty all real and imagined images of reality, even ones as seemingly solid and substantial as castles.[87] Kūkai versifies:

> Seeing a solemn castle over the sea
> Thronged with horses and people,
> Fools immediately think it is reality.
> The wise know it is temporary and empty.
> Heavenly halls, temples, earthly palaces
> That once looked real return to nothing.
> How laughable, how childish the astray are! Do not love blindly.
> Meditate earnestly and quickly live in the palace of Suchness.[88]

In this way, Kūkai undercuts all the imperial and palatial double entendres that he employed in addressing his imperial patrons or in making claims for Shingon Mikkyō's ability to protect the state. To say that all heavenly halls, temples, and earthly palaces of the world are temporary, empty, and ultimately return to nothing, is to dissolve all of the metaphorical and material constructions that he so skillfully set up throughout his life's written and wrought work (e.g., the Two World mandalas, Kōyasan and Tōji, the Daigokuden and *shinden* style residences, and so on). Kūkai's ultimate understanding of the emptiness of his conventional endeavors does not stop him from pursuing them, but it does put them into perspective.

Third, Kūkai's writings exhibit another internal inconsistency with regard to images and perception. On the one hand, Kūkai's commentary on chapter 20 of the *Golden Light Sūtra* urges a nondiscriminating eye that can see the ultimate emptiness of even the most frightening of appearances. He writes in the *Konshōōmyōkyō himitsu kada*:

> When beheld by the eye of enlightenment, the miraculously swift Yakṣas, the dark spirits, will reveal their secret identity. The reality of Hārītīs, child-eating demonesses, is nothing but emptiness. Do not become attached to names and forms of things that are but accidental. Forget names and forms and see their reality. You will then immediately arrive at nirvāṇa.[89]

In this passage, Kūkai urges the reader to see through samsara's worst *nāma-rūpa* illusions with the ultimate eye of enlightenment, and instead see their "secret identity," which is the *dharmakāya qua* emptiness. On a conventional level, however, at other times Kūkai is genuinely perplexed and scared by fearsome appearances. In a previously untranslated letter, Kūkai lists terrifying environmental and psychological effects that can be synchronous with the installation of ritual imagery and paraphernalia. He writes

> After establishing the altar, demonic activities can suddenly begin to happen even though all the images and accoutrements are new. Corpses start to rain down, or thunder and lightning (start to) shake the place immediately. The blackness of the smoke and flames (gathers) like clouds. In the altar, feces and defilements shower down and a horrible stench makes it unbearable. Skulls thrive on the drinks left in the (offertory) plates; their evil-looking faces are not like ordinary people at all. Figures grasping knives are terrifying, yet I still do not know exactly what causes it all. Or just as bright as daytime, fires can rain down and disasters occur. Or earthquakes tear up the ground and to our astonishment demolish dwellings. Rolls of thunder will suddenly roar and resound, lightning can (appear) shaped like a circle. Without

any reason at all, a strange wind will blow and scatter everything; it blows away the sand and uproots trees. Suddenly a beautiful woman will appear, different from any decent figure or ordinary person. [90]

It is improbable that Kūkai actually experienced all of these horrendous phenomena during actual ritual enactments, but rather took some poetic license in imagining or sampling tantric rhetoric about rituals going awry. What is interesting to note for the present discussion is the fact that this letter incidentally reveals Kūkai's presuppositions regarding new imagery. He writes that things can go wrong "even though all the images and accoutrements are new." This indicates that the production of new images and ritual objects should inversely prevent negative phenomena from occurring, though this inexplicably is not always the case. Other documents record him making new copies of the Two World mandalas and the *Dainichikyō* for the death anniversary of a dutiful child's mother[91] or copying the Great Samaya *Rishukyō* and displaying a dharma-mandala of Siddham *bījas* for the mother of his disciple Chūen.[92] Scholars rightly consider the copying of sutras and the making of mandalas to be merit-generating activities, but these documents also indicate another possible prophylactic motivation for creating new imagery as well. At least for memorial rites, Kūkai may have copied new texts and images to ensure against the negative karma and ritual defilement that is associated with death (*kegare*). These newly created images would ostensibly prevent Dainichi's most unwelcome manifestations from appearing, and instead invite only his purest, most enlightened aspects to be present. In the first memorial, Kūkai reports that after making the Two World mandalas, "the five buddhas rejoiced and did not withhold their presence" and that "all the bodhisattvas of the entire mandala ocean assembly, with unlimited compassion, in accordance with the wishes of this dutiful child, heard his unspoken prayers and granted mercy upon him."[93] This observation indicates that Kūkai occasionally suspends the ultimate nondiscriminating eye of nondualism and rather categorically distinguishes between good and bad on the conventional level.

These three examples occasion one final comment regarding Kūkai's double-level discourse and the role of skillful means (*upāya*). Kūkai takes his cue from the *Dainichikyō*, which first affirms that "enlightenment is free of form [and] all things are without form, for they are equal to the form of empty space."[94] Mahāvairocana, however, then preaches the dharma with a dizzying array of mandalic figures, colors, and voices, a practice to which Vajrasattva objects.

Mahāvairocana defends his reason for creating and teaching the mandala, announcing:

> As an expedient means of saving these [unenlightened, deluded] beings, by condescending to their proclivities, I have expounded this teaching (of the mandala). And yet in truth there is no time, no direction, no action and no creator in this teaching (of the mandala) for all things having form simply abide in their true form of emptiness.[95]

In this passage specifically referencing the status of the mandala image, Dainichi switches perspectives from conventional to ultimate reality and from soteriological concern to ontological understanding. In the first sentence, he descends to the conventional level and uses the myriad forms, figures, colors, sounds, and symbols of the mandalas to enlighten sentient beings. He somewhat deprecates the mandala as but a begrudging conceit or skillful pedagogical means that plays to the expectations and tendencies of the unenlightened. In the second sentence, however, he positively reevaluates these *upāya*-mandalas in light of the ultimate perspective. Seen in their true form, they are as nothing other than emptiness itself, the direct and supercondensed manifestations of the *dharmakāya*. He thus initially sets up divisions between conventional form vs. ultimate emptiness for pedagogical vs. philosophical purposes, but then collapses these distinctions into an enlightened expression of form = emptiness, signifier = signified (or in Dōgen's parlance, practice = realization).

For this reason, when the sutra elsewhere states that "Skillful means are the ultimate,"[96] it means that *upāya* such as the Diamond and Womb World mandalas can both lead to and are nothing other than the realization of emptiness itself.[97] This sentiment is echoed in Kūkai's own *Precious Key to the Secret Treasury*, when he outlines the five-part enlightenment process in terms of the letter *A* as previously mentioned. *Aḥ*, he writes, indicates the highest ideal of enlightenment, higher than even nirvana, because it combines wisdom with the skillful means to enlighten others. This is an expression of the bodhisattva ideal, which compassionately vows to enlighten all sentient beings. This vow, by extension and by necessity, involves a range of pedagogical approaches, visual aids included. As such, *upāya* such as the *Ajikan* visualization, the Two World mandalas, and other images are given positive valuation in the Mikkyō scheme.

Consequently, because esoteric images can operate on both the conventional and ultimate levels, Kūkai states in his *Catalogue* that the realization of suchness requires forms even though it technically transcends them. Alternately, in a more philosophically nuanced passage of the same text, Kūkai also asserts that the individual's level of awakening determines whether one sees visible or invisible truth, though enlightenment itself technically transcends the distinction between the two. Furthermore, because the mandalas can operate both on the soteriological and ontological levels, Kūkai claims that they can enlighten in a single glance and disclose the truth of the dharma even better than the scriptures can. This multivalent stance and these nuancing examples demonstrate Kūkai's ability to walk the tightrope of nondualism even as he accords unprecedented importance to the visual idiom.

Summary: Art as Enlightenment

In this chapter we have been almost overwhelmed with the complexity and vibrancy of the esoteric system. Kūkai's ability to synthesize and systematize the vast body of esoteric doctrinal, ritual, and artistic material was extraordinary. We have merely scratched the surface and introduced a few topics: his penchant for visual metaphors, his collapse of signifier/signified and perceiver/perceived, his theory of *monji* and *hosshin seppō* as expressed in and as the forms of the world, including his calligraphy, the *ajikan* meditation disk, and especially the Two World mandalas. We looked more closely at the sacred geography of the mandalas and their role in statecraft, their imperial iconography that spatializes the realm and the path of awakening, their interi-conic iterations at Tōji and Kōyasan, as well as Kūkai's important reminders about their ultimate emptiness. In this discussion, esoteric art has been seen as both ontological expressions of, and soteriological agents for, the realization of emptiness. As Mahāvairocana points out, it is precisely because the mandala's forms are empty that they can teach one to see all other forms as ultimately empty as well. As such, he asserts that the entire realm of real and ideal objects are all expedient means to enlightenment. For Kūkai, therefore, esoteric art is never a re-presentation of anything other than itself. Rather, like every other *monji* in the universe, it participates in the always-already nature of enlightenment. It does so, however, in superconcentrated form, as if all the energy of the universe were condensed into two painted images. Because they are so powerful, things can go horribly wrong, but conversely because they are so powerful, one glance at the mandalas can enlighten.

This is where Kūkai and Dōgen tend to part company. While Kūkai believed that the signifier *was* the signified and mandalas *were* tantamount to enlightenment itself, Dōgen still maintains a distinctly dualistic stance regarding representation and reality. More accurately stated, Dōgen believed that the visual re-presentation of the actual moment of realizing emptiness was fundamentally unsuited to the fixed visual format. For Dōgen, one could never spatially locate the ranging holochrony of time or the "just-now" moment of experiencing emptiness in a static picture. Let us turn now, therefore, to investigating Dōgen's take on the art of enlightenment.

4

Dōgen on the Art of Engaging

Introduction

NOW THAT WE have a better understanding of Kūkai's conventional and ultimate views of imagery, we are now in a position to consider Dōgen's equally nuanced views. At first reading, it is often difficult to discern whether Dōgen approves or disapproves of art. Within his writings, as well as within his own artistic production and collection, Dōgen's take on the problem of form is hard to pin down. Depending on the image under consideration or the audience he is addressing, Dōgen will at times reject an image out of hand, endorse its veneration wholeheartedly, or undercut it with text but let both text and image stand in nondual coexistence. A closer look at the specifics of his aesthetic theory and philosophy of form is therefore warranted.

As Roger T. Ames has observed, "the comparative approach is the best way to learn about anything."[1] In this spirit, the structure of this chapter will follow that of the last. For every topic heading in the previous chapter on Kūkai, this chapter will demonstrate that Dōgen extends but shifts Kūkai's themes to formulate his own unique view of imagery. This is not to say that Dōgen's thought is derivative in any way. On the contrary, he is perhaps one of the most original, innovative, and unique thinkers in all of Japanese religious history. His ideas, however, are directly juxtaposed here against Kūkai's in order to facilitate a more systematic comparative perspective.

In terms of representation and especially supercondensed representations of Buddhahood (e.g., *ajikan* and mandalas), Dōgen adopts Zen's iconoclastic rhetoric when he wants to make a point about practice-realization. A case in point is his analysis of Nāgārjuna's full-moon body *samādhi* in the *Buddha Nature* fascicle. This topic will be taken up in the section *On Full Moons, Rice Cakes, and the Inability of Art to Re-present Enlightenment.*

In terms of Kūkai's theory of *monji*, Dōgen shifts the emphasis away from Kūkai's notion of image-*as*-text and instead models his typical threefold process of image-*then*-text-*then*-both. Especially when discussing *chinzō* master portraits, Dōgen uses words about practice to undercut and therefore understand images of realization in an appropriate light. As he creates this dynamic tension, he skillfully mediates the dichotomy between text vs. image, practice vs. realization, experience vs. expression, and epistemological vs. ontological views. This topic will be taken up in the section on *What's Wrong with This Picture? The Treachery of the Image*

In terms of Kūkai's theory of *hosshin seppō*, a section entitled *Mujō Seppō and Objects-as-Actions* will address how Dōgen shifts the emphasis from objects-as-words to objects-as-verbs, from the dharma's basic building blocks to its total dynamic functioning (*Zenki*, the title of another of his *Shōbōgezō* fascicles).

In terms of perception, the section entitled *Zen Sights & Sounds* will address how Dōgen shifts the emphasis away from Kūkai's onto-lexicographical focus on sound, letter, and reality to a more intuitive epistemology that is obtained by "seeing through the ears" and "hearing through eyes." A further section on developing and refreshing the True Dharma Eye follows, for it is this enlightened perception that allows Dōgen to adjudicate if an image is valid or not. He obviously approved of several kinds of Buddhist figure portraits as evidenced by his Chinese praise poems of Ānanda and others in the *Eihei kōroku*, Dōgen's extensive record of sermons, poems, and other collected writings that date from the mid-1230s to his death in 1253.

In contrast to Kūkai's ubiquitous trope of imperial palace-cities, Dōgen considers his presence in the mountains of Echizen to be like a spiritual homecoming. He poetically links his urban youth with his rural adulthood through skillful alliteration and phonetic approximation, but ultimately collapses the distinction between city and country in his unique understanding of unobstructed time. It is also this unique temporal matrix that facilitates his intertemporal spin on "the house of the buddhas." This topic will be addressed in the section on *The Form of Enlightenment: Times*. The following section on *Intertemporality* will extend Kūkai's mandalic intericonicity to consider timeless buddhas and patriarchs and all concrete phenomena, which he also casts as interpenetrating being-times.

Finally, in terms of nuancing and deconstructing the master's views, Dōgen's uneasy relationship with imagery can be explained not only by ultimate and conventional perspectives as with Kūkai, but also by attending to his intended audience of either advanced or beginner students. This issue of audience will be addressed in the concluding section on *(Some Kinds of) Art as Experience; Experiencing Art (For Some Kinds of People)*. This last section serves as a final reminder that Dōgen's take on art, imagery, and the expression of enlightenment is contingent and can never be determined once and for all. In keeping with this Madhyamaka inheritance, Dōgen's sole insistence is on *not* insisting on any one point of view. Rather, he constantly strives to walk the tightrope of nondualism and tread the razor's edge between pro- and anti-imagistic discourse, depending on the circumstance. Let us begin with some of Dōgen's more outspoken passages and move on to his more nuanced nondualistic sentiments.

Of Full Moons, Rice Cakes, and the Inability of Art to Re-present Enlightenment

Like Kūkai before him, Dōgen is keenly interested in the problems of representation. Kūkai initially warns that inauthentic representation is as futile as sculpting in ice or painting on water, but ultimately comes to believe that his esoteric art forms, even more so than ordinary world forms, automatically manifest the universal presence and power of Buddhahood. Dōgen also questions the ability of art to re-presence enlightenment, but on occasion he does elevate a few special Zen icons as worthy of respect and reverence since he believes they authenticate one's realization of Buddhahood. This first section will introduce Dōgen's primarily negative views of images, such as Nāgārjuna's formless *samādhi* and Dōgen's own portrait, as he believes that spatially fixed visual metaphors are ill-suited to re-presencing the fundamentally ephemeral nature of the enlightenment experience. Later sections on the portrait of Dōgen's own master and other Buddha images, however, will further nuance and relativize this stereotypically Zen iconoclastic stance.

In general, Dōgen tends to invoke Zen's typical rhetoric against imagery when he wants to make a point about practice-realization. For example, Dōgen believes that a picture of Nāgārjuna's enlightened full-moon body on a monastery wall simply cannot capture the great event of the patriarch's enlightenment experience. In the *Buddha Nature* fascicle, Dōgen reports that he first saw a wall painting of Nāgārjuna's formless *samādhi* at Kuang-li-ssu (Jp. Kōriji) Ch'an temple on A-yu-wang-shan (Jp. Aikuō-zan) in 1223. Although no longer extant, this image apparently appeared on the western corridor of the main hall as part of a series of thirty-three portraits of Indian and Chinese Zen patriarchs. Dōgen calls these images transformation tableaux (*hensō*), as they purportedly depicted an enlightened aspect or transformative episode in the narrative hagiography of the thirty-three Buddhist patriarchs. At the time, Dōgen says that he initially did not understand what the simple, round, white, painted circle hovering above a dharma seat was intended to represent. It is only when he returns to Kuang-li monastery two years later in 1225 that he learns that it represents the episode in which Nāgārjuna reportedly "manifested a body of absolute freedom while sitting, [which] was just like the round full moon."²

Dōgen, however, bemoans the fact that painters interpreted this to mean that Nāgārjuna literally transformed his body into a full moon at the time of his enlightenment. He scoffs at the painting of a literal, big, white, round circle above a chair and sarcastically calls it nothing other than "a painting of a rice cake," the title of another fascicle dedicated to reality vs. representation (*Gabyō*). When Dōgen returns to the Kuang-li monastery, he specifically interrogates the monk in charge of guests and visitors about the image of Nāgārjuna. Dōgen asks Ch'eng kuei of Shu, "What transformation is depicted here?" The monk answers, "That's Nāgārjuna, bodily manifestating a moon-like shape." Dōgen comments, "But the noseholes in the face that uttered those words were drawing no breath; the words themselves were hollow in his mouth."³

In other words, when Dōgen inquired after this illustrated episode of Nāgārjuna's full-moon *samādhi*, he says that the monk answered him without any deep experiential understanding, as his nostrils lacked any breath and his words lacked any real substance. Dōgen then continues to probe his guide's level of understanding by asking, "Yes indeed, just like a picture of a rice cake, isn't it?" Here he assumes that his Chinese guide is familiar with one of Dōgen's favorite *kōans*, which he later discusses in the *Gabyō* fascicle, as well as in the fascicle on Ungraspable Mind (*Shinfukatoku*). Specifically, Dōgen references the famous case no. 4 in the *Blue Cliff Record* (Ch. *Pi-yen lu*, Jp. *Hekiganroku*) compiled in 1163. This *kōan* records the famous exchange between Te-shan Hsüan-chien (Jp. Tokuzan Senkan 780–865) and an elderly woman selling rice cakes. In this episode, the venerable Te-shan asks a simple laywoman for some rice cake refreshments (Ch. *dian xin* 點 心) known more commonly by its Cantonese variant *dim sum*. Hearing him boast of his accomplishments as a renowned intellectual, translator, and exegete of the *Diamond Sūtra*, the woman decides to take him down a notch and expose his deluded attachment to his own intellectual gifts and his own mind (which in truth is ungraspable). She simultaneously demonstrates her superior grasp of the scripture by utilizing a brilliant wordplay that stuns Te-shan into silence.

She craftily asks him "I have heard that the *Diamond Sūtra* says that past, present, and future mind is ungraspable. Which mind do you hope to somehow refresh with a rice cake?"[4] In landing this rhetorical jab squarely on the jaw of his false pride, the woman uses the term *dian xin*. This is a rare Chinese homonym that uses the same characters 點心 to indicate two meanings: (1) light refreshments like *dim sum* rice cakes that metaphorically provide one with "a little bit of heart"; and (2) a phrase that can be read literally as "pointing to the mind," which the *Diamond Sūtra* says is ungraspable since it flows ineffably through past, present, and future. In rhetorically asking him to pinpoint the mind (*dian xin*) that he wishes to refresh with a "little bit of heart" (*dian xin*), the woman's pun aims directly at the false source of his self-attachment. The added irony of the situation, of course, is that it is the *Diamond Sūtra* itself, the supposed area of his expertise, that teaches that the mind is ungraspable, and yet he obviously hasn't learned its lesson despite his supposed intellectual acumen. As a result, the woman automatically challenges Te-shan's reputed mastery of the scripture and reveals herself to be the true possessor of its enlightened meaning. By transforming a simple, tangible, graspable rice cake into an *upāya* for automatically revealing the intangible, ungraspable nature of mind, her witty turn of phrase strikes Te-shan speechless and she wins the bout.[5]

When Dōgen then rhetorically suggests that the painting of Nāgārjuna's full-moon *samādhi* looks just like a painting of a rice cake, he is deliberately and jokingly hinting that this visible, optically graspable, and fixed painting should ideally point to the ungraspable, ineffable emptiness of Nāgārjuna's experience. However, his Chinese guide doesn't seem to get Dōgen's humorous reference. Perhaps he was unfamiliar with Te-shan's rice cake *kōan*, or perhaps Dōgen's Chinese pronunciation left him unsure as to his meaning, or perhaps he was even offended by Dōgen's off-putting remark but nevertheless laughed politely. Regardless, Dōgen reports that the monk gave a loud laugh "but there was no edge on it. It couldn't have broken through a painted rice-cake."[6]

Thus when Dōgen further tries to engage the monk in a typical joust of Zen repartée and one-upmanship, the monk laughs but it has no Zen edge to it. Dōgen's crack about the painting resembling a rice cake is not itself cracked by the monk's laugh. In Dōgen's estimation, the exchange reveals the monk's lack of understanding and inability to distinguish between authentic and inauthentic expressions of enlightenment. It simultaneously reveals Dōgen's own disappointment with, and sense of superiority over, these simplistic monks, who nevertheless reside at one of the great temples of the Five Mountains of China. Dōgen's critique of the Chinese art thus serves to make a larger point about his superior wisdom, and one discerns that his ulterior motive in recounting this story is to establish himself as a legitimate authority and Zen master back in Japan. However, the way in which he makes his point speaks to his temporal-experiential priorities. Dōgen rants,

> For a long time people in the land of the Sung have endeavored to illustrate this episode in painting, but they have never been able to paint it in their bodies, paint it in their minds, paint it in the sky, or paint it on walls. In vain attempts to paint it with a brush tip, they have made depictions of a round mirrorlike circle on a Dharma seat, and made it out to be the moon-round shape of Nagarjuna's manifesting body. In the hundreds of years that have come and gone since then, these depictions have been like gold dust in the eyes, blinding people, yet no one has pointed out the error. How sad that matters have been allowed to go unremedied like this! If you understand that the round moon shape manifested by the body is an all-round shape, it is no more than a painted rice cake. It would be ludicrous in the extreme to divert yourself by playing with that.[7]

In Dōgen's estimation therefore, artists have objectified the episode without any true experiential realization; they paint it on the monastery walls, but they do not paint it in their bodies and minds through practice. Moreover, although they may graphically paint a scene on the wall with brush and ink, they can never truly "paint" in the sense of actualizing Buddha-realization through practice. Any static symbol or form that replaces the actual body-mind experiencing the fullness of *samādhi* is inadequate for Dōgen. All that counts is the experience, not its re-presentation. As Dōgen remarks in the *Gabyō* fascicle, "An old Buddha said: a painting of a rice cake does not satisfy hunger."[8]

For Dōgen, therefore, the combination of visual cues deceives the unenlightened, for it inaccurately depicts Nāgārjuna's body, unnecessarily mystifies his meditative state, objectifies his *sāmadhi* as something external or different or inaccessible to ordinary practitioners, and therefore actually hinders them from attaining this open, clear, and bright meditative state in their own real practice. As a corrective, Dōgen sets the record straight and insists that this episode has been grossly misunderstood to mean that Nāgārjuna literally transformed his body into a full moon. He is adamant that no miraculous bodily transformation occurred. "You should know without any doubt," he exhorts, that

> at that very time Nagarjuna was just sitting there on the high seat. The form in which he manifested his body was no different from the form of any one of us sitting here right now. Right now our own bodies are manifesting a round moon shape.... Although clearly and distinctly embodying the form of the full moon/Buddha nature, it is not a round moon shape set out on display.[9]

In this passage, one observes Dōgen's insistence upon seeing everyday forms in a transformed light. He urges his audience to see the normal body of Nāgārjuna as the manifestation of the whole realm of enlightenment, metaphorically referred to here as a full moon, or elsewhere as One Bright Pearl (*Ikka myōju*). From Dōgen's perspective, only those who have gone through the experience of awakening and acquired the True Dharma Eye can see the immaterial emptiness of material suchness. Only one who has tasted *shinjin datsuraku* can see, in the sense of "meeting" Buddha to Buddha, how Nāgārjuna's physical body can, like the round full moon, manifest the complete, transparent and full enlightenment of Buddhahood. For those who still have not experienced *shinjin datsuraku,* however, Nāgārjuna's formless experience is invisible and indistinguishable. Dōgen explains that "[t]hey could not see or hear it because their eyes and ears were obstructed. As their bodies had not yet experienced it, it was not possible for them to discern it."[10] For those like Dōgen, however, whose eyes and ears have opened and whose bodies and minds have experienced awakening for themselves, they already see the full-moonness of forms and no miraculous bodily transformation occurs.

In Dōgen's estimation, therefore, artists mistake simile for reality, the map for the terrain, and the menu for the meal. They imagine that external or objective appearance necessarily describes or recreates the description of an inner experiential state. Because of their delusion, he charges that their senses are obstructed and that they lack experiential discrimination. They vainly visualize it as an event external to themselves; they cannot render their own inner experience within an everyday outward form. They therefore literally depict a full-moon form, though this is actually a third-generation loss from the actual lived state of *samādhi* to its metaphorical verbal description to a graphic redescription of the literally taken metaphor.

By adopting this stance against images, Dōgen intimates that an enlightened painter perhaps could somehow be able to render directly within the outer form of a regular man's body his own personal inner experience of meeting Nāgārjuna's inner full-moonlike realization. Dōgen himself, as a self-avowed enlightened master, is reputed to have drawn his own likeness gazing at the full harvest moon (to be discussed presently), but in his writings Dōgen does not say anywhere how exactly this feat can or should be accomplished. He never explains what he means by painting a normal everyday figure in a direct, unmediated, enlightened fashion. Even if one could understand what it means to paint directly, immediately, with realization, Dōgen never outlines what that image might look like or what qualities it might have. Dōgen concludes:

> Things that are undepictable are best left unpainted. If they must be painted at all, they can only be painted straight to the point. Yet the body manifesting the shape of the round moon has never yet been painted.[11]

Dōgen does grudgingly accept in the *Summer Retreat* (*Ango*) fascicle, that if one is going to paint spring, for example, one should paint it directly. One should not use cliché symbols, such as peach or plum blossoms to signify the referent spring, but rather, simply paint it directly. Again, Dōgen in no way tells one how to do this in terms of technique, for he is not really talking about art here, but rather practice-realization. Thus, when he says to paint spring directly, he really means to practice *zazen* and see how it is already the awakened self.

This insistence on the identity of practice-realization is further echoed in his fascicle on *Painting of a Rice Cake*. Here Dōgen does acknowledge that the realization of Buddhahood would not be possible without an already established notion or image of Buddhahood in the mind's eye. As a result, he does recognize the value of depicting buddhas through stupas, through the thirty-two characteristic *lakṣaṇa* signs, a blade of grass, or even through the imagined idea of aeons of discipline. "Because a picture of a Buddha has always been drawn like this," he says, "all the buddhas are *picture-buddhas* and all *picture-buddhas* are buddhas."[12] That is, because the physical or mental representation of enlightenment already exists, one can conceivably toggle as he does between the post-enlightenment stance that nirvana is samsara, and the pre-enlightenment stance that samsara is nirvana. In this way, enlightenment and delusion, nirvana and samsara, ontology and epistemology, realizing practice and practicing for realization can all coexist (from the enlightened perspective) as coequal painted and actualized buddhas. All of Dōgen's remaining scriptural exegeses on the theme of pictures and rice cakes in this fascicle underscore this same nondual outlook.

Thus, Dōgen's aesthetic theory must always be read in light of his larger religious project, which focuses on living and engaging with life authentically. For Dōgen, *true* painting means living life authentically with full actualization of the body-mind of self and other through meditation. It means realizing the essential identity and difference of all the forms and colors swirling around one. It means not just being a part of the painting of life, but *being* the painting of life. For this reason, Dōgen says in the *Painting of a Rice Cake* fascicle "Unsurpassed enlightenment is a painting. The entire phenomenal universe and the empty sky are nothing but a painting."[13]

By reading the word "painting," not in the artistic sense, but with Dōgen's more existential spin on it, we can see that Buddha-nature itself is a free and expressive life-activity whose very open and formless unboundedness informs the realm of forms. Dōgen writes that the painting of this true, authentic existence in and through the realm of painted forms involves practice. If one is authentically going to "paint" enlightenment in the sense of truly manifesting and expressing realization, then one must practice with one's whole body and mind. If one is going to pursue the formless experience from within this realm of forms, one must sit zazen. As he articulates in the *Buddha-Nature* fascicle, "You must know that in [truly] painting the form of the body manifesting a round moon shape, the form of the manifesting body must be there on the Dharma seat."[14] Eyes must be half-closed and eyebrows raised and the body positioned in zazen meditation. If one sits in this way even for a short period of time as the *Bendōwa* fascicle says, then one will, without intention or human agency, become a Buddha and expound the dharma by one's very being. Anything less than this is deplorable and pointless for Dōgen. He writes in the *Buddha-Nature* fascicle:

> not to paint the body manifesting, not to paint the round moon, not to paint the full moon shape, not to trace the body of Buddhas, not to be *thereby expressing*, not to trace the preaching Dharma, (in short, not practicing zazen) and to trace in vain a picture of rice cake—what can possibly come of that?[15]

For this reason, Dōgen urges one and all: "Old Buddhas! New Buddhas! Encounter the real manifesting body! Do not waste your time admiring a painted rice cake!"[16]

What's Wrong with This Picture?
The Treachery of the Image

In addition to simply exhorting his students to practice zazen instead of venerating images, Dōgen also uses text to undercut the power of the visual. He inscribes accompanying verses to his own *chinzō* master portraits in accordance with the conventions of Sino-Japanese painting, but he subverts the realism of these paintings by asking rhetorical questions about their representative value. He also redirects the spectator/reader's attention away from the image itself and toward more abstract, poetic Zen metaphors, such as invisible full moons and unblinking (i.e., permanently awakened) fish constantly swimming in the deep waters of meditation. These kinds of textual strategies for deconstructing the image are well known in Ch'an/Zen, as evidenced by the witty satire evident in the inscription to the portrait of Dōgen's own master Nyojō, to be discussed below.

Before moving on to a text-image analysis of these specific examples, however, a preliminary observation and word of explanation are warranted. It is interesting to note that Dōgen's alternative textual strategies for dealing with imagery lie in sharp contrast to Kūkai's. Kūkai, it should be recalled, saw images *as* text and the forms of the world *as monji* that expressed and taught the dharma by their very existence. His mandala images were simply über-visual texts that automatically manifested and communicated the dharma faster and better than anything else. In the case of Zen master portraits, by contrast, Dōgen attempts to dissociate already-empty *monji* into two separate moments in which *mon* (patterns, forms, figures, and images) are directly followed by a devastating *ji* (text, words, letters, cracking jokes or verbal repartées that can demolish, empty out, deconstruct, and turn a revered Zen patriarch into a rice cake). Kūkai's ontological claims for his imagery collapse form and emptiness onto the same plane by virtue of his unobstructed spatial logic. This is the same presupposed logic that enables the reflexive *kaji* empowerment of self and Buddha as mentioned in chapter 2. Dōgen's more epistemological or experiential concern with imagery, however, recognizes that the typical unenlightened viewer does not see form-as-emptiness "in a single glance" as Kūkai claims, but rather simply tends to objectify and turn a hanging scroll of a Buddhist master, for example, into a mere poster child for awakening. Dōgen refuses to take the personalized image of the dharma at face value, so to speak, and consequently adds text to deconstruct it of any attempt at reification. Knowing that the average viewer sees the figure first and reads the verse second, Zen master portraits separate the form of the figure from the emptiness he embodies into two distinct moments. This is the same presupposed temporal logic that enables Dōgen's sequential assertion (image), negation (verse), and ultimately reaffirmation of self (both image and verse seen together) previously mentioned in chapter 2. This third uneasy coexistence of visual *mimesis* and its textually emptied *nemesis* in the end actively expresses the enlightened realization of nonduality. Consider the counterexample: a strict iconoclast would have simply and one-sidedly destroyed the image in an extreme intolerance for anything but the real thing. For Dōgen, by contrast, the best *chinzō* images are ones that can directly reveal this threefold enlightenment process and ultimately show its transformed, and ideally transformative, nondual view to the spectator-reader.

In juxtaposing image and text in this way, Zen master portraits create a dialectical tension at best, or cognitive dissonance at worst, between the visual and conceptual spheres as they wrestle with representation and reality. It is this same tension that René Magritte wrestled with in his painting entitled *The Treachery of Images* (*La Trahison des Images* 1928–29), which provides the anachronistic, yet nevertheless helpful, title for this section heading.

In figure 4.1, Magritte paints a realistic picture of a pipe, but directly below it also provocatively writes "This is not a pipe" (*Ceci n'est pas une pipe*). In keeping with semiotic theory, Magritte's combination of image and text underscores the gap between representation and reality and between images of pipes hanging on museum walls and real pipes that can be stuffed with

Figure 4.1. René Magritte *La Trahison des Images,* 1928–1929. Los Angeles County Museum of Art, Los Angeles. © 2011 C. Herscovici, London/Artists Rights Society (ARS), New York.

tobacco and actually smoked. It is in this same spirit of actually realizing one's internal Buddha-mind, not objectifying external Buddha-images, that Zen masters inscribe many of their own *chinzō* portraits.

In Dōgen's case, several extant inscribed portraits are said to survive from his lifetime, though some scholars question all but his 1249 moon-viewing self-portrait to be discussed presently.[17] Twenty verses about his own image called *jisan*, however, do survive in the earliest unrevised version of his *Eihei kōroku,* and thus can be attributed to Dōgen himself. In keeping with the *Yü-lu* Ch'an literary tradition, some of these verses by Dōgen are but thought-poems or word-pictures about his character, and therefore do not correspond to any literal image of him. Other verses, however, were deliberately composed by Dōgen himself as either poems of praise or as self-deprecating inscriptions for his own painted portraits.[18] Zen art historian Helmut Brinker further explains that this latter genre of *jisan* were usually brushed for a living sitter (*juzō*), and were probably not composed for any future posthumous effigy (*izō*). "In the case of contemporaneous portraits, [*jisan*] were composed and written on the scroll by the master himself (Ch. *zizan*, Jp. *jisan*), not rarely upon the request of his disciples, *confrères*, lay adherents or patrons."[19] On a side note, in his *Shisho* fascicle, Dōgen is highly critical of Rinzai Zen masters who peddled their inscribed portraits and calligraphy samples to anyone who asked or paid a donation for them, and Dōgen is equally disdainful of uninitiated priests parlaying these collected images into evidence for establishing their own temples, even though they hadn't truly received Zen transmission. As a result of his disdain for this then-common practice, we can deduce that Dōgen maintained a healthy regard for his own "brand identity" as an enlightened master so to speak, and guarded the integrity of both his texts and images fairly closely.

The first portrait of Dōgen to be considered is housed at Honmyōji temple in Kumamoto prefecture, Kyūshū (fig. 4.2). Although a late copy, this example provides evidence for the dating of Dōgen's earliest poem explicitly composed for portrait inscription, namely *jisan* no. 18 dated 1227.[20]

According to temple records, the figure itself is 54.6 cm x 26.5 cm and is a severely abraded Muromachi-period copy of an original portrait of the master from Ankokuji temple (no date or location given).[21] Above the Muromachi-period seated figure, there are two Edo-period colophon fields located in the upper register. The first inscription about opening a mountain is signed by the monk Sonkai, includes a pressed flower, and is dated to the sixth year of Meiwa (1770). The second inscription is also by Sonkai, or perhaps his same-named successor, and is dated to the seventh year of Bunsei (1825).

Figure 4.2. Dōgen portrait, Honmyōji, Kumamoto prefecture. Courtesy Honmyōji temple.

In this second colophon, Sonkai explains that he excerpted the extant original lines of Dōgen's poetic *jisan* no. 18 from the Ankokuji image and added them here. He then rewrites this poem of Dōgen's about a fish swimming in the deep waters of meditation, unperturbed by the snares of life. Before signing off with his own name, Sonkai finally writes, or perhaps copies from the Ankokuji image, the explanatory coda "Karoku 3 (1227), Dōgen *jisan*, Eiheiji's first patriarch's portrait."[22]

Even though it appears on a late copy, the poem's purported date of 1227 would place it precisely upon Dōgen's return from China. It is even possible that Dōgen wrote this poem for *chinzō* inscription in Kyūshū en route back up to his home temple of Kenninji in Kyoto. However, this *jisan* appears in vol. 10, no. 18 in Dōgen's *Eihei kōroku*. Since all the writings in the *Eihei kōroku* tend to date from the mid-1230s after he had established himself as a recognized Zen master at Kōshōji temple in southeast Kyoto, it is also possible that this inscription for a formal master portrait was not completed until sometime after Dōgen's return to the capital. Regardless, Dōgen explicitly composed the poem for his own portrait, and the juxtaposition of text and image creates an artistic tension that serves to both subvert and sustain Dōgen's image as a young Zen master. The poem reads:

> The cold lake reflecting the clear blue sky for thousands of miles
> A gold-scaled fish moves along the bottom in the quiet of night,
> Swimming back and forth while fishing poles snap off
> On the endless surface of water appears the bright white light
> of the moon.[23]

On the one hand, visually speaking, the formal *chinzō* image of a seated Zen master communicates the individual identity, solidity, and public face of the monastery. Poetically speaking, however, the text communicates the fluidity and private movements of the golden-bodied master hidden deep below the expanse of his fully illumined, white light moon-mind. In this case, the visual and poetic idioms simultaneously serve to concretize and dissolve the image of Dōgen as both an individual man and an abstract symbol of Zen awakening, as the fish is a stock metaphor for Zen enlightenment since it never blinks.[24]

In this regard, this example serves as an interesting comparative piece to Kūkai's calligraphic poem about the birds and fowl frolicking at the surface of Lake Masuda. Whereas Kūkai's poem lauds the joy and life-giving waters of the man-made irrigation lake, Dōgen here literally dives below the cold surface at night to the meditative depths below. He thus not only redirects one's attention from the image to the ideal, but also shifts the emphasis away from public works to private states, and from the calls of frolicking birds to the still, quiet coldness of night. How different this inscribed portrait is from the exuberance of Nāgabodhi's image at Tōji with its flying white *hihaku* script!

The second inscribed *chinzō* to be considered is definitively dated to 1249 (fig. 4.3). This reputed self-portrait by Dōgen at age forty-nine is said to capture a moment when he viewed the harvest moon in Echizen on the fifteenth day of the eighth month of 1249. Above his self-portrait, Dōgen brushes a Chinese poem that again invokes the stock images of harvest moons and fish swimming back and forth. It is modeled on a poem by Hung-chih Cheng-chüeh (Jp. Wanshi Shōgaku 1091–1157), the abbot of Tiantong monastery before Nyojō. Hung-chih was renowned for his silent meditation method,

Figure 4.3. Dōgen self-portrait viewing the harvest moon in 1249. Provided courtesy of Hōkyōji. Hōkyōji temple, Fukui prefecture. Used with permission.

but also for his *kōan* collections and poetry, which were much admired by Nyojō as well. Dōgen versifies in *jisan* no. 3 in the *Eihei kōroku*,

> Autumn is spirited and refreshing as this mountain ages.
> A donkey observes the sky in the well, white moon floating.
> One [the moon] is not dependent;
> One [*the well*] does not contain
> Letting go, vigorous with plenty of gruel and rice,
> Flapping with vitality, right from head to tail,
> Above and below the heavens, clouds and water are free[25]

In this enigmatic poem, the old mountain monk Dōgen initially sets up a standard Zen dichotomy between the reflected moon floating in well water and the real moon floating in the sky. This dichotomy denigrates representation over reality

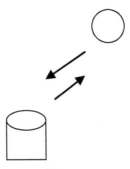

Figure 4.4. Dōgen's alternating views of the moon

and maligns the finger pointing to the moon instead of becoming the real moon itself, that is, imagining, talking, or thinking *about* awakening instead of actually experiencing awakening directly. He underscores the split between the moon's false illusion below and its true illumination above by saying that only a donkey (i.e., himself, perhaps)[26] gazes at the well instead of the real moon. Grammatically speaking as well, Dōgen intimates that asinine subjects-dualistically-perceiving-objects ("donkey observes the sky in the well") are inferior to simply floating in the sky of one's own accord ("white moon floating").

Subsequently, in the next two lines, however, Dōgen begins to break down this established bifurcation between reflection and realization, representation and reality, samsara and nirvana.

When he says that "one does not depend" and "one does not contain," he is toggling between two vantage points (fig. 4.4). In saying that "one does not depend," he means that the real moon above does not depend on the well below for its existence or appearance. Translated from Dōgen's poetic code speak, this means that satori realization does not need the well of samsaric forms below to manifest its full illumination, nor does it depend on gradual practice for its manifestation. For Dōgen, illumination is not the causal product or effect of practice, it already exists before, during, and after practice, though paradoxically one must practice zazen in order to realize this fact. Thus, in this line, Dōgen adopts an ontological stance that speaks from the bird's-eye enlightened perspective of the moon looking down unto the totality of existence. This vantage point automatically establishes, yet simultaneously collapses, the dualistic worldview of nirvana vs. samsara. Like the ubiquitous light of original enlightenment that it so aptly symbolizes, the full moonlight of the real moon already and everywhere just *is*.

In the next line, however, Dōgen adopts a more epistemological stance and says that "One (i.e., the well) cannot contain." This statement conversely speaks from the everyday unenlightened perspective of the well below aspiring upward toward the moon. From this vantage point, one cannot say that the well already contains the real moon of full realization, since the well really only contains but the moon's reflection. That is, one cannot say that one is already fully enlightened without practice. For Dōgen, therefore, realization does not need practice to exist, but cannot happen without it. They are nondual and coequal partners in the continual and paradoxical process of recovering what was never lost to begin with. Consequently, samsara and nirvana, or more poetically, well-floating reflections as well as sky-floating moons, freely appear suspended in the infinitely open water-sky of emptiness.

Thus, like a well-fed fish free to swim in the waters of contemplation, Dōgen frolics in the open expanse of this nondual space, while clouds above and water below float freely by him. He locates himself squarely in the samsaric realm as a fish swimming in water, but he nevertheless finds freedom and joy in his environment. He delights in the swirling moon-images floating in the water all around him and relishes the interfusion of moon (nirvana) and water (samsara) thoroughly. In this perfect realization of nonduality, "from head to tail, above and below the heavens, clouds and water are free."

The fact that "clouds and water" can also be read literally as *unsui* (雲水) or novice monk, expresses the typically Zen paradox that extols the recovered beginner's mind of a true master. It simultaneously constitutes a last-line self-deprecating jab at one who nevertheless has masterfully expressed his grasp of nondualism. The poem therefore follows Dōgen's threefold trajectory that progresses from an unenlightened donkey fixated on appearances, to a radical realization of emptiness that abrogates dualisms, to a third and final enlightened return that humbles one's sense of self-importance.

It is in this light that Dōgen self-referentially justifies yet qualifies this painted likeness of himself. Visually speaking, it is interesting to note that the portrait itself only depicts the figure of Dōgen. No picture of the moon, whether suspended in air or in water, is shown. This implicitly indicates that the moon lies above and beyond the contours of the hanging scroll, and analogically speaking, connotes that real lived practice-realization lies above and beyond formal representation or stock symbolism. True to his earlier critiques of Nāgārjuna's full-moon body, he does not paint a white circle on a dharma seat, but rather shows the suchness of his anthropomorphic form even as he communes with the moon. It is further interesting to note that Dōgen's gaze points directly upward as he looks above into the night sky. Despite his nondual rhetoric, his upturned line of vision indicates that he nevertheless prefers to be pictured in his fully enlightened aspect, and not mired in mirages like the unenlightened downward facing donkey. The overall combination of the textual and visual impressions implies that Dōgen himself embodies the freedom, detachment, and effortless weightlessness of the very full harvest moon rising before his enlightened gaze. In this case, therefore, the text both undergirds and undercuts the treachery of the image, which both is and is not emblematic of his enlightenment experience.

Finally, and theoretically speaking, the text-image tensions created in this case would ideally trigger the realization of nondualism in the open space between the actual reader-spectator and the *chinzō* itself. Knowing that the majority of people viewing his portrait and reading his verse would be unenlightened novices in the monastery, Dōgen strategically delivers his poetic punch line about *unsui* floating freely to inspire them. The invocation of their own inferior rank at the climax of his verse would automatically wake them up, attract their attention, perhaps generate a fleeting thought of dissent or resentment that they were *not* free in the monastic regimen, but then (again, ideally) dissolve such feelings in the paradox of freedom within discipline, and realization within practice.

The final Dōgen *chinzō* to be considered is figure 4.5, housed at Eiheiji. It demonstrates the difference between actualizing enlightenment instead of envisioning it, and realizing practice/practicing realization instead of just showing it as a mandala. Scholars debate whether the portrait itself may have been completed posthumously, but Dōgen's Chinese verse definitely appears as *jisan* no. 10 in the *Eihei kōroku*. In this accompanying verse, Dōgen deconstructs the validity of his own likeness when he self-deprecatingly versifies,

> Recognizing this [portrait] as true, how can this be reality?
> Upholding this portrait, how can we wait for the reality?
> If you can see it like this, what is this body hanging in emptiness?
> Fences and walls are not the complete mind.[27]

In this verse, Dōgen takes up the old conundrum of reality and representation in the form of three conditional questions. First, he rhetorically asks which is more real, himself or a picture of himself. This automatically calls into question the ontological status of both the painting and the sitter himself. Second, he rhetorically asks whether displaying his portrait now can somehow lead others to realization later on. This more functional, temporal, and epistemological query automatically destabilizes the then-current assumption that venerating the master's painted "double" could help advance

Figure 4.5. Dōgen *chinzō*. Eiheiji temple, Fukui prefecture. Used with permission.

one's practice.[28] Third, he rhetorically asks if the enlightened eye viewing the portrait in a correct, nondualistic, and emptied-out way can really discern the nondualism of form and emptiness. That is, by asking if one can perceive this image of Dōgen in the enlightened sense of "seeing" a Buddha eye-to-eye, then "this body hanging in emptiness" itself is called into question. "Body in emptiness" can refer to the painted figure suspended on the wall, to

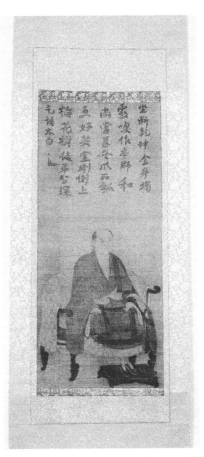

Figure 4.6. *Chinzō* portrait of Dōgen's Master Nyojō. Provided courtesy of Hōkyōji. Hōkyōji temple, Fukui prefecture. Used with permission.

the spectator's body floating before it, to the living Dōgen hanging in emptiness like Nyojō's bell already discussed in chapter 2, or to form and emptiness more generally. Combined with doubting the value of viewing his double in the previous line, the entire matter of form and emptiness itself remains uncertain, which after all, is Dōgen's main objective. The final line of Dōgen's verse does nothing to resolve matters either. His cryptic allusion to fences and walls literally leaves the reader-viewer hanging as well. Here he refers to Nan-yang Huichung's (675–775) response about the mind of ancient buddhas being "fences, walls, tiles and pebbles."[29] He calls his realization only partially complete, but does not say what complete realization would be. In the end, the verse is designed to destabilize his students and remind them not to mistake the painting for the real thing or somehow substitute the representation for the experience. When it comes to representing himself, therefore, Dōgen is happy to let imagery stand, as long as he can use text to undercut its treachery.

Another Zen master portrait provides an alternative textual strategy for deconstructing image-attachment: the biting power of satire and parody. A humorous inscription appears not on one of Dōgen's *chinzō* this time, but rather on the *chinzō* of Nyojō himself, the Zen master under whom Dōgen achieved enlightenment while in China (fig. 4.6). Dōgen reputedly brought this inscribed portrait of his master back to Japan from China in 1227 along with his *shisho* transmission certificate and his master's robe. Despite Dōgen's typically Zen rhetoric of returning empty-handed, Dōgen did return fully equipped with these authenticating seals confirming his awakening. This image is currently housed at Hōkyōji in Fukui prefecture, Japan.[30]

This *isuzō* seated portrait depicts Nyojō sitting in his abbot's chair (*kyokuroku*), with a sumptuous textile (*happi*) draped over the back. His legs are folded in the *kekkafuza* meditation pose, and his monk's slippers appear below on his *fumidoko* stand. He appears here in three-quarter profile view facing to the right, which is a standard convention that suggests that this was a living portrait and not completed posthumously. Art historians continue to argue over this latter point, however, as a later Yüan dynasty source says that this pictorial convention is meaningless.

In the upper third of the hanging scroll, the inscribed *san* reveals an interplay of text and image that both substantiates and subverts Nyojō's image of authenticity.

> Uninterrupted sitting lasts as long as heaven and earth
> And reveals the golden body.
> This is what distinguished my master.
> But what should a monk look like?
> A Chinese watermelon? An eggplant? A bottle gourd?
> Even funnier—a vajra monk
> Hanging upside down from a plum tree.
> —Written in earnest for disciple Je-chen [also] of Mt. T'aipai[31]

In this verse, Nyojō opens with a poetic line expressing the eternity of practice, which produces golden-bodied patriarchs such as his own former master Chikan, and by extension, himself, pictured here sitting on his dharma seat. In the context of this painted portrait, however, Nyojō immediately questions this lofty golden ideal, and rhetorically asks what a monk should really look like. He crashes from the sacred to the profane in a single line by suggesting that the various bald, shiny, shaven heads of individual monks resemble the various shapes and sizes of melons, gourds, and eggplants in the market. He suggests that his own funny vegetable-shaped monk-head depicted here looks even sillier than real vegetables, ostensibly because it is dressed up in serious Zen robes and posed on a chair. He concludes by imagining an even more hilarious scene: a plum tree that yields monk-heads like fruit, dangling down from on high. This last image can be read as Nyojō simply extending the metaphor of monk-heads resembling various fruits and vegetables, or it can be read as an even deeper deconstructive parody of himself and of his own likeness. The plum tree was a more indigenous Chinese substitute for the Buddha's bodhi tree of enlightenment, so this line obliquely suggests that as a vajra or diamond monk, he has obtained the full fruit of enlightenment. At the same time, however, he imagines himself hanging upside down from this tree, without any lofty ideas or ideals about enlightenment but with his gaze set firmly on the ground. He literally seeks to overturn or upend any preconceived notions about the appearance of awakening. In typical Zen style, therefore, Nyojō's text follows the threefold sequence that presents him as a Zen master, negates him as a self-deprecating eggplant head, and represents him as enlightened precisely because he is so down-to-earth and funny. As a result, his combination of formal image and amusing text validates yet also undercuts the image of enlightenment, overturns conventional expectations, and relegates the realm of heaven and the sublime to the realm of the humble squash. Even his signature line "Written in earnest for disciple Je-chen [also] of Mt. T'aipai" contains a twist. T'aipai-shan, literally meaning Grand Old White Mountain, is one of the five famous Gozan temple mountains in China,[32] but "T'aipai" can also literally mean "potato" in Chinese. Given the content of the preceding inscription, this double entendre could suggest that he is simultaneously signing off on his portrait as both the esteemed abbot of one of China's most prestigious temples, as well as signing off as Zen Master Potato Head. In light of such parody and satire, the treachery of the image doesn't stand a chance. No wonder Dōgen held the portrait of his master in such high esteem.

Thus, despite Dōgen's protests in his *Buddha-Nature* fascicle that "things that are undepictable would best be left unpainted," he was keenly interested in artistic depictions of fully realized beings. He writes two poems praising the image of Śākyamuni Descending from the Mountains, which is a Chinese pictorial convention that reimagines how Buddha emerged from his first meditative realization of nirvana. Dōgen also writes a prose poem on the first

Zen patriarch Bodhidharma, a seven-line verse on Buddha's close disciple Ānanda, and one on Myōzen, Dōgen's own Zen companion and fellow traveler in China.

Ānanda's poem serves as a final case in point. In the first four lines of verse, Dōgen referentially summarizes the hagiography of this eminent disciple of the Buddha, and in the last three lines, reminds the spectator of the treachery of his image.

> He overturned the banner before the gate.
> Sitting on the river, he considered others in allotting his body.
> Within a dream, Ānanda broke through the great barrier.
> Before, he'd protected the Tathāgata during and after his life.
> Caution!
> Don't keep your eyes on this painting.
> With sincere mind make prostrations and give homage.[33]

In this poem praising Ānanda's portrait painting, the first line explains that according to the *Mumonkan* or *The Gateless Gate*, Ānanda removed the flag of dharma debate after Mahākaśyāpa refused to tell him what the Buddha transmitted to him in his famously silent flower sermon. The second and third lines explain that according to the *Transmission of the Lamp* (Ch. *Ching-te Ch'uan teng lu*), Ānanda broke through the great barrier of life and death along the Ganges river between two rival kingdoms so that both sides could share equally in his relic-remains. The fourth line explains that in the past, Ānanda served the Buddha both before and after his *parinirvāṇa* as both the Buddha's attendant and the credited source of all of his reported sayings in the sutras, which have lived on to the present day.[34] These first four lines thus establish Ānanda as truly a nondual figure. He transcended both speech and nonspeech, and even within samsara's dream of life and death, broke through the great barrier between the two, straddled both sides of the Ganges, and facilitated the dharma both during and after Buddha's lifetime.

In the last three lines, however, Dōgen jolts the spectator awake with an alarming "Watch out!" (*totsu!*) and then treads the razor's edge between eschewing and embracing the form of the painted figure. This coda to the poem follows Dōgen's characteristic tripartite deconstructive and reconstructive strategy. That is, after asserting the everyday hagiographic view of Ānanda in the first four lines of the poem, Dōgen then empties it out before reasserting its venerable position in Buddhist lore and practice. He empties the image of meaning by telling the viewer not to fixate on Ānanda's physical image appearing before the eyes, for it is not a portrait *per se,* but rather a mere anachronistic imagining of the figure. In the very next line, however, he then encourages the viewer to venerate this image of Ānanda with a sincere mind and make prostrations before it. Some Protestant-inspired exegetes might interpret this to mean that Dōgen wanted the viewer to venerate the *idea* of Ānanda, or see him as a symbol, exemplar, or role model of nondualism to be emulated. This is certainly true on some level, but on a deeper, more experiential and existential level, Dōgen here is himself modeling and expressing the process for achieving a truly nondualistic stance. This process can both reject, but then also reclaim, the form of the figure in all but the same breath. This polarizing ambivalence of the inscription, when paired with the actual figure of Ānanda himself, would simultaneously reinforce both the treachery and the attraction of the image. It would thus show Dōgen's skillful negotiation of false dichotomies to be on a par with Buddha's closest disciple, and would ideally elicit the realization of nondualism within the viewer himself.

Kūkai's Legacy: Mujō Seppō and Objects-as-Actions

As demonstrated above, Dōgen dissociated Kūkai's *monji* image-letters into a self-sabotaging, yet highly illuminative, tension between arts and letters. In a similar way, he also inherits Kūkai's doctrine of *hosshin seppō* but dynamically reworks it into what he calls *mujō seppō* or "the insentient preaches the dharma."[35]

Like Kūkai before him, Dōgen believes that even the natural forms of the world "speak" or incessantly preach the dharma. Dōgen believed that all form-events in the universe *are* Buddha-nature. In the *Buddha Nature* fascicle, for example, Dōgen inverts the standard Mahāyāna reading of "all sentient beings have Buddha-nature" to "entire being *is* Buddha-nature."[36] His creative rereading of the standard Chinese grammar collapses the dualism of subjects (sentient beings) possessing objects (Buddha-nature), and instead reveals a holistic worldview wherein subjects and objects mutually inform one another. This "total dynamic functioning of the universe" articulates a vision of coarising, copresencing *dharmas* that equally "receive and use"[37] one another to disclose truth.

More specifically, however, Dōgen explicitly explains that seemingly inanimate objects, such as mountains and rivers, directly unfold the Buddha way. In his *Mountains and Rivers* fascicle (*Sansuikyō*), Dōgen says that "these mountains and waters of the present manifest the way of the old buddhas" and "Wherever buddhas and patriarchs are, water is, and wherever water is, buddhas and patriarchs manifest."[38] In Dōgen's temporalized worldview, Kūkai's word-forms become dynamic verb-forms. Kūkai's static, discreet *monji* instead now move and flow and unfold the truth in a continual process of impermanence and change. Even mountains can move forward and backward in ranging time, for "walking ahead does not oppose walking back, walking back does not oppose walking ahead. This virtue is called flowing mountain; mountain flowing."[39] Dōgen's surprising claim that mountains are flowing and his even more surprising counterclaim that rivers are still, only makes sense when one considers shifting viewpoints within the universe's total dynamic functioning. That is, Dōgen believes that mountains and rivers, and ultimately everything else in the entire universe, are all moving and thereby unfolding the truth. However, like viewing a moving train, it depends whether one perceives this flow from the outside (in which case the train appears to move from point A to point B on the horizon) or whether one sees it from the inside (in which case it doesn't feel like the train is moving at all). As a result, when viewed from afar, mountains can be seen as part of the unfolding truth of becoming, and seen from within, flowing river water doesn't seem to move at all as long as one moves perfectly along with it. It is in this sense that there is both ranging or flowing being-time (*kyōryaku*), as well as temporarily abiding or dwelling being-times (*nikon*). This sentiment of the world-as-a-verb, heightened by Dōgen's attention to relative perspective, impermanence, and coarising of being-times, puts a unique spin on Kūkai's original theory of *monji* and *hosshin seppō*.

Moreover, given Dōgen's epistemological concern with experience and the acquisition of enlightened perception, he believes that it is not enough to simply state ontological truths or articulate doctrines, such as *hosshin seppō*, as Kūkai does. What counts for Dōgen is the actual realization of such truths through the acquisition of the enlightened perception of the True Dharma Eye.

Dōgen reasons in the *Mujō seppō* fascicle that if nature was always and everywhere already preaching the dharma as Kūkai states, then no one could fail to see it and everyone would awaken instantaneously. This is obviously not the case. Although the Mahāyāna *hongaku* doctrine of universal original enlightenment theoretically teaches that everything already is enlightened on a fundamental level, it is nevertheless obvious that on the practical level, sentient beings cannot awaken using ordinary perception. As a result, Dōgen proposes that only zazen practice-realization can lead to the kind of enlightened vision that can perceive the world in this illumined manner. The ordinary, visible form of nature may remain the same, but from the awakened perspective, the light in which it is perceived is altered.

Dōgen also emphasizes the need for direct experience over doctrinal speculation in the *Bendōwa* fascicle. Here, Dōgen directly responds to a hypothetical interlocutor who asks the difference between Shingon and Zen. After diplomatically stating that true Buddhists do not quibble over sectarian distinctions, he essentially agrees with Kūkai that insentient forms preach the dharma and have led some to enlightenment, that *monji* make up the entire universe, and that the dharma is holographically contained in every molecule. However, Dōgen cautions against becoming caught up in doctrinal complexities and linguistic traps. He even self-deprecatingly deconstructs his own spin on Kūkai's teachings, saying that *sokushin zebutsu* and *sokuza jōbutsu* are but indicative mediations, not direct actualizations of the dharma. He writes,

> Some have entered into the stream of the Buddha's truth at the invitation of grass, flowers, mountains, and rivers. Some have received and maintained the stamp of Buddha by grasping soil, stones, sand and pebbles. Furthermore, the Vast and Great Word (*kodai no monji*) is even more abundant than the myriad phenomena. And the turning of the great Dharma-wheel is contained in every molecule.
>
> This being so, the words *Mind here and now is the Buddha* (*sokushin zebutsu*) are only the moon in water, and the idea *Just to sit is to become Buddha* (*sokuza jōbutsu*) is also a reflection in a mirror. We should not be caught by the skillfulness of the words.[40]

In this passage, Dōgen goes on to advocate Śākyamuni's original practice of seated zazen meditation for the automatic manifestation of inherent realization. Those who engage in zazen practice-realization, he argues, can experientially grasp how the being-times of nature manifest truth, but those who do not can only intellectualize it as a theory. This difference between describing ontological structures and experiencing them directly through zazen is at the heart of Kūkai's and Dōgen's spatial and temporal systems, respectively.

Zen Sights and Sounds

Dōgen's emphasis on experience over intellect, and practice over theory is also made evident elsewhere in the *Mujō seppō* fascicle. Dōgen first quotes and then comments upon the poem by his lineage's founding patriarch Great Master Tung-shan Liang-chieh [Jp. Tōzan Ryokai (807–869)]:

How very wonderful! How very wonderful!
The [insentient] preaching of the dharma is a mystery.
If we listen with the ears, it is ultimately too difficult to understand.
If we hear the sound through the eyes, we are able to know it.[41]

In the Sino-Japanese context, the ear traditionally represents intellectual understanding, whereas "hearing through the eye" indicates the True Dharma Eye, that is, the intuitive understanding that comes from real experience.[42] Commenting upon this last line, Dōgen disparages certain individuals who mistakenly believe that seeing "the activity of grass, trees, flowers, and birds" with the human eye is the same as intuitively *hearing sound through the eyes*. He says,

> This point of view [i.e., equating unenlightened with enlightened perception] is completely mistaken and is not the Buddha-Dharma at all. The Buddha-Dharma has no such theory. When we learn in practice the founding Patriarch's words *hearing sound through the eyes,* the place where the sound of the [insentient] preaching the Dharma is heard, is the eyes themselves, and the place where [it] is realized, is the eyes themselves.[43]

Dōgen here is urging his students to hear and realize intuitively the dharma-preaching-world in each of their own eyes. One can tentatively call this intuitive perception that accompanies meditative experience, transensory perception.

This transensory synesthesia of sound and sight is not unlike Kūkai's conflation of language and image in *monji* patterns of name and form (*nāma-rūpa*). The difference however, between Kūkai's notion of *monji* image-letters and Dōgen's intuitive "hearing through the eyes," is that the former is presented as an ontological reality; the latter is urged as an intuitive activity. Dōgen's two stock examples for sudden intuitive realization, in fact, are the two famous episodes when Hsiang-yen Chih-hsien achieved enlightenment by hearing a ceramic roof tile strike bamboo, and when Ling-yun Chih-ch'in awakened when viewing plum blossoms. Dōgen deliberately chooses these two examples and regularly invokes them together to show, like *monji*, that hearing and seeing *nāma-rūpa* correspond. In doing so, Dōgen was able to appeal to his audience as a whole as some individuals tend to be more disposed toward sound (temporally oriented hearing types) or sight (spatially oriented seeing types).

Figure 4.7. Shokanzeon Kannon, seated image in the Dharma Hall, Eiheiji. temple, Fukui prefecture. Used with permission.

The transensory and intuitive experience of "hearing through the eyes" is also present in the *Kannon* fascicle. In this text, Dōgen comments upon the compassion of "the regarder of the sounds of the world" Shokanzeon, which over time has come to be displayed in the dharma hall of Eiheiji monastery (fig. 4.7). This bodhisattva's compassion is so great that he/she intuitively hears or sees the cries of the world even before they are uttered. With regards to this bodhisattva, Dōgen favorably assesses a famous dialogue between two dharma brothers Ungan and Dogo:

UNGAN SAYS: "The whole body (henshin) is hands and eyes."
DOGO SAYS: "Your words are nicely spoken. At the same time, your expression of the truth is just eighty or ninety percent of realization."
UNGAN SAYS: "I am just like this. How about you, brother?"
DOGO SAYS: "The thoroughly realized body (tsūshin) is hands and eyes."[44]

Nishijima and Cross point out that the terms *henshin* and *tsūshin* both mean "whole body," but that Dogo's dynamic kanji *tsū* (通) describes active movement or passage, as opposed to Ungan's more general *hen* (徧), which literally means "everywhere on the surface." This is another interesting instance in which a spatial term is less effective than a temporal one in expressing Zen's process-oriented vision. A whole body that is "everywhere" is only 80 or 90 percent as effective as one that actively "passes or moves through" reality. For this reason, *henshin* is translated as "whole body," but *tsūshin* is translated as "thoroughly realized body" in the sense that there is thorough permeation and activity of "hands and eyes." Because Dōgen's lineage descends from both of these dharma brothers, he does not take sides, but rather declares that both are appropriate expressions of Kannon's "limitless abundance" (*nyokyota*). The point here, however, is that Dōgen believes that Kannon's enlightened vision involves the intuitive perception of and active participation in the world. For him, this perceptive and dynamic dharma eye does not see the forms of the world objectively as something other than oneself. Rather, because one has gone through the *shinjin datsuraku* experience and been confirmed by all *dharmas*, the resultant enlightened vision is an intimate, wise, and compassionate understanding that allows one to intuit perfectly where and how to engage with forms.

The Role of Perception: The True Dharma Eye

Thus, Dōgen's entire project arguably hinges on developing, maintaining, and transmitting fully enlightened vision. Dōgen calls this ability to correctly discern reality the True Dharma Eye, a term that Bhāvavivka first coined in the sixth century to describe how one saw the world after the rigors of his threefold experiential paradigm. As heir to Bhāvavivka's Madhyamaka tradition, Dōgen accordingly entitles his major life's work The Treasury of the True Dharma Eye (*Shōbōgenzō*). In this collection of fascicles[45] written in vernacular, yet idiosyncratic, Japanese between 1231 and Dōgen's death in 1253, Dōgen lays out the essentials of Zen theory and practice, which all center around correctly perceiving and engaging with the world. In one fascicle called "Enlightened Vision" (*Ganzei*), for example, Dōgen explains that there is a difference between ordinary and enlightened vision, and says that "'Diamond enlightened vision' is in both the continuous rain and the beautiful sky, and in the singing of bullfrogs and worms."[46] Rainy vs. clear skies and singing frogs vs. silent worms are usually separate and distinct categories, but Dōgen says that enlightened vision can take in both together.

Like Kukai, Dōgen in the *Shōbōgenzō* often invokes the stock image of the Buddhist mirror of the enlightened mind, which reflects reality wholly and without distortion. However, whereas Kūkai prefers to focus on grasping the totality of spatially fixed objects, such as elephants and dragons, Dōgen stresses how this mirror of the enlightened mind can take in the totality of unobstructed time. This mirror-mind, he claims, perceives and reflects all the other buddhas and patriarchs throughout unobstructed time, just as the *shisho* transmission certificate indicates. In addition, whereas Kūkai's interresonating bell of Dainichi self-echoed its own dharma truth throughout the valley, Dōgen stresses that the wind bell ringing out wisdom hangs in emptiness, which allows all the myriad buddhas and patriarchs to view one another (i.e., view themselves) across the aeons. In this way, Dōgen puts his typical temporal spin on the mirror metaphor, which he appropriately calls The Eternal Mirror (*Kokyō*).[47] In this eponymous fascicle, Dōgen writes:

> What all the buddhas and all the patriarchs have received and retained, and transmitted one-to-one, is the eternal mirror. They have the same view and the same face, the same image and the same cast; they share the same state and realize the same experience. A foreigner appears, a foreigner is reflected—one hundred and eight thousand of them. A Chinaman appears, a Chinaman is reflected—for a moment and for ten thousand years. The past appears, the past is reflected; the present appears, the present is reflected; a Buddha appears, a Buddha is reflected; a patriarch appears, a patriarch is reflected.[48]

In this passage, Dōgen claims that all buddhas effectively have the same experience and therefore resemble one another in the eternal mirror of the mind. Chinese masters and foreign disciples, such as Dōgen himself, have the same face and the same shape, he says, and both the quantity and duration of such buddhas and patriarchs extend throughout the world and throughout time. "One hundred and eight" is a stock Buddhist numerological moniker for "many," or in contemporary parlance, "millions" of reflections in time's endless hall of mirrors. Buddhas and patriarchs appearing "for a moment and forever" recall again the characteristic notion of embedded momentary *nikons* nested within the wide-ranging *kyōraku* of being-time. This great and eternal self-reflective mirror of enlightenment, furthermore, can be infinitely recast and replicated, for "Buddhas are the cast image of the great round mirror."[49] This metaphor of the mirror's mold shaping generation after generation of buddhas in its own image indicates the creative repeatability of the enlightenment experience. This poetic expression does not negate the agency or potency of the individual Zen practitioner relying on his own efforts (*jiriki*), nor does it indicate that anything is transmitted, transferred, or taken away from one mirror to the next. Adding one more layer to the eternal hall of mirrors simply adds another endless interreflection.

To further clarify and distinguish his unique understanding of the mirror metaphor from Kūkai's, however, later in the *Kokyō* fascicle Dōgen specifically makes clear that "The great round mirror is neither wisdom (*chi*) nor principle (*ri*), neither the underlying essence or nature of things (*shō*) nor their formed aspects (*sō*)."[50] He thereby distinguishes Zen's mind-to-mind and eye-to-eye reflective vision from Mikkyō's by the well-known Two World mandalas of wisdom and principle in the noumenal Diamond or phenomenal Womb Worlds. In addition, he distinguishes Zen's great round mirror from the notions of essence and formed aspect that Kūkai reputedly calligraphed in the Ten Factors of Existence/Ten Examples of Suchness (*jūnyoze*; see chapter 3, figs. 13a, b, c). Dōgen thereby implicitly posits the superiority of Zen vision over and against codified Mikkyō imagery. This is because Dōgen believes that Zen's dynamic insight is reached only through real experience; it should not be theorized or even visualized in esoteric images. It should only be continually renewed and shared over time.

The importance of refreshing one's True Dharma Eye is indicated in the *Ganzei Enlightened Vision* fascicle. Here Dōgen recounts his late master's stay at Zuiganji temple, in Chekiang Province, eastern China. He says that Nyojō entered the dharma hall there and said:

> Pure the autumn wind, bright the autumn moon; Earth, mountains, and rivers are clear in the Eye; Zuigan blinks and we meet afresh; Sending staffs and shouts [*katsu*] by turns, they test the patch-robed monk.[51]

Dōgen likens Nyojō's renewed vision at Zuiganji to "blinking" (*tenkatsu*), indicating that even an enlightened master's dharma eye needs to be continually refreshed. The temporary cleansing of blindness *katsu* (瞎) is also phonetically linked to the homonym *katsu* (喝), the special kind of Zen shout that can either express or elicit the mind of enlightenment. One thereby learns that opening the dharma eye after *shinjin datsuraku* is not a one-time event, especially when considered in conjunction with the many Zen stories of enlightened masters continually checking students' level of realization. Rather, after the dharma eye is opened, one's enlightened vision needs to be renewed with the same kind of momentary freshness that blinking produces, and tested or manifested with the kind of force that Zen shouts express. Only then can one approach the permanent awakening that characterizes the unblinking fish idealized in Dōgen's *chinzō* inscriptions discussed above. Furthermore, every time one blinks, one sees Buddhahood anew, for as Dōgen writes, "Renewing our vision is the same as meeting"[52] in the sense of meeting or seeing eye-to-eye with all the other buddhas in time again. Dōgen concludes that when this happens, "They meet like thunder and lightning."[53]

This moment of seeing eye-to-eye with Buddha is further explained in the *Kenbutsu Seeing the Buddha* fascicle already mentioned in chapter 2. The subtext to this fascicle is the well-known Zen *kōan,* which admonishes "When you see the Buddha, kill him! When you see the Patriarch, kill him!" This anti-imagistic, anticonceptual tool is designed to empty the mind of any preconceived attachments to obtaining enlightenment, so that one can in fact, realize emptiness and obtain enlightenment.[54] Dōgen, however, in this fascicle heartily asserts that buddhas and patriarchs can see their realized interactivity in an eye-to-eye, mind-to-mind, or shoulder-to-shoulder meeting. For Dōgen, this enlightened meeting of dharma eye vision can only be used in connection with special zazen practice-realization, as one enlightened master-buddha sees it in another enlightened student-buddha. In the context of this mind-to-mind transmission, which is better described as a meeting of minds in what Yuasa calls the "symmetry of time,"[55] the dharma eye of practically realized Buddhahood can only be recognized after the third movement in Dōgen's Logic of Not. Only after a zazen practitioner experiences the threefold enlightenment process can one see the world in light of the True Dharma Eye; only now can one properly and moreover experientially see how each and every bright leaf-time, blade of grass-time, tree-time, flower-time, and self-time reciprocally manifest the dharma teaching.

Forms of Enlightenment: Times

In contrast to the imperial palace-cities and all the architectural metaphors that so characterized Kūkai's oeuvre, Dōgen's emphasis naturally shifts to the flux and flow of nature's total dynamic functioning. The temporal life stream and positional relativity of Dōgen's *Mountains and Rivers* fascicle discussed above, for example, resists the highly structured symbolic objectification that characterizes even Kūkai's mountain project at Kōyasan. That is, Kūkai may also have embraced mountain settings for their ascetic training potential just as Dōgen did, but he mandalicized the landscape. Dōgen rode it.

Kūkai had lived in an age of centralized, state-sponsored religious institutions dedicated to the pacification and protection of the state. Dōgen, however, lived in an age when Heian's imperial monopoly on state Buddhism was splintered by a growing landed gentry in the provinces, a military shogunate ruling through the Hōjō regents in the new northern capital of Kamakura, and to a negligible degree, the puppet emperor still residing in the old capital of Heian. After his return from China in 1227, Dōgen spent sixteen years in and around the old capital of Heian, but spent the last ten years of his life far removed from the city. He followed the centripetal forces of other Kamakura Buddhist movements in 1243 when he accepted Lord Hatano Yoshishige's land grant in Echizen province (present-day Fukui province, far to the northwest of Heian and west/southwest of Kamakura). It is debated whether Dōgen's move to the remote mountains was by choice or by virtue of necessity, as Enni Bennen's growing Rinzai competition at Tofukuji Temple, not far from Dōgen's own Kōshōji temple, may have made city life unbearable for Dōgen. Nevertheless, in his writings Dōgen rationalizes his move by quoting his teacher Nyojō's entreaty to retreat from the crowds of the city, retire deep into the mountains, educate just a few elect disciples, and continue the transmission of the true dharma.[56]

In one poem written while traveling in these mountains, Dōgen rejoices that he has finally found his original abode, a Mahāyāna Buddhist metaphor for recovering one's original Buddha-nature. Inspired by a well-known *kōan* about one's original face before one's parents are born, Dōgen writes a *waka* traditional Japanese poem about the Echizen mountains entitled "True Body Before Father and Mother's Birth" (*Fubo shoshō no mi* no. 13-J).[57]

Tazune hairu	Seeking the Way
Miyama no oku no	Amid the deepest mountain paths
Sato nareba	The retreat I find
Moto sumi nareshi	None other than
Miyako nari keri	My primordial home: satori![58]

Doctrinally speaking, Dōgen's poem says that seeking the Buddha Way in the mountains is nothing other than a spiritual homecoming. He says that traveling among the venerable and deep mountains (*miyama* みやま, 御山、深山) has brought him back to his primordial home, where he can recover the body of his original enlightenment. His return to his idealized home village or *sato* deep within the mountainous landscape thus automatically invokes satori, or realization.

At the same time, however, his last line explodes this rural idyll with an astonishingly unexpected word choice. In contrast to Echizen's mountains (*miyama* み や ま), Dōgen says that his primordial home is actually nothing other than the old capital of Heian itself (*miyako* 京), where Dōgen was, in fact, born and raised. That is, after hinting that he has returned home and regained the spiritual insight of a child in the mountains, he now says that his true birthplace was actually none other than the metropolitan center. The apparent contradiction between city and country, however, is nonetheless immediately dissolved again through Dōgen's poetic alliteration and wordplay. As Steven Heine points out, when the syllables are broken up, *mi-yama* literally means "the body of mountains" 身山 and *mi-ya-ko* literally means "body and child 身 や 子." The alliterative resonance of the words *miyama* and *miyako* thus conflate the body of mountains with the body of his childhood in the capital, and signal the rediscovery of his original nature in the rural present through the recovery of his urban past. Dōgen's word choice thus links the rugged with the refined, the mountains with the metropolis, and even cursive Japanese *hiragana* with the more formal Chinese *kanji* writing. It simultaneously and importantly points to the recovery of all the time that has passed from his childhood to the present.[59]

In Dōgen's case, therefore, his true homecoming and rebirthing in the mountains is not without its urban references. However, all of his metropolitan hints and wordplays serve the purpose of highlighting the timeliness of the trek, the collapse of linear time frames, and the fusion of childhood bodies in the city with their now-adult bodies in the mountains. His take on the city that so structured Kūkai's thought and activity is now fundamentally temporalized and relativized within the larger flux and flow of nature, human-nature, and Buddha-nature.

Dōgen elsewhere invokes the architectural spaces so typical of Kūkai, but again, temporalizes them in his writings. Dōgen does, in fact, recommend placing oneself into "the house of the Buddhas" in order to be enlightened. In his *Shōji* fascicle on *Life and Death*, Dōgen says,

> when you simply release and forget both your body and mind and throw yourself into the house of the buddhas, and when functioning comes from the direction of Buddha and you go in accord with it, then with no strength needed and no thought expended, freed from birth and death, you become Buddha. Then there can be no obstacle in any man's mind.[60]

This house of the buddhas can be seen as an esoteric inheritance, but the main thrust of Dōgen's message is a very Taoist-inspired going in accord with the functioning of the buddhas. It is this laissez-faire forgetting of the self à la Chuang Tzu that allows one to effortlessly escape the cycle of birth and death. Dōgen scholar Takahashi Masanobu states that the phrase "the house of the Buddha," in fact, should be understood

> within the context of the fundamental assertion raised in the *Busshō*, namely, the question of the Buddha-nature itself. What on earth is this house? We may define it as "the place of departure and return," that is, a place of rest... in the chapter *Yuibutsu-Yobutsu* (The Relation of Buddha to Buddha) of the *Shōbōgenzō*, Dōgen brings out the question of from where man comes and to where he returns, that is, the eternal question of the beginning and end of life.... We have come from the house of the Buddha and will return there again... the house of Buddha can be found everywhere in the Cosmos.[61]

In this regard, Dōgen's "house of the Buddha" is not so different from Kūkai's description of Dainichi's universal palace. In Kūkai's case, the buddhas of past, present, and future reside *in* the palace; however in Dōgen's case, they *are* the palace itself. The spatial is again subordinate to the temporal. It is the very coming and going of sentient beings that is associated with the house itself. This shift from encapsulated containment and possession to pure unbounded becoming in, through, and as time also marks Dōgen's most famous rereading of the *Nirvāṇa Sūtra*. As mentioned previously, in his *Buddha-Nature* fascicle, Dōgen famously states that all beings don't possess or have Buddha-nature, but that rather, *are* nothing other than Buddha-nature itself. Furthermore, as he reiterates in the *Busshō* fascicle, "If you wish to know the Buddha-nature, you must realize that it is nothing other than temporal conditions themselves."[62]

Intertemporality

Kūkai and Dōgen may see eye to eye, so to speak, in perceiving how forms preach the dharma, and may agree that special condensations of the dharma, such as mandalas and *ajikan* disks, or inscribed *chinzō* or *shisho* certificates are particularly efficacious in revealing truth. However, given Dōgen's highly dynamic and temporalized vision of the universe, he prefers that these forms not be fixed in space as they are in Kūkai's scheme. If, as Ryūichi Abé suggests,

"Kūkai's deconstructive strategy is a path by which he constructs and reconstructs a concrete model of the universe," then as Steven Heine declares, Dōgen "uncompromisingly situates the absolute in the relative world of ephemeral phenomena and language."[63] Even the concrete images that Dōgen invokes in his more poetic moments are fundamentally temporal in nature. The opening poem to the *Uji Being-Time* fascicle, for example, references mountains, oceans, buddhas, demons, staffs, hossu fly whisks, stone lanterns, people, the earth, and sky. Although each object is prefaced by the phrase "there is a time" or "for the time being" (*uji*), are not all these images concrete spatialized forms?

A hint from classical Chinese tells us otherwise. Dōgen knew this idiom well and often employed it in his *kanshi* Chinese poems. As Abé suggests, in classical Chinese, horizontal and vertical indicated space and time, respectively.[64] Because verticality was equated with temporality in classical Chinese, it is no wonder that Dōgen evokes entirely vertical images to explicate his fundamentally temporal vision of reality. The opening poem of the *Uji* fascicle reads:

> For the time being, I stand astride the highest mountain peaks.
> For the time being, I move on the deepest depths of the ocean floor.
> For the time being, I'm three heads and eight arms [i.e., a demon]
> For the time being, I'm eight or sixteen feet [tall, i.e., a Buddha]
> For the time being, I'm a staff or a whisk.
> For the time being, I'm a pillar or lantern.
> For the time being, I'm Mr. Chang or Mr. Li [i.e., somebody or other]
> For the time being, I'm the great earth and heavens above.[65]

This emphasis on verticality (from mountain peaks to the bottom of the ocean, from the vast earth to the endless heavens above) means that for Dōgen, all space is fundamentally temporal. All being is fundamentally time, or rather, all beings are fundamentally times, and since they all interpenetrate one another in an unobstructed fashion, one can appear as any one of these concrete phenomena "for the time being." Envisioning reality[66] as vertical (i.e., temporal) existences means that spatial considerations are relegated to temporal ones and physical properties are subsumed under the rubric of time. This is the exact inverse of Kūkai, who placed all buddhas of past, present, and future into Dainichi's universal palace, thereby subsuming temporal considerations under spatial ones.

Furthermore, this vertical time in Dōgen's poem transcends all dualities. It envelops all distinctions between good and evil (e.g., eight-armed demons vs. sixteen-feet-tall buddhas) and between animate or inanimate objects (the upright bodies of ordinary people like Chang or Li vs. stone pillars or lanterns). Even vertical staffs and *hossu* fly whisks, symbols of Buddha's enduring enlightenment from mind to mind, are fundamentally impermanent being-times. All these vertical forms compel the reader to "Look! Temporal conditions. [See the] transcendence of conditions. Look! Buddha-nature. [See the] emancipated suchness of Buddha-nature."[67]

Summary: Nuancing Dōgen's Views (Some Kinds of) Art as Experience; Experiencing Art (for Some Kinds of People)

After considering all the evidence above, one might well ask how Dōgen could maintain such contradictory viewpoints throughout his writings. Why does Dōgen think that the representation of Nāgārjuna's *samādhi* is inauthentic, but the representative robe and *shisho* certificates themselves are the manifestation of the way of the buddhas? Why does a picture of a moon constitute nothing but a rice cake, but a picture of a master constitute a trace of enlightenment? Why did Dōgen revere his master Nyojō's *chinzō* portrait, but chastise his students for revering his own? Why did he denigrate the painting of spring, but paint his own self-portrait of himself admiring the harvest moon?

It seems that Dōgen's experiential dualism played out into an artistic double standard: it was acceptable for him, a self-avowed enlightened master, to paint his own full-moon body directly, but not any other Sung painter, whose enlightenment was suspect. Likewise as a spectator, it was acceptable for him to assess Nyojō's *chinzō* as a direct trace of enlightenment, but he cautions his own unenlightened students not to revere his own likeness without doubt. He never outlines specifically how a spectator might be able to recognize the difference between an authentic, immediately painted figure as opposed to an inauthentic, mediated one. He simply assumes that awakened individuals, such as himself, can discern it with the True Dharma Eye. He does not spell out whether enlightened spectators alone can see, in the sense of "meeting," enlightened painting, or whether unenlightened spectators can also get a glimpse of realization somehow, as was the case with Kūkai's mandalas. Dōgen's visual theory is altogether lacking in this regard, for in fact he doesn't believe it can be done artistically. He claims that one really cannot ever represent the experience of nondualism, only approximate it through graphic and textual means.

Dōgen's double standard and inconsistent view of images, however, can be better understood when one accounts for his shifting vantage points and intended audiences. On the one hand, Dōgen distinguished between unenlightened and enlightened ways of seeing. This means that from the unenlightened or pre-enlightened perspective, there is an experiential dualism between pre-enlightenment and post-enlightenment views. On the other hand, however, like Tao-sheng (c. 360–434) before him, Dōgen maintains that from an enlightened perspective, practice is realization, aspiration is attainment, and the path is the goal. This means that ultimately, no essential difference exists between unenlightened seekers and accomplished, enlightened masters. It seems that Dōgen affirms distinctions with one hand, even as he denies distinctions with the other.

One must conclude that Dōgen's iconoclasm was not a wholesale one, but rather a qualified and selective one. He simply privileged some images and repudiated others. This characterizes a similar preferential tendency in other religious movements of the Kamakura period (e.g., Hōnen and Shinran's preference for *nembutsu* scrolls over figural images of Amida Buddha, or Nichiren's exclusive devotion to his own brand of *Lotus Sūtra* imagery).[68]

In addition, and perhaps most importantly, the *way* in which one approached imagery was paramount for Dōgen. If one possessed, to use the postmodern expression, a healthy hermeneutic of suspicion for the treachery of the image, then one could fruitfully engage in wordplay, Zen one-upmanship and a shared understanding of the pitfalls of representation. If one did not possess this discerning True Dharma Eye, and if one merely approached an image at face value so to speak, then one was in a sense doomed to fall for the optical illusion that mistakes representation for the primary presentation of real, lived experience.

Thus, in a sense like Kūkai, Dōgen also believed that there were certain forms that were better at presencing the dharma than others. In Kūkai's case it was the forms of mandalas, sculpture halls, and ritual activities, such as mantra and mudra that condensed universal truth. In Dōgen's case, it was any seal or emblem that materially condensed the immaterial form of mind-to-mind dharma transmission: the robe, a bowl, a *chinzō* portrait, a *shisho* transmission certificate. These highly privileged fixed objects, however, could not be viewed correctly and certainly could not be obtained until one had fully dropped off body-mind of self and other in meditative practice-realization, allowed the ten thousand *dharmas* to rush back in, and confirm the self as but one of many. It is obvious that Dōgen believed that he himself was worthy of seeing these privileged forms in the correct Zen spirit.

At other times, Dōgen's attitude toward imagery is more accommodating to those who have not yet experienced *shinjin datsuraku*. When speaking to an audience of laypersons or novices, Dōgen endorses the veneration of Buddhist images because it is beneficial for these beginning students. This primarily derives from his early Tendai training in the *Lotus Sūtra*, which says in chapter 2, "If someone with a confused and distracted mind should take even one flower and offer it to a painted image, in time he would come to see countless Buddhas."[69] In the following passage taken from Dōgen's *Zuimonki* talks, it seems that Dōgen is speaking with the beginning practitioner in mind. He straightforwardly urges his audience to revere images of the Buddha, for they are emblematic of the first of the three jewels (i.e., the Buddha, the dharma, and the sangha). They therefore are worthy of veneration, regardless of their aesthetic qualities. That is, for Dōgen, (1) the Buddha is evidenced in even crude images; (2) the dharma teaching is evidenced in even low quality scriptural texts; and (3) the sangha monastic community is evidenced in even wayward monks. He writes,

> Even though it may be a crude statue made of sticks and mud, as an image of the Buddha, reverence it. Even though it may be a poorly written scroll with yellow paper and red holders, as a sacred scripture, venerate it. Even though a monk breaks the precepts and knows no shame, respect him as a member of the sangha.... If the precept-breaking, the shameless monk, the crude image of the Buddha, and the shoddy scripture cause you to lose faith and withhold respect, you will without fail be punished. In the laws left behind by the Tathāgata, we find that Buddhist images, the sacred texts, and the priesthood bring blessings to men and devas. Therefore, if you venerate them, benefits will always accrue.[70]

With specific regard to crudely fashioned Buddha statues, it is worth noting that Dōgen himself may have modestly aspired to carving a Buddha statue with his own hands. In 1244, Dōgen laid out the Buddha Hall at Daibutsuji, later renamed Eiheiji in 1246, and reportedly said, "As a vow of my lifetime, I am determined to carve a statue of Shākyamuni Buddha with my own hands. I am not certain how long I will live, but this is my intention. It might not be exquisitely crafted but my intention is to carve it with my own hands, even if it takes many years."[71] Dōgen scholar Kazuaki Tanahashi notes that this main Buddha statue of Dōgen's had indeed been completed by 1249, though it did not survive Eiheiji's devastating fire of

1473.[72] Furthermore, an extant copy of Dōgen's *Omens of the Sixteen Arhats* (*Jūroku rakkan genhitsugi*) attests to the fact that during his lifetime, Eiheiji was vibrantly decorated with medieval Zen Buddhist statuary and imagery. Written in Chinese, dated to 1249, and currently housed at Kinryūji in Ibaragi Prefecture, this copy of Dōgen's writing notes that "In front of the Buddha statue there appeared especially wonderful and beautiful flowers" and that "they also appeared in front of all the wooden images of the sixteen arhats, as well as all the painted images of them."[73] Knowing how influential the *Lotus Sūtra* was to Dōgen's thought, it seems that Dōgen took chapter 2 of the scripture to heart, for it promises that "If there are persons who for the sake of the Buddha fashion and set up images, carving them with many distinguishing characteristics" and "If they employ pigments to paint Buddha images, endowing them with characteristics of hundredfold merit, If they make them themselves or have others make them, then all have attained the Buddha way."[74]

From this evidence, we can conclude that Dōgen was in no way a strict iconoclast. Rather, he seems to have been keenly interested in the Buddhist imagery and symbolism, even noting in his *Hōkyōki* journal that Nyojō's Lecture Hall in China was decorated with painted white lions on the floor in front of his dharrma seat and a symbolic lotus canopy overhead. In his journal entry no. 37, Dōgen notes that Nyojō distinguished between lions with white manes (i.e., his students who had received full transmission) and those lions who still only had blue manes (i.e., those who had not yet awakened to the dharma as expounded from his seat). In the next sentence he abrogates this dualism by noting that the Lotus canopy over the seat symbolizes the single suchness of the world and the dharma.[75]

When speaking to his own novices, moreover, Dōgen avoids the topic of iconoclasm altogether. As he continues his *Zuimonki* talk, he glosses over a famous iconoclastic episode of a Ch'an practitioner in China, perhaps because he does not think his audience ready to grasp its deeper lessons. The full episode of this story narrates that the ninth-century Tan-hsia T'ien-jen (Jp. Tanka Tennen, 739–824) burned a wooden Buddha to stay warm. When upbraided by his master, he countered that he was only trying to obtain the ashes of the Buddha. When asked how he was going to get such highly venerated relics from a mere piece of wood, he replied, "if it's nothing but a piece of wood, why scold me?" In another version of the story, he responds, "Then may I have another to burn?"[76] Tan-hsia's anti-image antics strove to highlight the nondualism of sacred and profane, but Dōgen does not elaborate on this for his beginning audience. Instead, he launches into a very Confucian reflection on Tan-hsia's hidden virtues and the maintenance of the proprieties, omitted here. Dōgen only remarks:

> The Zen Master Tan-hsia T'ien-jen burned a wooden image of the Buddha. Although this appears to be an evil act, it was meant to emphasize a point in his teaching.... If this is so, how can we not render homage to anything representative of the Three Treasures?[77]

One final example taken from the *Zuimonki* talks adds another dimension to Dōgen's views on art and imagery. Simply put, this other dimension is the necessity of adapting to circumstances. No hard and fast rule should be mandated about either revering or destroying images. Although it is good for beginners to revere the Buddha, in some cases it is also acceptable and even admirable to treat the Buddha's image less than honorably. Dōgen relates the story of a poor man living near Kenninji, his old training monastery in Kyoto. The poor man asks the Abbot Eisai for help, but the temple itself was without adequate food or funds at the time. Eisai gives him a scrap of leftover copper from the halo that was being made for the temple's main image of Yakushi Buddha, and tells him to exchange it for food. Eisai's students asked, "Isn't it a crime to make personal use of what belongs to the Buddha?" Eisai replies that they are correct, but that saving people from starvation is worth committing such an egregious crime and falling into hell. Dōgen remarks, "Students today would do well to reflect on the excellence of Eisai's attitude. Do not forget this."[78]

With regard to such temple images, it is interesting to note that Eisai's Kenninji is reputed to have been installing a Yakushi Medicine Buddha, and not the standard Mañjuśrī images associated with Zen monasteries. This either compels us to reevaluate our understanding of medieval Zen imagery, or of the *Zuimonki*, or both. A propos, Dōgen, too, is reputed to have solicited funds for the installation and consecration of a Mañjuśrī image in his proposed Monks' Hall at Kannondori in Fukakusa south of Heian in 1235, but the Chinese letter attributed to him only appears in a late biography of the master dated to 1754 and is therefore questionable. He supposedly writes, "a sacred figure of Mañjuśrī will be enshrined in the center of the hall.... We will acknowledge the gifts by installing the donors' names inside the sacred image of Mañjuśrī. The enshrined names will form myriad syllables as seeds of wisdom illuminating everyone."[79] The mention of the mantric value of the donors' enshrined names, and the esoteric assumption that they could serve as *bīja* seed syllables that would help enlighten the monks within the hall, may be the result of Keizan Jōkin's (1268–1325) later esotericizing influence on Sōtō Zen.[80] Given the shifting sands of Dōgen's views on art and imagery, one would be hard-pressed to conclude precisely how he viewed Buddhist art once and for all. Rather, Dōgen's inconsistent views on imagery seem to alter with his changing audience and changing circumstances. It is as Masunaga declares:

> Such inconsistencies develop in part, perhaps, from the different levels from which Dōgen talks; at times he is the mentor to virtual beginners, and his approach is the simple one that explains the requisites for study; occasionally [however], he is the accomplished Zen Master, who has transcended all dualisms [a]nd he speaks from the level of that accomplishment.... [I]t is often a trap for the unwary reader that is to be found in most Zen writings, since the standpoint from which the Master speaks is frequently difficult to ascertain.[81]

Fundamentally as an enlightened master, Dōgen adopts an anti-image stance because he believes that experience is not representable except in some very special cases like the *shisho*, or with a little textual deconstruction, *chinzō* portraits. Alternately, however, as a teacher attuned to the needs and capacities of his audience, he is pro-image, since he deems them beneficial to beginners. Finally, however, no definitive rule for images can be fixed for all time and circumstance for Dōgen. These considerations are the only way to make sense of all the apparent contradictions in his visual theory.

5

Concluding Remarks

IF, AS THE critical theorist Theodor Adorno observed, "art is the magic delivered from the lie of being truth,"[1] then this study has demonstrated that religious art, in a sense like magic, can both be and not be true. For Kūkai, the magic of art meant graphically constructing, but also poetically deconstructing, the absolute truth embodied in the Two World mandalas. For Dōgen, it meant embracing select Zen icons, but also using text and time to qualify the treachery of the image. For both, ultimately speaking, perception was reality.

In reconsidering our opening questions, therefore, it is necessary to keep these nuanced perspectives in mind.

In response to our first question, "Do images help or hinder the realization of Buddhahood?" the answer is an equivocating Yes. Both masters believed that images could help but also hinder one's realization of emptiness, though their emphases differ. Kukai's esoteric art could trigger awakening in a single glance and also express the entirety of the dharma better than words, but ultimately speaking, even the mandalas had to be emptied of their doctrinal value and substance. Ajikan visualizations could well facilitate the religious experience of *kaji,* and proximity to the mandalas or their intericonic rearrangements could automatically empower one's spatial location with the microcosmic palace of Dainichi in all of his personified aspects, but Kūkai's poetry also recognizes the ultimate ineffability of these provisional castles in the air. For Dōgen, conversely, Zen art could mislead as easily as it could inspire practice-realization. Full moons reflected in well water were as problematic as full moons resembling rice cakes painted on Chinese temple walls, and master portraits had to be paired with nondualizing text so that they could stand as enigmatic emblems of emptiness. At the same time, however, even crudely fashioned Buddha statues could inspire beginners, and other select Zen icons such as the *shisho* could trigger profound understanding in the spectator. For both masters, therefore, the end result is a similar nondual understanding of form and emptiness, though their emphases and approaches differ.

In response to our second question, "Does the experience of awakening involve the imagination or not?" the answer is far more polarized. Kūkai definitely engages the active imagination in visualizing the mutually empowering state of *kaji* when "Buddha enters me, I enter Buddha." By contrast, Dōgen's experience of *shinjin datsuraku* explicitly drops off body and mind, which naturally includes all imaginative content. If Kūkai's religious experience of *kaji* was understood to be the spatialized interbeing of self and *dharmadhātu* facilitated through esoteric art, then Dōgen's religious experience of *shinjin datsuraku* was understood to involve the temporalized interbecoming of buddhas and patriarchs throughout ranging time that was facilitated not by art or ritual, but rather by "just sitting." These unitive and purgative mysticisms, or active and passive meditational techniques to borrow neurotheological terminology, worked with the mind's spatio-temporal orientation faculties in different ways. Like the early Indian *kaṣina maṇḍala* meditations that he inherits, Kūkai's *via positiva* deliberately mobilizes the natural image-making activity of the mind in a positive way to ultimately expand the spatial contours of any form (oneself included) to both embrace and be enveloped by the entirety of the universe. This is experienced as a special unobstructed space that is a self-illuminating, self-revealing palatial realm of enlightenment. In contrast to Kūkai's kataphatic model, Dōgen's more apophatic *via negativa* is heir to the early Indian meditative ideal of absolute cessation (*nirodha samapatti*) in that he takes that same image-making activity of the mind but quiets it, empties it of imaginative content and drops it off along with the sensation of one's own being. Letting go of the spatial thinking that even mental images require means that from the momentary self-negating deafferented state of "no thought, no image" (*munen musō*), a self-as-world reaffirming experience can occur in, through, and as a special sense of unobstructed time. In this open temporal matrix of the ever-present now, the supposedly irreversible "arrow of time" mysteriously becomes reversible and transhistorical. It is able to flow both forward and backward to animate mountains and rivers and to awaken "buddhas alone, together with buddhas," so that each patriarch's unique satori instant is linked with all the others across the ranging aeons. Thus, Kūkai's primarily spatial, and Dōgen's primarily temporal interpretations of Kegon philosophy provide the framework for their unitive and purgative paradigms for awakening.

Their space-time interpretations also incidentally influence how they view the relationship between form and emptiness in general. Kūkai's spatial-reflexive reading of the *Heart Sūtra's* "form is emptiness, emptiness is form" sets him up for *kaji*, becoming a Buddha in this very body and the embrace of forms *as* emptiness. By contrast, Dōgen's temporal-sequential reading of form, then emptiness, then form again sets him up for the imageless void of *shinjin datsuraku*, one's subsequent enlightened perception with the True Dharma Eye, and one's post-experiential realization that this very mind already *is* Buddha and that practice already *is* realization. Both masters agree with the Mahāyāna maxim that samsara equals nirvana and that worldly forms (including even insentient ones) self-express and self-reveal the dharma. For Kūkai, however, this truism is self-evident to all, but for Dōgen, only those with his kind of deep religious experience can truly see it. As a result, from Mikkyō's perspective, Zen's undue emphasis on the void is mistaken since it forgets that all forms are inherently pure and enlightened as the *Rishukyō* states. From Zen's perspective, conversely, Mikkyō's accumulative obsession with intericonic symbolism and "smells and bells" ritualism is equally misguided, since all that counts is experience. Kūkai and Dōgen thus represent the inheritance of two distinct Buddhist poles of ontological thought and soteriological practice regarding the nature of enlightenment.

Finally, our third question, "Can art ever represent the experience of enlightenment itself?" again receives an equivocating Yes. Both masters alternately claim that religious art can and cannot be tantamount to awakening, but it depends on the image under consideration, the political or ecclesiastical priorities of each Buddhist master, and whether they assume ultimate/ontological or conventional/pedagogical standpoints appropriate to advanced or beginner audiences.

When one recognizes the collapse between signifier and signified in Mikkyō's symbol system, one appreciates that for Kūkai, art can be the direct expression of awakening. Because Kūkai understands that form and emptiness are already coterminous and nondual, he sees no problem with (empty) images whatsoever. He transcends the old early Buddhist problem of *nāma-rūpa* and makes the *monji* image-letters of reality the very basis of (empty) reality. His intericonic reservoir of forms allows for their inexhaustible recombinatory potential, and he is thereby able to convey specific esoteric doctrines visually, sculpturally, and architecturally at Tōji, Kōyasan, and the Shingon'in New Year's ceremonial hall. For Kūkai, therefore, expedient means such as the mandalas are the ultimate, the signified is the signifier, art can convey truth, and one glance can enlighten. The soteriological potential of form for Kūkai, therefore, cannot be overlooked or denied. Rather, it must be engaged with, channeled, and used as fuel for enlightenment as the

Rishukyō states. For Kūkai, therefore, all forms of the world can potentially be vehicles to awakening as they all disclose the dharma, but there nevertheless are some esoteric art forms that do it faster and better than others. The *ajikan* disk is a case in point, and the Two World mandalas, as well as all the painted and sculpted versions of its figures at key Shingon sites were considered to be the most efficacious images for illuminating anyone present in their proximity. Therefore, when speaking publicly to the court on the level of conventional truth, Kūkai makes unprecedented claims for his newly imported images to gain political favor over his predecessor Saichō. In his more private poetry, however, he speaks from the standpoint of ultimacy and deconstructs the images' value and power to enlighten. His deconstructive writings appear separately from the impact of his imagery, however, and to the average viewer, the overwhelming power of his elaborate iconographic system remains the method par excellence for representing the dharma.

Dōgen, by contrast, believes that images like Nāgārjuna's full-moon body can be extremely misleading, and he repeatedly cautions students that symbolic representations of spring, for example, are but mere stereotypes, not the actual prototypes. These examples demonstrate his disdain for imagery, since it can never reproduce the lived experience of *samādhi* or spring itself. At the same time, however, these apparently anti-image cautionary tales need to be read with a grain of salt. In these fascicles, Dōgen presents himself to his students as more enlightened than Chinese monks and better able to discern direct painting than anyone else, and as such, may have been told with ecclesiastical motivations in mind. That is, they should not be read only as evidence of Dōgen's iconoclastic tendencies, but also as a means for institution building centered around himself as superior. He therefore uses anti-image rhetoric to make a larger point about his ability to establish, lead, and extend his master's lineage in Japan. Given this fact, and Dōgen's active engagement in image-inscription and arguably even image-production, one is compelled to reassess Zen's purely iconoclastic reputation. For Dōgen, some extraordinary Zen images can re-present enlightenment provided that one see and read them with the True Dharma Eye and the kind of experiential, synesthetic sensibility that "seeing with the ears" and "hearing with the eyes" affords. This is certainly the case with the *shisho* certificate, which Dōgen says, made the ageless dharma transmission visible and present to him in a mysterious moment of illumination by the myriad compassionate buddhas. It is also the case in Dōgen's *chinzō* portraits and inscribed patriarch pictures, wherein he masterfully walks the tightrope of nondualism between public face and private moment, reflected and real moons, conventional and ultimate reality. He does not think that this art can ever replicate the experience itself, but it can approximate it and ideally even inspire unrealized beginners and advanced viewers alike to practice-realization.

Thus, Kūkai and Dōgen's enlightenment experiences do differ according to their unitive or purgative models, but their views on imagery and the nonduality of form and emptiness are fairly close in the end. In Kūkai's ontology, form and emptiness are by nature nondual, that is, forms already everywhere are empty of inherent essence, but he occasionally slips into more or less conventional or ultimate voices to stress the images' efficacy or emptiness, respectively. Dōgen does not believe the average viewer sees form as already empty, however, so his soteriology insists on emptying out conventional forms (oneself included) first before they can be perceived in that same ultimately nondual light. As a result, Kūkai emphasizes the primacy of already empty esoteric art forms to trigger and illustrate enlightenment. Dōgen first concentrates on the trigger experience itself, so that the image's ability to illustrate enlightenment in the end depends upon whether the beholder has that experientially gained True Dharma Eye or not. Kūkai concentrates on forms as already and everywhere empty, Dōgen concentrates on emptiness, which then ideally can be seen as concretized in and as form.

Significance to the Field

In posing and addressing these questions, this study has attempted to break new scholarly ground in several ways. Above all, it has furthered the comparative studies of Kūkai and Dōgen by focusing specifically on their views of imagery and its role in meditative experience. Increased scholarly attention on esoteric visual culture and revisionist scholarship deconstructing Zen's iconoclasm compel us to reevaluate the role that images played in Japanese Buddhism. Largely in reaction to charges of logocentrism, visual studies as it pertains to religion have developed as a distinct interest in the academy.[2] However, to date, no one has brought the fields of religious studies and art history to bear on a systematic comparative study of Mikkyō and Zen, arguably two of the most image-oriented sects in Buddhist history, in either its affirmative or negative light. This study is an attempt to remedy this lacuna in scholarship. More specifically, however, this study has accomplished several objectives. First, it is only the second in-depth study to compare Kūkai and Dōgen's thought, but the first since the 1980s to engage their texts and images together. These, I argue, must be considered together to understand their ideas about enlightened perception and art's ability or inability to re-present awakening. Second, it liberates Kūkai and Dōgen from sectarian scholarship, which has pigeon-holed them into iconographic/ritual vs. philological/philosophical categories. Third, its methodology restores the historical symbiosis between religious thought and artistic expression, before the academic disciplines of religious studies vs. art history were invented in the nineteenth century. Fourth, it does not rely on Western European philosophical frameworks as previous scholarship has done, but rather locates the common denominator for analysis within the Buddhist tradition itself. Finally, its comparative approach relativizes the dominance of Zen scholarship in America, and it offers a nuanced understanding of how Japanese Buddhists themselves viewed the role of imagery vis à vis awakening. Given these considerations, we can draw several interrelated conclusions about the art of enlightenment in Japanese Buddhism in terms of both form and content.

Space/Time

First, in terms of form or methodology, this comparative study has sought to break new methodological ground by proposing space and time as organizing principles for analyzing both meditative experience as well as visual and material culture. In this way, it has attempted to find a kind of "middle path" between the old insights of phenomenology and the more recent scholarly focus on the sociology of religion. Scholarship on the phenomenology of religion emerged from the late nineteenth- and early twentieth-century "inward turn," that is, the overarching concern with inner psychological states and supranormal consciousness. Consequently, Shingon became "Tibetanized," that is, *all* mandalas were understood to be visual aids for blissful personal awakening, and Zen became "Zenified," that is, idealized as the epitome of self-realization through an impossible and ritually myopic economy of means. Recent revisionist scholarship focusing on the social, political, material, and altogether constructed nature of religion, however, has debunked much of this old scholarship. Robert Sharf, for example, has demonstrated that Shingon's Two World mandalas are *not* actively visualized by meditators in contemplation as in Tibet, but rather function primarily to empower ritual space.[3] In addition, Steven Heine and Dale Wright have recovered the many historical, political, and sociological aspects of Zen ritual that D. T. Suzuki either consciously or unconsciously omitted in his reverse-Orientalist presentation of Zen minimalism to the West.[4] As a result of this latest pendular swing in academe, the baby (i.e., religious experience) has been thrown out with the bathwater so to speak. This study, however, attempts to resuscitate the role of meditative experience in the discussion of socially constructed religion in all its visual and material aspects.

In terms of content, moreover, looking at the shared inheritance of Kegon Buddhist philosophy, as opposed to European theoretical models, has demonstrated that Kūkai's and Dōgen's understandings of interpenetrating space and time correspond to both the kind of meditative experience they have and to the kind of imagery they favor. Kūkai's notion of spatial interpenetration is not only reflected in the reflexivity of *kaji* (Buddha enters me, I enter Buddha), but it also finds expression in the spatial mapping of two nondual mandalas. By contrast, Dōgen's understanding of temporal interpenetration is reflected in the process (not place) of awakening (study the self, forget the self, confirm the self), and also finds expression in the nonlinear time frame of the *shisho*. Certainly, the mandalas hint at the process of enlightenment, and the *shisho* is a material object occupying space, but in terms of *relative* emphasis, one can talk about spatialized time in Kūkai's case and temporalized space in Dōgen's. For this reason, Kūkai prioritizes becoming a Buddha in this very body (quickly), and Dōgen prioritizes the mind-to-mind realization that this very mind is Buddha (with the body seated in *zazen*). Enlightenment can be a where or a when, a thing or an event, a noun or a verb that is experienced as a sacred "betweenness" in space or as an eternal moment in time's symmetry.

Text/Image

Second, in terms of methodology, this study has attempted to use text and image analysis, that is, the traditional tools of religious studies scholars, as well as art historians, to make Mikkyō and Zen Buddhist art and doctrine accessible and understandable to audiences today. This interdisciplinary approach makes good common sense given the nature of Buddhism itself, which was promulgated throughout the pan-Asian sphere as a teaching of images. This combined hermeneutical approach, which situates Kūkai and Dōgen along India's two parallel strains of imagistic and nonimagistic meditative traditions, has helped to relativize, or at least contextualize, Suzuki's overblown claims for the superiority of Zen over all other kinds of Buddhism. Certainly every Buddhist sect ranked themselves first in their *kyōhan* doctrinal classifications; Kūkai's masterful *Ten Stages of Mind* is no different in this regard. What is different, is the disproportionate reception that Suzuki's Zen has enjoyed in the American popular imagination, and the ways in which he was able to capture America's Protestant predilection for biblical text over image, and individual charism over priestly ritual mediation. This legacy of Zen's reception in American scholarship necessitates not a knee-jerk debunking of Zen as other scholars have done, but rather a more reasoned and balanced assessment of *both* Kūkai's *and* Dōgen's views on imagery.

In terms of content, moreover, this religio-artistic analysis has revealed that Kūkai's and Dōgen's respective reputations for iconicity and iconoclasm are certainly understandable, though hopefully now more qualified and nuanced than before. By looking closely at Kūkai's and Dōgen's philosophies of form and by analyzing their writings and projects related to religious imagery, we come to understand how and why they alternately embraced and rejected the visual power of fixed images.

Expression/Experience

Finally, in terms of methodology, this study concurs with Katz's position that context, or the inherited expressions of a religious tradition, will influence what kind of mystical experience one has. It further elaborates on his central argument, however, by highlighting the important role that imagery plays in priming the subject for a particular experience. In Kūkai's case, viewing the Diamond and Womb World mandalas in China and ritually establishing a karmic tie with Dainichi pictured in the center was a crucial step or initiation that was designed to lead the adept into a much deeper, broader and sustained ritual-meditative practice for *kaji*. By comparison, in Dōgen's case, we have shown that viewing the circular format *shisho* certificates in Sung dynasty China were essential to shaping his understanding of the eternal dharma transmission, and thus to facilitating his transhistorical claims about the *shinjin datsuraku* experience. His *Hōkyōki* note distinguishing different colored lions under Nyojō's one dharma lotus canopy was also a key image for him, as he also toggles between experiential dualism and One Bright Pearl monistic rhetoric in his writings.

This careful attention to voice, as well as to context, intended audience, and motivating intent, is crucial to understanding Kūkai's and Dōgen's views, not only of imagery, but also of enlightenment itself. The term enlightenment or Buddhahood can equally refer to a state of mind, a description of the universe, a process of awakening, or a means of perception. It is important to recognize which mode of meaning Kūkai, or Dōgen, or any other Buddhist writer for that matter intends when analyzing their views. The ontological *ordo essendi* or ultimate perspective is descriptive, it is an expression of the equality and reflexivity of form and emptiness as it acknowledges the nonduality of all apparent dichotomies. The more soteriological *ordo cognoscendi* is prescriptive, it is concerned with epistemology and the experiential ways in which wisdom can be gained. Both Kūkai and Dōgen adopt these voices at different times, and it is important to attend to them especially when they speak of form, emptiness, and the nondistinction between the two.

This study has also attempted to extend Katz's reasoning even further by asserting its inverse as well. That is, not only does inherited tradition inform experience, but new experiences can also transform tradition in a dynamic feedback loop of religious thought, practice, experience, and expression. That is, religious experience is not only the byproduct of one's priming, but also the basis for new visual and verbal religious expression, which in turn becomes the received knowledge for the next generation of practitioners to inherit and experience. Katz's contextualist model leaves little room for innovation or dynamic evolution within a given religious tradition; for him mystical experience can only reinforce received tradition. This is hardly the case with Kūkai and Dōgen. As we have seen, both Buddhist masters were heirs to their Mikkyō and Sōtō traditions, respectively, but continued to transform and grow their lineages in unique ways once back in Japan. Kūkai may have displayed the Two World mandalas together for the first time, he rearranged iconic figures from the mandalas in sculptural form, created a new esoteric Buddhist New Year's ceremony, and systematically explained the sprawling corpus of esoteric Buddhist thought and practice for the Japanese. Dōgen's innovative hermeneutical moves completely revolutionized the meaning of Buddha nature, recontoured the limits of time, resignified the insentient world of mountains and rivers, and made just sitting the apotheosis of realization. Such contributions indicate that both Kūkai and Dōgen were highly original thinkers who used their meditative insight to invent entirely new visual and verbal vocabularies for understanding and transforming their worlds.

Looking Beyond Kūkai and Dōgen, or Not

In the process of investigating issues of iconicity and iconoclasm in premodern Japanese Buddhism, this study has touched upon a variety of related topics that might be considered in any religio-artistic analysis. Specifically, one might study the inherited philosophical legacies of form as expressed in text and image, and recognize that these expressions of philosophical ideas inform religious experience and vice versa. Second, studying the relative status of space and time in the arts and letters of a tradition can help determine whether that tradition's experience of the sacred, however it may be defined, will be described as either a divine union or a moment of absolute negation. Third, in considering the above, a fuller appreciation for the tradition's graphic-sculptural-architectural constructions in space or actional, performing arts in time can be gained. Finally and perhaps most important, it is essential to discuss these considerations evenhandedly and with attention to ultimate or conventional standpoints of the speakers, so as to avoid the pitfall of privileging one kind of philosophical discourse, religious experience, or specific kind of art form over another. In the Buddhist tradition alone, as this study demonstrates, there is a long and varied discourse regarding form, formlessness, and the nondistinction between the two. When viewed comparatively as has been done here, almost any world religion at one time or another might be shown to exhibit a similar range of tendencies as well.

Beyond the contours of this comparative study, therefore, several new directions in the study of icons and iconoclasm may be suggested beyond the scope of Kūkai's and Dōgen's oeuvres. Indeed the space-time analytical model, the text-image methodology, and the expression-experience feedback loop advanced here may have significant implications for the study of mystical experience and artistic expression in other religious traditions as well. In Sufism, for example, the imagery used to describe divine union with the Beloved in the secret garden of the soul vs. the experience of *fanā* and *baqā* (complete annihilation of the self in, and return from, the eternal timelessness of God) might prove to be a fruitful comparison. Detailing the spiritual marriage with Christ in the center of St. Teresa of Avila's mandalalike *Interior Castle*, and contrasting that with the *via negativa* of St. John of the Cross's *Ascent of Mount Carmel* might make for another interesting pair. Juxtaposing the spiritual trajectories and associated arts of other kataphatic and apophatic examples may well be illumined by a similar approach.

That being said, this study makes no pretensions that the Buddhist context is universally applicable. The problem of rendering visible that which is invisible, and the subsequent pitfall of fetishizing those forms of faith, explains why many religious traditions throughout the world at one point or another have tried to deconstruct their images of the absolute. However, each tradition is philosophically motivated by completely distinct theological and doctrinal models. For example, the monotheistic rationales for Jewish-, Muslim-, or Protestant-inspired iconoclasm, which are being relativized and nuanced by scholars today, are wholly disparate from the reasons behind Zen Buddhist iconoclasm, which we have shown, does not necessarily even apply to Dōgen's case. That is, questions of blasphemy, idolatry, or *shirk* (the sinful "association" of Allah with any lesser entity or limited concept) may explain some of the world's monotheistic iconoclasms, but Zen iconoclasm is primarily motivated by the urge to demonstrate one's grasp of impermanence and emptiness by not attaching to any reified image of Buddhahood. There is no strict dogma to adhere to in Zen, other than perhaps the imperative to eschew dogma itself.

Moreover, the ways that Russian Orthodox or Roman Catholic icons function theologically have little to no relation to the ways that animated Shingon Buddhist icons functioned in Japan. Byzantine icons in the Christian tradition functioned as two-way windows onto the divine, that is, they permitted the human to gaze upon the face of God and conversely, they allowed the light of God, materially rendered as gold leaf or silver plate, to be discerned visually on Earth. Japanese icons, by contrast, were usually sculpted and consecrated as "living images," that is, ritually animated with relics, scriptures, or preceptor-name rolls to symbolize the Buddha, the dharma, and the sangha community of practitioners. Their function to provide "this-worldly benefits" (Jp. *genze riyaku*) for healing, rainmaking, state protection, and other practical effects is a far cry from Christianity's theological and doctrinal rationales for making the likeness (Gk. *eikon*) of God.

Thus, the limited scope but potential relevance of this comparative study hopefully will spark new interdisciplinary research and deeper methodological insights into the questions of iconicity and iconoclasm in religious studies, art history, and studies of mysticism, and visual culture. These interrelated fields have much to gain and much to give to one another. Kūkai and Dōgen's shared leitmotif of nondualism, therefore, might serve here as a helpful reminder that such disciplinary distinctions both are, and are not, useful categories. Each area of inquiry certainly provides its own expertise and methodological rigor, but ultimately, these disciplines can and should be brought together into conversation with one another. Otherwise, to borrow Kūkai's old Indian analogy, we risk resembling the blind men discerning only but a part of the entire elephant. Far better, it would seem, to be like Dōgen's "buddhas alone, together with buddhas," so that each individual scholar, in unobstructed collaboration with others, might pool their unique talents, resources, and enthusiasms to see the one bright pearl of imaged experience.

Notes

INTRODUCTION

1. All images can be viewed in the print version of this publication.
2. See Benjamin, "The Work of Art In the Age of Mechanical Reproduction."
3. For more on cultural criticism, see Horkheimer and Adorno, "The Culture Industry: Enlightenment as Mass Deception." For more on *hibutsu*, see Rambelli, "Secrecy in Japanese Esoteric Buddhism," 107–129.
4. John 20:29 (The New Oxford Annotated Bible).
5. Arnheim, *Visual Thinking*.
6. For more on Gandhāran syncretism, see Rosenfield, "Prologue: Some Debating Points on Gandhāran Buddhism and Kuṣāṇa History," 16.
7. Yoritomi locates the roots of esoteric Buddhist culture in the southeast Indian region around Orissa in the sixth to seventh centuries. See Yoritomi, *Indo bukkyō*; Yoritomi, *Dainichikyō nyūmon*, 47–60. Ch'an/Zen's origins are traditionally traced back to Bodhidharma's sixth-century introduction of *dhyana* meditation to Shaolin monastery, China.

CHAPTER I

1. Matsunaga and Matsunaga, *Foundation of Japanese Buddhism*, vol. 1, 204–7; Matsunaga and Matsunaga, *Foundation of Japanese Buddhism*, vol. 2, 2–3. For more on constructions of Kūkai, see Nicholoff, *Sacred Kōyasan*, 31–74; Reader, *Making Pilgrimages*, 42–45.
2. Matsunaga and Matsunaga, *Foundation of Japanese Buddhism*, vol. 2, 4–7; Kitagawa, *Religion in Japanese History*, 126–28. For more on constructions of Dōgen, see Heine, *Did Dōgen Go to China?*
3. See Shaner, *The Bodymind Experience in Japanese Buddhism*; Yuasa Yasuo, *The Body: Toward an Eastern Mind-Body Theory*, 111–56.
4. Hakeda, *Kūkai Major Works* 145–46; KDZ 2:553.
5. 海外求道虚往實帰, Hakeda, *Kūkai Major Works*, 52; KZ 5:433–34.
6. Dōgen's empty-handed return is found in chapter 1 of the *Dōgen oshō kōroku.* DZZ 2: 18 n. 48. For more on this, see Kodera, *Dōgen's Formative Years in China*, 75–78; Heine, *Did Dōgen Go to China?* 260 n. 85.

7. Originally, Kūkai only used the term "world" in reference to the Diamond World mandala (*kongōkai*金剛界), not to the Womb Treasure Ocean mandala (*taizōkai*胎蔵海). However, the twin homonyms for world (*kai* 界) and ocean (*kai*海) and the mandalas' ubiquitous twin displays soon collapsed this distinction and led to the convention of calling them the Two World mandalas.

8. Hakeda, *Kūkai Major Works*, 148; KDZ 2:558.

9. Matsunaga and Matsunaga, *Foundation of Japanese Buddhism*, vol. 2, 239.

10. Mention of Myōzen's relics is found in the *Shari sōdenki* (DZZ 2:235–36). Mention of Ju-ching's portrait, Fu-jung's dharma robe and the two texts appear in the 1753 publication of Kenzei's (1417–1474) *Biography of the Founder Dōgen of Eihei* (*Eihei kaisan gyōjō kenzei-ki*), also known as the *Kenzei-ki*, though this late source should be considered with care. For more on this text, see Kawamura, *Eihei kaisan*. Mention of Fu-jung's robe also appears in the *Shisho* fascicle (Nishijima and Cross, *Master Dōgen's Shōbōgenzō*, 1:196; DZZ 1:342), the *Hōkyōki* (Kodera, *Dōgen's Formative Years in China*, 132; DZZ 2:384) and in the *Eiheiji sanso gyōgōki* (DZZ 2:398). No mention of receiving Nyojō's *shisho* certificate actually appears in the *Shisho* fascicle, but Dōgen explains that Nyojō cautioned against bragging about one's succession. Nishijima and Cross, *Master Dōgen's Shōbōgenzō*, 1:195; DZZ 1:342. For more on this, see Kodera, *Dōgen's Formative Years in China*, 75–78; Heine, *Did Dōgen Go To China?*, 24–26, 50, 260 n. 86.

11. By the Kamakura period, Kūkai's phrase for becoming a Buddha in this very body had become well-known in the esoteric strain of Tendai (*taimitsu*) monasteries on Mount Hiei where Dōgen studied.

12. DZZ 1:735

13. おのれをしるとき、密行をしるなり. DZZ 1:395.

14. Dōgen's enlightenment experience may have been the result of miscommunication and/or insightful wordplay. He may have heard his master encouraging his students either to "cast off the dust of the mind" (心塵脱落, Ch. *hsin-chen t'o lo*) or "cast off body-mind" (身心脱落, Ch. *shen-hsin t'o lo*). Both are pronounced *shinjin datsuraku* in Japanese.

15. Otto, *Mysticism East and West;* Underhill, *Mysticism*, 125–48. Underhill also proposes a third type of pilgrim mystic.

16. Weber, *The Sociology of Religion*, 166.

17. Kohn, *Early Chinese Mysticism*, vii.

18. d'Acquili, Newberg, and Rouse, *Why God Won't Go Away*, 28.

19. Ibid., 117–23.

20. Ibid., 121.

21. Ibid., 118.

22. Davidson, "The Physiology of Meditation and Mystical States of Consciousness," 386.

23. d'Acquili, Newberg, and Rouse, *Why God Won't Go Away*, 122.

24. Ibid., 118.

25. Ibid., 119.
26. Ibid., 120.
27. Suzuki, *Zen Buddhism,* 29, 30..
28. Yamasaki, *Shingon,* 119.
29. Abé, *The Weaving of Mantra,* 143–44; T 18, 207c–208a.
30. Yamasaki, *Shingon,* 119–20.
31. Hakeda, *Kūkai Major Works,* 196; KDZ 2:83.
32. Ibid.
33. For more on this see Harvey, *An Introduction to Buddhism,* 248; Sharf and Sharf, *Living Images,* 154–55.
34. Harvey, *An Introduction to Buddhism,* 252–53.
35. Williams, *Mahāyāna Buddhism,* 44.
36. Sharf and Sharf, *Living Images,* 5.
37. deBary, *The Buddhist Tradition in India, China and Japan,* 110–22.
38. Bhattacharyya, *An Introduction to Buddhist Esotericism,* vii.
39. Sharf, "Visualization and Mandala in Shingon Buddhism,"192.
40. David Morgan deconstructs the very presupposition that Protestant Christianity necessarily indicates an iconoclastic or at least anti-image sentiment. He demonstrates that American Protestants actively and effectively used a great deal of imagery in their missionary activity, in their constructions of domestic virtue and vice, and in their educational campaigns, where they even substituted American flag veneration for Bible veneration in schools in the last decade of the nineteenth century. See Morgan, *The Sacred Gaze,* 230–40. Jess Hollenbach, furthermore, effectively argues against the dominance of apophatic mysticism studies by resurrecting the importance and validity of visionary experience in an exhaustive study of Teresa of Avila's *Interior Castle* and Black Elk's *Great Vision.* See Hollenbach, *Mysticism,* 25, 155–79, 305–606.
41. Hakeda, *Kūkai Major Works,* 145–46; KDZ 2:553.
42. Sharf, "Visualization and Mandala in Shingon Buddhism," 188.
43. Suzuki, *Zen Buddhism,* 84.
44. Katz, "Language, Epistemology and Mysticism," 26–27.
45. Sharf instead argues that the Two World mandalas serve rather as agents of spatial empowerment. See Sharf, "Visualization and Mandala in Shingon Buddhism," 189. Other images in the Shingon repertoire, however, are actively visualized (e.g., during *ajikan* meditations).
46. Other passages in the *Shōbōgenzō,* however, support the idea of complete eradication of ordinary cognition during *shinjin datsuraku.*
47. See especially chapter 13 "Ritual Antiritualism" in Faure, *The Rhetoric of Immediacy;* Foulk and Sharf, "On The Ritual Use of Ch'an Portraiture in Medieval China," 149–220.
48. Faure, *Visions of Power,* 19.
49. Sharf and Sharf, *Living Images,* 7.

50. For more on the history of religion and art in the academy, see DeConcini, "Crisis of Meaning."

51. It is important to note, however, that not all art historians were provenance-hunters and all religion scholars philologists. Art historians like Soper intimately knew images' associated texts, and religion scholars such as Maspero, Tucci, and Eliade saw the connections between religious art and scriptural ideas.

52. See for example, Payne, *Tantras in East Asia*; Orzech, *Esoteric Buddhism and the Tantras in East Asia*; Abé, *The Weaving of Mantra*; Unno, *Shingon Refractions*; Sharf and Sharf, *Living Images*; Nicholoff, *Sacred Kōyasan*; Ruppert, *Jewel in the Ashes*; Rambelli, *Buddhist Materiality*.

CHAPTER 2

1. See Corbin, *Temple and Contemplation*; Eliade, *The Sacred and Profane*.

2. Abé, "Mandala as a Time Machine: Sexual Symbolism and the Figuration of Time in Shingon Buddhist Iconography"; Leighton, *Visions of Awakening Space and Time*.

3. *Chronos* is not an ideal word choice since it presupposes a linear time line. Nevertheless, it can be used to connote both an ongoing duration of temporal activity, as well as an instantaneous moment (e.g., a chronic condition that both extends throughout time and flares up at particular points in time). This double sense can provide a helpful subtext to understanding Dōgen's "ranging" (*kyōryaku*) and "just-now" (*nikon*) times, provided one discards the linear temporality that *chronos* presupposes.

4. Yamasaki, *Shingon*, 86–89; Abé, *The Weaving of Mantra*, 221–27.

5. Abé, *The Weaving of Mantra*, 211, 428.

6. Yamasaki, *Shingon*, 88; *KZ* 1:719. For more on Mikkyō's two-transmission theory, see Abé, "Capturing the Dharma."

7. It is unclear whether the esoteric and exoteric Nāgārjunas refer to the same figure, however. See Abé, *The Weaving of Mantra*, 231.

8. A purely psychosymbolic reading of this episode would indicate that it is necessary to overcome the wild fears and forces in the waters of the subconscious in order to obtain profound wisdom. In Asian mythology, *makaras* are specifically associated with the *svādhiṣṭhāna cakra* or lower *tanden* located near "the waters of the body," that is, the urogenital tracts. As a result, these ichymorphous symbols of sexual, procreative energy must be surpassed if one is to obtain profound wisdom in meditation. A full discussion of this topic, however, exceeds the confines of this investigation.

9. See Yampolsky, *The Platform Sūtra of the Sixth Patriarch*, 6 n. 8; T 50, 297–322.

10. While the Gaṇḍavyūha section of the sutra metaphorically describes young Sudhana's visit to over fifty good friends as a pilgrimage through a spiritual landscape, Kūkai adopts a more vertically oriented "heavenly ladder" paradigm of ascent

to Buddhahood. This upward directionality is an important factor in envisioning Kūkai's enlightenment paradigm.

11. See Fontein, *The Pilgrimage of Sudhana* for illustrations of Sudhana's pilgrimage in Chinese, Japanese, and Javanese art and architecture.

12. Williams, *Mahāyāna Buddhism*, 125.

13. For a clear presentation of the interpenetrating nature of Kegon cosmology, see Sadakata, *Buddhist Cosmology*, 143–57; Prince, "The Hua-yen Vision of Enlightenment."

14. Hakeda, *Kūkai Major Works*, 244–45; KDZ 2:288–89; T 10, 32a, 30a, 36b.

15. Hakeda, *Kūkai Major Works*, 245; KDZ 2:289.

16. Ibid., 217; KDZ 2:128.

17. Ibid., 256 (brackets mine); KDZ 2:324.

18. Elsewhere in the *Sokushin jōbustugi*, Kūkai spatializes this temporal expression by explaining, "Everlasting means immovable, indestructible, etc." Inagaki, *Kūkai's Principle of Attaining Buddhahood with the Present Body*, 23; KDZ 2:235.

19. Hakeda, *Kūkai Major Works*, 226; KDZ 2:223.

20. The Five Ranks of Bodhisattvahood group the fifty-two (or fifty-four) levels of spiritual advancement into five groups of ten plus two (or four) enlightened Buddha stages. These are comprised of:
    1. the ten stages of faith (*jūsshin*);
    2. ten stages of security or abodes (*jūjū*);
    3. ten stages of practice (*jūgyō*);
    4. ten stages of devotion (*jūekō*); and
    5. ten stages of development (*jūji*), which are described as *bhumi* lands.

    The stage approaching Buddhahood (*tōgaku*) and the stage of Buddhahood (*myōgaku*) are the last two enlightened Buddha stages. *Nichiei bukkyō daijiten*, 82.

21. Hakeda, *Kūkai Major Works*, 213; KDZ 1:603.

22. Ibid., 269; KDZ 2:361–62. Kūkai's mention of water and gold here references two major Kegon masters: Tu-shun (557–640) used the metaphor of water and waves, and Fa-tsang (643–712) used the metaphor of a golden lion to explain the interpenetration of universal and particular, emptiness and form.

23. Yuasa mentions this in conjunction with the philosopher Henri Bergson in his chapter on "Space-Time and Body-Mind Integration." See Yuasa, *Overcoming Modernity*, 185.

24. Abé, *The Weaving of Mantra*, 225; KZ 1:45–46; T 39, 808a.

25. Robert Sharf deconstructs as textually unfounded previous assumptions regarding the practitioner's visualized progress through the Shingon mandalas. He further underscores the importance of the mandalas as ritual agents of spatial empowerment, not personal enlightenment. He argues that in the Shingon ritual context, there are too many figures, too many morphing shapes, and too little time to do anything but ritually intone the liturgical instructions to perform deity yoga with

each Buddha or bodhisattva. He further argues that the mandalas' automatic ability to transform the ritual hall into a pure land (and hence anyone in its presence into a Buddha) means that the presence of the mandalas "does not so much serve as an aid for visualizing the deity as it abrogates the need for visualization at all." Sharf, "Visualization and Mandala in Shingon Buddhism," 192.

26. The order for discussing the nine halls of the Diamond World mandala follows Gengō's (914–95) clockwise spiral analysis outlined in the *Kongōkai kuemikki*. Gengō, however, also provides a counterclockwise analysis starting in the lower right-hand corner and ascending up and around to the left.

27. Kūkai first articulates Dainichi's four modes of self-expression in his *Becoming a Buddha in This Very Body,* but Kūkai invokes these four categories of Dainichi's enlightened nature elsewhere, as well. In the opening invocation and culminating poem of *The Precious Key to the Secret Treasury* (*Hizō hōyaku*), for example, Kūkai first takes refuge in Dainichi, then in his silence and his syllables (*dharma-mandala,* secret of speech), his symbols (*samaya-mandala,* secret of mind), his personifications (*mahā-mandala,* secret of body), and his activities (*karma-mandala,* summary of all secret activities). In the concluding poem summarizing the tenth and ultimate stage of mind, Kūkai likewise invokes Dainichi of the Diamond and Womb Worlds (*mahā-mandala*), his mantras that represent and communicate reality (*dharma-mandala*), and his symbols of his mind-power, such as vajras and swords (*samaya- mandala*). We are able to be enlightened in this very body, he concludes, if we can but realize these ubiquitous activities of his (*karma-mandala*) (Hakeda, *Kūkai Major Works,* 217 n. 222; KDZ 2:128). The Diamond World mandala puts all of these associated teachings into visual format, though it rearranges their order (Yamamoto, *Introduction to the Mandala,* 30).

28. *The Interpretations of the Six Kinds of Mandalas* (Jp. *Rokushu mandara ryakushaku*), which the Tendai monk Enchin (814–889) brought back to Japan in 858, is a two-fascicle oral commentary on the six-hall Diamond World that is based on Śubhākarasiṃha's earliest translation of the *Kongōchōkyō.* The *gobushinkan* scroll of iconographic drawings predating 855, also imported by Enchin, further illustrates the deities of the Buddha, Vajra, Ratna, Padma, and Karma halls and concludes with Śubhākarasiṃha's portrait. See Ono, *Bukkyō no bijutsu to rekishi,* chap. 4. Ono Genmyō (1883–1939) first discovered the six-mandala oral commentary at Shōren-in in Awata, Kyoto. The *gobushinkan* is preserved today at the Emman-in sub-temple of Onjōji temple in Shiga Prefecture.

29. Lokesh Chandra and other scholars theorize that Kūkai's nine-hall version may reflect Vajrabodhi's later translation of a short version of the *Kongōchōkyō* completed after Śubhākarasiṃha's and may have been designed to conform to Chinese ideals of imperial and sacred space. For more on this, see Winfield, "Mandala as Metropolis."

30. ten Grotenhuis, *Japanese Mandalas,* 45–46.

31. Komine, "Satori no tenkai," 142.

32. As a result, such jewel vases are often used in ritual *kanjō* (Skt. *abhiṣekha*) initiations to carry the water of pure transmission; and consequently, as mentioned above, are also pictured in esoteric patriarch portraits.

33. Yamamoto, *Introduction to the Mandala,* 17.

34. Earth (Skt. *Pṛthivī*), Fire (Skt. *Agni*), Air (Skt. *Vāyu*); Water (Skt. *Varuṇa*).

35. Kiyota, "Shingon Mikkyō's Twofold Mandala," 102; *Nichiei bukkyō daijiten,* 78l.

36. Nishijima and Cross, *Master Dōgen's Shōbōgenzō,* 175 (italics mine); DZZ 1:264.

37. Kasulis, "Uji (Being-Time)," 2; DZZ 1:190.

38. Ibid., 4–5 (italics mine); DZZ 1:191.

39. British astronomer Arthur Stanley Eddington first coined this phrase during his 1927 Gifford Lectures. See Eddington, *The Physical World,* chap. 6.

40. The *Lotus Sūtra* passage reads in full, "Buddhas alone, together with buddhas, can perfectly realize that all *dharmas* are real form." Nishijima and Cross, *Master Dōgen's Shōbōgenzō,* 1:52 n. 13; DZZ 1: 780–86; T 262.9, 5c11.

41. Nishijima and Cross, *Master Dōgen's Shōbōgenzō,* 1:156–57 (italics mine); DZZ 1:292.

42. 3000 worlds = 1000 worlds (10 worlds with 10 distinguishing characteristics each) X 3 periods of past, present, and future.

43. Kodera, *Dōgen's Formative Years in China,* 69. See Heine, *Did Dōgen Go to China?,* 160 n. 85.

44. Kasulis, "Uji (Being-Time)," 4; DZZ 1:191.

45. Nishijima and Cross, *Master Dōgen's Shōbōgenzō,* 1: 200; DZZ 1:345.

46. Ibid., 192; DZZ 1:339.

47. 佛祖命脈證契即通、道元即通。大宋法寶慶丁亥,住天童如淨.

48. Nishijima and Cross, *Master Dōgen's Shōbōgenzō,* 1:200; DZZ 1:345.

49. Ibid., 191 (italics mine); DZZ 1:338.

50. Kodera, *Dōgen's Formative Years in China,* 46 (brackets in original); DZZ 1: 337.

51. Nishijima and Cross, *Master Dōgen's Shōbōgenzō,* 3:215; DZZ 1:494.

52. Nishijima and Cross, *Master Dōgen's Shōbōgenzō,* 1:192–93; DZZ 1:339–40.

53. Kodera, *Dōgen's Formative Years in China,* 73–74, 160 n.186.

54. Ibid., 71; DZZ 1:338.

55. Heine, *Did Dōgen Go to China?,* 236.

56. Tanahashi, *Enlightenment Unfolds,* 201; DZZ 1:561.

57. DZZ 1:12.

58. Nishijima and Cross, *Master Dōgen's Shōbōgenzō,* 1:29; DZZ 1:12. Another commentary on the verse that further stresses the formlessness of the bell's emptiness appears in Dōgen's *Hōkyōki* journal, which he supposedly kept during his studies in China from 1223–1227. *Hōkyōki* entry no. 38 reports a clarifying exchange between Dōgen and his Chinese master. Dōgen rhetorically asks, "The so-called emptiness does not refer to the form of emptiness, does it? Skeptics always think of emptiness as a form. Today's students…see the blue sky and call it emptiness. I truly feel sorry for them." Ju-ching replied with compassion: "What is called

emptiness is *prajñā*, and not the emptiness as in the form of emptiness....Not one of the abbots in all corners of the world realizes even the nature of forms; how much less can they illuminate emptiness?" Kodera, *Dōgen's Formative Years in China*, 135. For the questionable dating of this journal, see Heine, *Did Dōgen Go to China?*, 36–38.

59. Yuasa, *Overcoming Modernity*, 188.

60. Sharf, "Visualization and Mandala in Shingon Buddhism," 183.

61. KDZ 3:483.

62. In this expedient visual metaphor, the negative node above indicates a state of no-mind, the positive node below indicates gathering one's vital energies at the lower *tanden,* which prevents so-called Zen sickness. The eighteenth-century Rinzai monk Hakuin Ekaku (1686–1768) was one of the most famous sufferers of Zen sickness. Hakuyū's prognosis was: "Your meditation has been too unmeasured and your asceticism too strict....Facing your previous overmeditation, you are now seeing severe sickness....Gather together the flames of your heart and place them under your navel and below your feet, then your whole chest will become cool....Energetically fill the lower part of your body with spiritual energy, this is essential for nourishing life." Addiss, *The Art of Zen*, 105.

63. Nagatomo, "The Logic of The Diamond Sūtra." Okumura, *Realizing Genjōkōan*, iii.

64. Eckel, *To See the Buddha*, 29.

65. Waddell and Abe, "Genjōkōan," 129–30; DZZ 1:7–8.

66. Ibid., 130; DZZ 1:8.

67. DZZ 1:480. Given Dōgen's particular temporal framework, the term for form (*sō*) is better translated as aspect-phases, so that Tathāgata indicates a "whole state of action." Nishijima and Cross, *Master Dōgen's Shōbōgenzō*, 3:191 n.2.

68. Waddell and Abe, "Genjōkōan," 128; DZZ 1:7.

69. Dumoulin, *Zen Buddhism*, 86.

CHAPTER 3

1. These three modes or dimensions of Dainichi's self-expression, as well as the fourth summative dimension of Dainichi's combined activities (*karma-mandala*) are pictured in the first four mini-mandalas of the Diamond World outlined in chapter 2.

2. I adapt this phrase from Kitagawa, who relies on Haas to describe the Neo-Confucian shogunate of the Edo period. See Kitagawa, *Religion in Japanese History*, 154, n. 54.

3. Hakeda, *Kūkai Major Works*, 145–46; KDZ 2:552–53.

4. Hakeda, *Kūkai Major Works*, 128; KDZ 6:83.

5. Hakeda, *Kūkai Major Works*, 234; KDZ 2:253. Originally, mirrorlike wisdom is associated with Yogācāra's deepest eighth *ālayavijñāna*, which enables access to the enlightened wisdom of the *dharmadhātu*.

6. KDZ 2:307–308, 341 n. 24.

7. Scholars have debated for centuries whether this text is incomplete, but this is improbable as Kūkai considered it required reading for his Sanskrit students. It is also possible that Kūkai only focused on objects of sight after his analysis of language in order to bridge the relationship between text and image, sound and form, *nāma-rūpa* in a fully developed theory of *monji*.

8. In phenomenological terminology, *nōen* refers to the noetic act and *shoen* refers to the noematic content. Shaner, *The Bodymind Experience in Japanese Buddhism*, 108.

9. Hakeda, *Kūkai Major Works*, 246; KDZ 2:293–94.

10. Ibid., 229–30; KDZ 2:234–36.

11. *Kyōhan* is an abbreviation of the term *kyōsō hanjaku*, which refers to the "classification of the various tenets of Buddhism from some particular sectarian standpoint." *Nichiei bukkyō daijiten*, 190L–191R.

12. Yogācāra identifies three sources for the arising of existences: imagination (Skt. *parikalpita*), dependent origination (Skt. *paratantra*), and perfect existence or suchness (Skt. *pariniṣpanna*). See Hakeda, *Kūkai Major Works*, 197 n. 128.

13. KDZ 2:106

14. KDZ 2:127.

15. Kūkai was influenced by two very different language systems: ideographic Chinese, as well as alphabetic Sanskrit. He mastered classical Chinese under his maternal uncle Atō and at the state university in Nagaoka c. 791, and was familiar with China's *I-ching* philosophy that symbolically condensed the world's yin/yang energy combinations into microcosmic diagrams and trigrams. Kūkai specifically mentions the *Eight Trigrams of Fu-hsi* in the opening lines of his earliest known work, the *Indications of the Goals of the Three Teachings* (*Sangō shiiki*), written c. 727 at age twenty-four. Hakeda, *Kūkai Major Works*, 101–39; KDZ 6:5–121. Yet Kūkai also studied Sanskrit and Siddham calligraphy under the Indian masters Prajñā and Muniśrī while in Chang'an from 804–806, and Indian *mantrayāna* that condensed universal energies into microphonic sound bites. His *Catalogue of Imported Items* stresses the need for maintaining the original pronunciation of the Sanskrit mantras, as transliterating their sounds into Chinese characters can only approximate or mix up the long and short vowels, thereby warping their meaning and ultimate efficacy. Hakeda, *Kūkai Major Works*, 144; KDZ 2:549. Finally, Kūkai absorbed the ancient Chinese and Vedic theories that Chinese characters and Sanskrit *bīja* sound syllables actually exist on a suprahuman plane. According to Chinese mythology, written characters emerged from the primordial waters of creation on the back of a world-bearing tortoise, and according to Vedic lore, the Hindu goddess of speech, Vac, first uttered the primordial mantras of creation when she spoke the world into being. Kūkai's familiarity with these mythologies is evidenced by his commentary on the *Heart Sūtra* written in 834, the year before he died. In the *Secret Key to the Heart Sūtra* (*Hannya shingyō hiken*), Kūkai proclaims that the scripture's words are tantamount to the characters that appeared on the shell of the primordial

tortoise, the signs on divination stalks, the interpenetrating nodes of Indra's net, or of Sanskrit grammar that contains myriad meanings. Hakeda, *Kūkai Major Works*, 265; KDZ 2:352–55.

16. Rambelli, *Buddhist Materiality*, 88–128.

17. An interesting analogy can be drawn with Psalm 19:1–4, which states that "The heavens declare the glory of God; the skies proclaim the work of his hands. Day after day they pour forth speech; night after night they reveal knowledge. They have no speech, they use no words; no sound is heard from them. Yet their voice goes out into all the earth, their words to the ends of the world" (New International Version). It can also be compared with the late nineteenth-century European literary and artistic movement of Symbolism, which theorized the direct expression of ideas through signs. As the art critic Albert Aurier wrote in March of 1891, "in the eyes of the artist, that is, the one who must express absolute beings...[objects] can only appear to him as signs. These are the letters of an immense alphabet which only the man of genius knows how to spell." Aurier, "Le Symbolisme en Peinture: Paul Gaugin," 160. Conversely, the Symbolist poet Saint-Pol Roux also saw words as "setting sail for sculpturality." See Delevoy, *Symbolists and Symbolism*, 80.

18. Abé, *The Weaving of Mantra*, 339; KZ 1:251–52.

19. KDZ 2:274.

20. Hakeda, *Kūkai Major Works*, 145; KDZ 2:552.

21. Hakeda, *Kūkai Major Works*, 150; KDZ 2:563.

22. See Gardiner, "Kūkai and the Beginnings of Shingon Buddhism in Japan," for a detailed analysis of this text.

23. T 16, 525b.

24. This text is a one-hundred-fascicle commentary on the *Mahāprajñāpāramitā sūtra*, attributed to Nāgārjuna and translated by Kumarājiva. T 25, 13c.

25. Hakeda, *Kūkai Major Works*, 247; KDZ 2:302; T 39, 656a.

26. KDZ 6:163. My translation of the last two lines is more literal than Hakeda's poetic interpretation, which reads: "It is open or closed depending on how we look at it;/ His silence or eloquence make incisive tongues numb." Hakeda, *Kūkai Major Works*, 91. Hakeda's interpretation would suggest that our own level of enlightenment determines our reading comprehension of the book of life, and the experience of reading between the lines of Dainichi's silence and speech itself cannot be put into words.

27. This notion that words are tantamount to real forms gave rise to at least one medieval miracle tale in which Kūkai ends a devastating drought. He traces the character for "dragon" on the water surface of a dwindling creek bed, and the fluid character magically transforms into an actual rain-bearing dragon. See Tanabe, "Kōbō Daishi and the Art of Esoteric Buddhism," 410. This gives a new twist to Kūkai's earlier admonitions against water-painting, for in the Shingon context, mantras and other power-words (in this case, dragons) can fully mirror and manifest their actual referents.

28. KDZ 2:128.

29. Abé, *The Weaving of Mantra,* 129–30 (brackets in original); KZ 2:40–41.

30. The analogy of Mount Sumeru as brush and the earth as ink differs from the *Seireishū* analogy of mountain brushes and ocean ink. It makes sense, however, if one is familiar with illustrations of traditional Buddhist cosmology, in which the tip of an inverted Sumeru mountain dips down into the earth and its pool of concentric oceans. KDZ 2:325.

31. The *ten* seal-style calligraphy had first emerged under Ch'in Shih Huang-ti during the Warring States Period and *rei* squared writing standardized it during the Han dynasty. I am grateful to Professor Kishida Tomoko of Kōyasan University for her illuminating lecture on "*Kōbō daishi to chugoku no bunka*" at Osaka's Taiyūji Temple on September 13, 2001. For more on Kūkai and lexicography, see Bailey, "Early Japanese Lexicography."

32. Tanabe, "Kōbō Daishi and The Art of Esoteric Buddhism," 411, citing Nakata, *The Art of Japanese Calligraphy,* 68.

33. *Kōbōdaishi to mikkyō bijutsu,* 92.

34. Rinne, *The 53rd Annual Exhibition of Shōsōin Treasures,* 10.

35. The term *nyoze* in Japanese is most commonly recognized as the set phrase, "Thus have I heard," a standard opening line in many Buddhist sutras. The term *jūnyoze* can accordingly be translated as the Ten Factors of Existence or, more generally, as the Ten Examples of Suchness.

36. *Nichiei bukkyō daijiten,* 153 *l.*

37. *Kōbō daishi ten,* n.p.

38. Ibid.

39. Payne, "*Ajikan*: Ritual and Meditation in the Shingon Tradition," 223–24.

40. Kiyota, *Shingon Buddhism,* 72.

41. Payne, "*Ajikan*: Ritual and Meditation in the Shingon Tradition," 228–31.

42. Hakeda and Payne explain that this can indicate the union of body and mind and/ or the linking of right and left thumbs to form the *vajrāñjali mudrā.* See Hakeda, *Kūkai Major Works,* 220 n. 230; Payne, "*Ajikan*: Ritual and Meditation in the Shingon Tradition," 228.

43. Hakeda, *Kūkai Major Works* 220–21 (brackets in original, parentheses mine); KDZ 2:136.

44. Ibid., 219–20; KDZ 2:135–36. The fifth mantra is spelled *Āṃḥ* in KDZ.

45. See Ruppert, *Jewel In The Ashes.*

46. When describing the *Dainichikyō* in the *Daibirushana jōbutsukyō shomonshitai,* Kūkai says that the text itself illuminates the great mind, explains all-knowing wisdom and the equality of wisdom and method. See KDZ 3:543. Likewise, when discussing the *Kongōchōkyō* in his 830 *Precious Key to the Secret Treasury,* Kūkai states that the methods of *samādhi* described therein are so powerful that they should be strictly reserved for *kanjō* initiates only lest one die young, invite afflictions, or be reborn in hell. See Hakeda, *Kūkai Major Works,* 223; KDZ 2:143. Also, when discussing the *Kongōchōkyō* in the *Kongōchōkyō kaidai,* Kūkai describes the text that

outlines but the tip of Dainichi's iceberg, literally calling its descriptions but "the antennae of a snail" (*kuwakaku*). See KDZ 3:139.

47. KDZ 2:558.

48. As mentioned earlier in the Introduction, Hakeda mitigates this claim by translating it as "the sight of them *may well* enable one to attain Buddhahood." Hakeda, *Kūkai Major Works* 145–46.

49. Sharf, "Visualization and Mandala in Shingon Buddhism," 187–88. DeBary translates this last sentence, "Art is what reveals to us the state of perfection." deBary, *The Buddhist Tradition*, 138; KDZ 2:553.

50. Hakeda, *Kūkai Major Works*, 150. KDZ 2:563. The ambivalence regarding visibility of the dharma reflects Madhyamaka influence; the image of the recovered gem in the dirt and opening one's spiritual eyes is an expression of Tathāgatagarbha thought. Dōgen's *One Bright Pearl* (*Ikka myōju*) also references this *Lotus Sūtra* episode in which a poor man remains oblivious of a precious pearl sewn into the lining of his coat by a dharma friend. T 262, 9, 1c3.

51. Various versions of this sutra had been used for over a century to refresh the four deva kings' vow to safeguard the four corners of the land from calamity and illness by virtue of the Buddha's golden purifying light. Specifically, Emperor Shōmu first issued ten copies of the latest version of *The Sūtra of the Victorious Kings of the Golden Light Ray* (*Konkōmyō saishōōkyō*) to every province in the twelfth month of 728. *Kokubunji*, 147.

52. Ruppert, *Jewel in the Ashes,* 103–4 (brackets in original); KZ 3:518–19.

53. Yamaori, *Wandering Spirits and Temporary Corpses,* 155.

54. The anonymous *Origin and Practice of the Mishuhō* (*Goshichinichi mishuhō yuisho sahō*) describes how Tōji's Abbot Kangen performed the ritual in 921, and the *Diary of the Mishuhō at the Imperial Mantra Chapel in the Second Year of Eichi* (*Eichi ninen shingon-in mishuhōki*) describes how the Tōji Abbot Kanjin (1084–1153) performed the ritual in 1142. Abé, *The Weaving of Mantra*, 349. The Shingon'in Mishuhō arrangement is illustrated in Scroll 6, section 4 of Sumiyoshi Jokei's seventeenth-century copy of Tokiwa Mitsunaga's late twelfth-century *Handscroll of Annual Ceremonies* (*Nenjū gyōgi emaki*). See figure 158, Mason, *History of Japanese Art*, 135.

55. This parallel confrontation model, in which the two mandalas are hung parallel to the hall's side walls facing each other with altars extending out into the open space of the room, has been a standard Shingon arrangement for initiations since at least the founding of Murōji's Kanjōdō in 1308. Fowler, *Murōji*, 120. It continues to be set up today at Kongōbuji's Golden Hall for the annual *kechien kanjō* (Skt. *abhiṣekha*) lay initiation rituals, which alternate between the two mandalas every May (for Womb World initiations) and October (for Diamond World initiations).

56. For more on this, see Ruppert, *Jewel in the Ashes.*

57. For more on the Mishuhō see Abé, *The Weaving of Mantra*, chap. 8; Ruppert, *Jewel in the Ashes*, chap. 4; Yamaori, *Wandering Spirits and Temporary Corpses* chapter 5; Mack, "A Reconsideration of the Goshichinichi mishuhō." For rare

photographs of how this secret annual ritual is arranged at Tōji today, see Tōji soken issen-nihyakunen kinen shuppan hensan iinkai, *Shin tōbōki,* 119–23.

58. Duara, *Culture, Power and The State,* 146.

59. KDZ 2:532.

60. The *Kongōchōkyō* was translated into Chinese by both Vajrabodhi (Ch. Chin-kang chih; Jp. Kongōchi, 671–741) and his disciple Amoghavajra (Ch. Pu-k'ung Chin-kang; Jp. Fukū kongō, 705–74) in the mid-eighth century. The *Dainchikyō* is a mid-seventh-century text translated into Chinese in 724 by Śubhākarasiṃha (Ch. Shan Wu-wei; Jp. Zemmui, 637–735) and I-hsing (Jp. Ichigyō, 684–727).

61. ten Grotenhuis, *Japanese Mandalas,* 53–57.

62. For more on this see Winfield, "Mandala as Metropolis."

63. Steinhardt, *Chinese Imperial City Planning,* 109–18.

64. For more on the role of these scriptures in East Asian statecraft, see Orzech, *Politics and Transcendent Wisdom*; Osabe, *Tenno wa doko kara kita ka*; Yoritomi and Tachikawa, *Chūgoku mikkyō,* 141–53.

65. For more on this text, see Abé, *The Weaving of Mantra,*193–204; KDZ 4:321–53; KZ 2:157–72.

66. KDZ 4:328; KZ 2:156.

67. Abé, *The Weaving of Mantra,* 195.

68. Hakeda, *Kūkai Major Works,* 53; KZ 3:476.

69. For an example of this, see Hershock, *Liberating Intimacy.*

70. Bogel, *With a Single Glance,* 322.

71. This pentad selects one bodhisattva from each of the five moon disks in the Diamond World's central Perfected Body Hall (nos. 1, 5, 9 and 13 from figure 2.13). Dainchi's Kongōharamitsu (Skt. *Vajrapāramitā*) in the center functions metonymically for all four perfection (*pāramitā*) bodhisattvas in the center disk of the Diamond World mandala. Ashuku's Kongōsatta (Skt. *Vajrasattva*), Hōshō's Kongōhō (Skt. *Vajtaratna*), Amida's Kongōhō (Skt. *Vajradharma*), and Fukūjōju's Kongōgō (Skt. *Vajrakarma*) are four select great bodhisattvas who function metynomically for all sixteen great bodhisattvas in the four cardinal disks of the Perfected Body Hall of the Diamond World mandala.

72. At Tōji, Fudō Myōō (Skt. *Acalanātha*) is surrounded by Kongō yasha (Skt. *Vajrayakṣa,* alt. *Vajrahūṃkara*), Gozanze (Skt. *Trailokyavijaya*), Daiitoku (Skt. *Yamāntaka*), and Gundari (Skt. *Kuṇḍali*). Technically, in the Womb World mandala, Fudō appears to the extreme right of Hall 3, Hannya bosatsu (Skt. *Prajñāpāramitā*) appears in the center and Gundari does not appear at all.

73. Ashuku Hōshō, Fukūjōju, Muryōju.

74. Gardiner, "Mandala, Mandala on the Wall," 255.

75. Gardiner, *Kōyasan,* 25.

76. *Tanjō garan to okunoin,* 123.

77. Ibid., no. 46, 118–22.

78. Sawa, *Mikkyō no bijutsu,* 19.

79. Hakeda erroneously identifies these figures as "the Mahāvairocana of the Diamond Realm, surrounded by the four buddhas of the Matrix (Womb) realm placed to the east, south, west, and north." Hakeda, *Kūkai Major Works,* 50.

80. Dōmoto, *Dōmoto Inshō: gushōga hen,* 286. Dōmoto only specifies consulting *The Precious Key to the Secret Treasury* and *The Catalogue of Imported Items,* but in preparing his sketches he also consulted *zuzō* iconographic manuals.

81. Abé, *The Weaving of Mantra,* 280.

82. These two levels of perceiving the world technically derive from Nāgārjuna's middle way school of Madhyamaka, or, more specifically, from its Svātantrika subsect, which asserts that *dharmas* exist on the conventional level but cannot be said to exist as discrete *dharmas* on the ultimate level.

83. KDZ 2:294.

84. Hakeda, *Kūkai Major Works,* 99; *KZ* 3:554.

85. Gibson and Murakami, *Tantric Poetry of Kūkai (Kōbō Daishi), Japan's Buddhist Saint,* 23–34; KDZ 6:677–88. This list originally appears in the *Mahāvairocana sūtra's* section on Entering the Shingon Gate: The Mind for Staying There. T 18, 3b.

86. Kūkai also references this list of empty analogies when discussing Yogācāra in the sixth stage of mind of the *Precious Key to Secret Treasury.* Hakeda, *Kūkai Major Works,* 200; KDZ 2:93.

87. Kūkai's intended reader here is Master Kōchi (770–?) of the Eastern Mountains (*tōzan*) in Shimotsuke Province (present-day Tochigi prefecture). Kūkai is also known to have sent Kōchi the *Vajraśekhara sūtra* and the *Kanensho* appeal for disseminating esoteric texts twelve years earlier in 815. See Gardiner, "Kūkai and the Beginnings of Shingon Buddhism in Japan," 34, 48–51; "Transmission Problems."

88. Gibson and Murakami, *Tantric Poetry of Kūkai (Kōbō Daishi), Japan's Buddhist Saint,* 28; KDZ 6:683–84.

89. Abé, *The Weaving of Mantra,* 338; KZ 1:830.

90. Letter 84, KDZ 4:207–8.

91. KDZ 6:511–12.

92. Ibid., 513–14.

93. Ibid., 512.

94. Abé, *The Weaving of Mantra,* 132; T 18, 1c.

95. Ibid., 133 (parentheses in original, brackets mine); T 18, 4c.

96. Enlightened mind is the cause, great compassion is the foundation, and skillful means are the ultimate. Yamasaki, *Shingon,* 105; T 18, 1c.

97. Yamasaki, *Shingon,* 105; T 18, 1c.

CHAPTER 4

1. Remarks delivered at the American Philosophical Association Eastern Divisional meeting, Philadelphia, PA, 2003, in response to a panel dedicated to his *Focusing the Familiar.*

2. Waddell and Abe, *The Heart of Dōgen's Shōbōgenzō*, 77; DZZ 1:22; T 51, 2076

3. Ibid., 83; DZZ 1:26.

4. 金剛經云。過去心不可得。現在心不可得。未來心不可得。上座欲點那箇心; T2003.048.0143c06-c07.

5. Heine, *Opening a Mountain*, 94–96.

6. Waddell and Abe, *The Heart of Dōgen's Shōbōgenzō*, 83; DZZ 1:26.

7. Ibid., 81–82; DZZ 1:25.

8. Nishijima and Cross, *Master Dōgen's Shōbōgenzō*, 2:278; DZZ 1:210.

9. Waddell and Abe, *The Heart of Dōgen's Shōbōgenzō*, 79; DZZ 1:23.

10. Ibid., 81; DZZ 1:24.

11. Ibid., 84; DZZ 1:26.

12. Nishijima and Cross, *Master Dōgen's Shōbōgenzō*, 2:280; DZZ 1:212.

13. Tanahashi, *Moon in a Dewdrop*, 136; DZZ 1:212.

14. Waddell and Abe, *The Heart of Dōgen's Shōbōgenzō*, 82; DZZ 1:25.

15. Ibid.

16. Ibid.

17. Thanks are due to Shohaku Okumura for clarifying Ingen's (1592–1673) seventeenth-century inscription on a famous Dōgen portrait housed at Kōshōji (personal communication with the author, 7/17/11). Ingen's inscription on this later portrait reads, "the appearance of 'appearance as no appearance' can't be seen visually but can only be known by means of wisdom. Therefore, not using the mind to look for reality is awareness." Thanks to Prof. Grace Lin of Elon University for her assistance in reading Ingen's highly abraded and stylized calligraphy.

18. Many thanks to Taigen Dan Leighton for this clarification (personal communication with the author, 6/29/11).

19. Brinker and Kanazawa, *Zen Masters of Meditation in Images and Writings,* 161.

20. This portrait from Honmyōji in Kumamoto should not be confused with another image that Leighton reports seeing at Honmyōji in Kumamoto in 1992. According to Leighton, he saw what "indeed looks like a young Dōgen, a bit more round-faced than the later portraits, but recognizably the same monk." Leighton and Okumura, *Dōgen's Extensive Record,* 42. That image was signed "Monk Dōgen of Kenninji, Karoku 3," and was a brighter line-drawn image of a smiling Dōgen with *jisan* no. 18 inscribed in calligraphy attributed to Dōgen's own hand (personal communication with the author, 8/14/11). This author's efforts to locate that image at Honmyōji in Kumamoto were unsuccessful.

21. *Honmyōji*, 23. The Ankokuji temple system for national pacification was created by the Ashikaga shōgunate between 1362–1367, but like its Nara-period Kokubunji predecessors, many already extant temples throughout the country simply changed their names. Without further information from Sonkai, therefore, it is all but impossible to determine the date or the location of this Ankokuji reference with any certainty.

22. *Honmyōji*, 24.

23. Heine, *Did Dōgen Go To China?*, 123; DZZ 2:188. Also translated in Leighton and Okumura, *Dōgen's Extensive Record*, 608; Tanahashi *Enlightenment Unfolds*, 29.

24. For this reason a fish-shaped hollow wooden drum (*mokugyō*) is traditionally suspended and struck outside of the monks' hall to signal the start and end times of meditation.

25. Leighton and Okumura, *Dōgen's Extensive Record*, 602 (italics mine); DZZ 2:187.

26. Heine, *Zen Poetry of Dōgen*, 130–31 and Genryū Kagamishima's 1988 edition of the DZZ omits the donkey reference, but Tanahashi, *Enlightenment Unfolds*, 260 also includes it. Leighton and Okumura explain that the character for donkey may have been added later, and that Manzan's revision of the verse in his edition of the *Eihei kōroku* invokes Ts'ao-shan's exchange about donkeys and wells observing each other. Leighton and Okumura, *Dōgen's Extensive Record*, 602 n. 15.

27. Leighton and Okumura, *Dōgen's Extensive Record*, 605; DZZ 2:188. Heine translates this verse alternately:

    If you take this portrait of me to be real, Then what am I, really? But why hang it there, If not to anticipate people getting to know me? Looking at this portrait, Can you say that what is hanging there [on the wall] Is really me? In that case your mind will never be Fully united with the wall (as in Bodhidharma's wall-gazing meditation cave) Heine, *Zen Poetry of Dōgen*, 131 (brackets mine).

28. For more on *chinzō* veneration in Sung China, see Foulk and Sharf, "On the Ritual Use of Ch'an Portraiture."

29. Leighton and Okumura, *Dōgen's Extensive Record*, 605 n. 30

30. Ju-ching's portrait was located at Eiheiji according to an entry in the *Honkō kokushi nikki* dated 1611, and according to Itō Keidō, this may have been moved to nearby Hōkyōji in Echizen Province. Other versions of this *chinzō* exist at Kōshōji in Uji and in the private collection of Okazaki Masaya of Tokyo. Kodera, *Dōgen's Formative Years*, 77.

31. Many thanks to Profs. Sun Lixia (Dalian University) and Grace Lin (Elon University) for their translation help.

32. Ning-tsung (r. 1194–1224), an emperor of the Southern Sung dynasty, determined the rank of the five major monasteries of the Lin-chi School of Ch'an, modeling after the five major *vihāras* of India: (1) Hsing-sheng Wan-shou monastery on Mount Ching; (2) Ching-te Ling-yin monastery on Mount Pei; (3) T'ien Tung Ching-te monastery on Mount T'aipai; (4) Ching-tz'u Pai-en-kuang shiao monastery on Mount Nan; and (5) Kuang-li Monastery on Mount Ayu wang. Kodera, *Dōgen's Formative Years in China*, 152 n. 23.

33. Ibid., 600–601: DZZ 2:186.

34. Ibid., 600–1, n. 6–9.

35. Nishijima and Cross translate this title and catch-phrase as The Non-Emotional Preaches the dharma, maintaining that "nature can only teach us the truth when we ourselves are balanced (non-emotional)." Nishijima and Cross, *Master Dōgen's Shōbōgenzō*, 3: 115. I, however, prefer the traditional translation of "the insentient preaching of the dharma." I have therefore replaced "non-emotional" with "insentient" in citations from the *Mujō seppō* fascicle.

36. Waddell and Abe, *The Heart of Dōgen's Shōbōgenzō*, 61; DZZ 1:14. See also Kim, "'The Reason of Words and Letters': Dōgen and Kōan Language."

37. Nishijima and Cross, *Master Dōgen's Shōbōgenzō*, 1: 12; DZZ 1:737. This is a favorite set phrase of Dōgen's in the *Bendōwa* and other fascicles.

38. DZZ 1:258, 264.

39. DZZ 1:259.

40. Nishijima and Cross, *Master Dōgen's Shōbōgenzō*, 1: 9 (parentheses mine); DZZ 1:735.

41. Nishijima and Cross, *Master Dōgen's Shōbōgenzō*, 3:117 (brackets mine); DZZ 1:400.

42. Ibid., 117 n. 15.

43. Ibid., 122; DZZ 1:403.

44. Nishijima and Cross, *Master Dōgen's Shōbōgenzō*, 2: 212; DZZ 1:169.

45. For more on the various twelve, twenty-six, sixty, seventy-five, or ninety-five fascicle *Shōbōgenzō* collections, see Heine, *Did Dōgen Go to China?*, 70.

46. Nishiyama and Stevens, *Shōbōgenzō (The Eye and Treasury of the True Law)*, vol. 2, 102; DZZ 1:497.

47. For more on Dōgen's source material for this fascicle, see Heine, *Did Dōgen Go to China?*, 120.

48. Nishijima and Cross, *Master Dōgen's Shōbōgenzō*, 1:239–40; DZZ 1:175.

49. Ibid., 241; DZZ 1:176.

50. DZZ 1:176.

51. Nishijima and Cross, *Master Dōgen's Shōbōgenzō*,3:215; DZZ 1:494. Nishiyama and Stevens translate this as "The autumn breeze is pure and fresh, the autumn moon is clear and bright. With enlightened vision we can see the real form of the great earth, mountains and rivers. Staying at Zuiganji has renewed my vision. The sound of the stick and the shout of a *katsu* are again lively as we test each other." Nishiyama and Stevens, *Shōbōgenzō (The Eye and Treasury of the True Law)*, vol. 2, 99.

52. Nishiyama and Stevens, *Shōbōgenzō (The Eye and Treasury of the True Law)*, vol. 2, 99; DZZ 1:494.

53. Ibid.

54. See McFarland, "If You Meet the Patriach, Kill Him! Dispensing With Bodhidharma."

55. Yuasa, *Overcoming Modernity*, 191

56. For more on Dōgen's move to Echizen, see Heine, *Did Dōgen Go to China?*, 155–72.

57. Ōkubo notes that the character for body 身 *mi* can also be read as the character for eye 眼 *manako*. See note at bottom of DZZ 2:412. Heine accordingly translates

the alternate title *Fubo shoshō no manako* as "True Seeing Received At Birth," a title which references two *Lotus Sūtra* passages about returning to one's original home. See Heine, *The Zen Poetry of Dōgen*, 84, 102, 170 n. 11. However, given all of the poem's corporeal double entendres, I have chosen to translate Dōgen's original character more literally to capture his sentiment of recovering his original nature or "true body" before his parents were born.

58. Heine, *The Zen Poetry of Dōgen*, 84. DZZ 2:412.

59. Ibid., 84–85.

60. Waddell and Abe, "Genjōkōan," 79; DZZ 1:779.

61. Takahashi, *The Essence of Dōgen*, 41–43.

62. Waddell and Abe, *The Heart of Dōgen's Shōbōgenzō*, 66; DZZ 1:16.

63. Abé, *The Weaving of Mantra*, 280; Heine, *A Blade of Grass*, 6.

64. "[T]he term *sūtra* was translated into Chinese as *ching* (Jp. *kyō*), [meaning] 'vertical (or temporal) thread,'…[Buddhist sutras were thus the] 'temporal thread' preserving the names impregnated with rectifying power given by the sages of ancient India." Abé, *The Weaving of Mantra*, 316. This lends further import to Kūkai's claim in the *Sokushin jōbutsugi*, for example, that "All of these existences (i.e., the three kinds of symbols: letters, signs, and images) are interrelated horizontally and vertically without end, like images in mirrors, or like the rays of lamps." Hakeda, *Kūkai Major Works*, 232.

65. Waddell and Abe, *The Heart of Dōgen's Shōbōgenzō*, 48 (brackets mine); DZZ 1:189. Brackets inspired by Kasulis and Nagatomo's unpublished 1976 translation, which reads:

> An old Buddha says:
> There is a time [I am] standing on the highest mountain peak;
> There is a time [I am] roaming about in the depths of the sea.
> There is a time [I am] a three-headed, eight-armed [demon];
> There is a time [I am] a sixteen-foot tall [Buddha].
> There is a time [I am] a staff or hossu;
> There is a time [I am] a pillar or stone lantern.
> There is a time [I am] just somebody or other
> (Mr. Chang or Mr. Li)
> There is a time [I am] the vast earth or endless sky.

66. Here it should be noted that I use "reality" as a convenient collective singular for the plurality of *dharmas* that are constantly coming and going out of existence. It should be noted that Dōgen choses to itemize particular moment-beings in time and does not fix or reify them into any overarching noun.

67. Waddell and Abe, "Buddha-Nature Part I," 103; DZZ 1:16.

68. See Stone, *Original Enlightenment*, 272–88 for more on Nichiren's *daimoku gohonzon* and related imagery. See Dobbins, "Portraits of Shinran," 22–25 for more on Shinran's use of calligraphic scrolls invoking the illustrious name of Amida Buddha.

69. Watson, *The Lotus Sūtra,* 40.

70. Masunaga, *A Primer of Sōtō Zen,* 55.

71. Tanahashi, *Enlightenment Unfolds,* xlix, 200; DZZ 2:405. This account appears in the 1753 publication of Kenzei's (1417–1474) *Biography of the Founder Dōgen of Eihei (Eihei kaisan gyōjō kenzei-ki).* It is possible that the eighteenth-century editor of the biography and/or the fifteenth-century Kenzei put these words into thirteenth-century Dōgen's mouth, so this account should be considered with care.

72. Ibid., xlix.

73. Ibid., 259; DZZ 2:399.

74. Watson, *The Lotus Sūtra,* 39.

75. Kodera, *Dōgen's Formative Years in China,* 135.

76. McFarland, "If You Meet the Patriach, Kill Him! Dispensing With Bodhidharma," 14

77. Masunaga, *A Primer of Sōtō Zen,* 55–56.

78. Ibid., 27–28.

79. Tanahashi, *Enlightenment Unfolds,* 48.

80. For more on Keizan, see Bodiford, *Sōtō Zen in Medieval Japan;* Faure, *Visions of Power.*

81. Masunaga, *A Primer of Sōto Zen,* 2

CHAPTER 5

1. Adorno, *Minima Moralia,* 222.

2. For example, at the American Academy of Religion Annual Conference, moderator Gary Laderman (Emory University) introduced a panel on "Icons, Idols and Objects: Facets of Materiality in East Asian Buddhism" by saying "This panel on Buddhist materiality is intended, in part, to remedy the logocentric emphasis on texts and ideas in religious studies" (Nov. 22, 1999).

3. Sharf, *Living Images,* 151–97.

4. Heine and Wright, *Zen Ritual.*

Glossary

Aikuō-zan	阿育王山
ajikan	阿字観
Amida	阿弥陀
Amida	阿弥陀 (alt. Muryōju)
Ango	安居
Ankokuji	安國寺
Ashikaga	足利
Ashuku	阿閦
Atō	阿刀
Awata	栗田
A-yü-wang-shan	See Aikuō-zan
Bendōwa	辨道話
Benkenmitsu nikkyōron	弁顕密二教語
bettō	別当
Birushana	毘盧舎那
bodaboji	勃陀勃地
Bodaidaruma	菩提達磨
Bumpitsu ganshinshō	文筆眼心抄
Bunkyō hifuron	文鏡秘府語
Busshō	仏性
byōdōshōchi	平等性智
Ch'an	See Zen
Ch'ang-an	長安
Ch'eng kuei of Shu	西蜀の成桂知客
Ch'ing-pien	See Shōben
Ch'ing-yüan	See Seigen
Changlegong	長楽宮
Chao Wu	趙呉
chi	智
Chih-chien	See Chikan
Chikan	智鑑
chiken-in	智拳印

Ch'in Shih Huang-ti	秦始皇帝
Ching	See kyō
Ching-shan	徑山
Ching-te Ch'uan teng lu	景德傳燈錄
Ching-te Ling-yin ssu	景德靈印寺
Ching-tz'u Pai-en-kuang shiao ssu	浄慈法報恩光孝寺
Chin-kang chih	See Kongōchi
Chin-kang fa-chieh-kung	See Kongō hokkaigū
chinzō	頂相
Chou li	周禮
Chuang Tzu	莊子
Chūen	忠延
Chūtai hachiyōin	中台八葉院
Daibirushana jōbutsukyō shomonshitai	大毘廬遮那成仏経疏文次第
Daibutsuji	大仏寺
Daichidoron	大智度語
daienkyō chi	大圓鏡智
Daigokuden	大極殿
Daiitoku	大威徳
daimoku gohonzon	題目御本尊
Dainichi	大日
Dainichi nyorai	大日如来
Dainichikyō	大日経
Dairi	内裏
Daruma-shu	達磨宗
Den-e	伝衣
dianxin	點心
Dōgen	道元
Dogo	道吾
Dōmoto Inshō	堂本印象
Echizen	越前
Eichi ninen shingon-in mishuhōki	永治二年真言院御修法記
Eihei kaisan gyōjō kenzei-ki	永平開山行状建撕記
Eihei kōroku	永平広録
Eiheiji	永平寺
Eiheiji sanso gyōgōki	永平寺三箇靈瑞記
Eikyūji	永久寺
Eisai	榮西
Ejō	懷奘
Ekan	懷鑑
emaki	絵巻
Emman-in	閻魔院
Enchin	円珍

Enni Bennen	圓爾辯圓
Enō	惠能
ensō	円相
Fa-tsang	法藏
Fubo shoshō no mi	父母初生身
Fudō Myōō	不動明王
Fu-fa-tsang yin yüan-chuan	See *Fuhōzō innenden*
fugen shinden	普賢心殿
Fugen	普賢
Fuhōzō innenden	付法蔵因縁伝
Fu-hsi	伏羲
Fujiwara Munehiro	藤原宗弘
Fu-jung Tao-kai	See Fuyō Dōkai
Fukakusa	深草
Fukū kongō	不空金剛
Fukui	福井
Fukūjōju	不空成就
fumidoko	文床
Fuyō Dōkai	芙蓉道楷
Fu-yung	芙蓉`
Gabyō	画餅
Ganzei	眼睛
garan	伽藍
Gekongōbu	外金剛部
Gengō	元杲
Genjōkōan	現成公案
genze riyaku	現是利益
Gikai	義介
Gisho	義湘
gobushinkan	五部心観
godaimyōō	五大明王
gong	工
gorintō	五輪塔
gorintō	五輪塔
goshichinichi mishuhō	後七日御修法
Goshichinichi mishuhō yuisho sahō	後七日御修法由緒作法
Gozanze	降三世
gū	宮
Gundari	軍荼利
gyōsho	行書
haisha	拝写
hake	刷毛
Hakuin Ekaku	白隠慧鶴

Hakuyū	白幽
Han	漢
Hannya bosatsu	般若菩薩
Hannya shingyō hiken	般若心経秘鍵
happi	法被
Hatano Yoshishige	波多野義重
Heian	平安
Heijō	平城
Heizei	平城
Heizei tennō kanjōmon	平城天皇灌頂文
Hekiganroku	碧巖録
Henchiin	遍知院
Henjō hakki seireishū	偏照発揮性霊集
henshin	徧身
hensō	変相
hibutsu	秘仏
Hiei-zan	比叡山
hihaku	飛白
Himitsu mandara jū jūshinron	秘密曼荼羅十住心語
himitsu shōgon shin	秘密荘厳心
hisō	非相
Hizō hōyaku	秘蔵宝鑰
Hizōki	秘蔵記
Hōdō	宝幢
Hōgen	法眼
Hōharamitsu	宝波羅密
Hōharamitsu	法波羅密
hokkai taishō chi	法界體性智
hokkaigū	法界宮
hokkaitaishō chi	法界體性智
Hōkyōji	宝慶寺
Hōkyōji	宝慶寺
Hōkyōki	寶慶記
Hommyō	本妙寺
Hōnen	法然
hongaku	本覺
Honkō kokushi nikki	本光国師日記
Honmyōji	本妙寺
honzon	本尊
Hōshō	法生
Hōshō	宝生
hosshin seppō	法身説法

Hossō	法相
Hsiang-yen Chih-hsien	See Kyōgen Chikan
hsin-chen t'o lo	心塵脱落
Hsing-sheng Wan-shou ssu	興聖万寿寺
Huang-long	黄龍
Huang-po	黄檗
Hua-yen	See Kegon
Hua-yen jing	See *Kegonkyō*
Hui-kuo	惠果
Hui-neng	See Enō
Hung-chih Cheng-chüeh	See Wanshi Shōgaku
I Ching	易経
Ichigyō	一行
I-hsiang	See Gisho
I-hsing	See Ichigyō
I-ichi Seido	惟一西堂
Ikka myōju	一顆明珠
Ikkyū Sōjun	一休宗純
Ingen	隠元
inka	印可
isuzō	椅子像
itto jōbutsu	一覿成仏
izō	遺像
ji	字
jijimuge	事事無礙
jiju hōraku	自受法楽
Jimyōin	持明院
Jingoji	神護寺
jiriki	自力
jisan	自賛
jissō	実相
Jizō	地蔵
Jizōin	地蔵院
jō-in	定印
Jōkaishō	除蓋障
Jōkaishōin	除蓋障院
jōshosa chi	成所作智
jōshosa chi	成所作智
Ju-ching	See Tendō Nyojō
jūekō	十廻向
jūgyō	十行
jūhachidō	十八道

jūji	十地
jūjū	十住
Jūjūshinron	十住心語
jūnyoze	十如是
Jūroku rakkan genhitsugi	十六羅漢現瑞記
jūsshin	十信
jūyukan	十喩觀
juzō	壽像
juzu	数珠
Kaifukeō	開敷華王
kaji	加持
Kamakura	鎌倉
Kamei kotsuji	仮名乞児
kami	神
Kanensho	勧縁流
Kangen	観賢
Kanjin	寛信
Kanjiten	歓喜天
Kanjizai	観自在
kanjō	灌頂
Kanjōdō	灌頂堂
Kanjōin	灌頂院
Kannon	観音
Kannondōri	観音導利
Kannonin	観音院
kanshi	漢詩
Karoku	嘉禄
katsu	喝
katsu	瞎
Katsumaharamitsu	磨波羅密
kechien kanjō	結縁灌頂
kechimyaku	血脈
kegare	汚れ
Kegon	華厳
Kegonkyō	華厳経
keiseki	経籍
Keizan Jōkin	螢山紹瑾
kekkafuza	結跏趺坐
Kenbutsu	見仏
Kenbutsu	見仏
Kenninji	建仁寺
Kenzeiki	See *Eihei kaisan gyōjō kenzei-ki*

Kenzei	建撕
Kinryūji	金龍寺
kōan	公案
Kōchi	広智
kodai no monji	広大の文字
Kōkō	光孝
Kokū	虚空
kokubunji	国分寺
Kokūzō	虚空蔵
Kokūzōin	虚空蔵院
Kokyō	古鏡
Kōmyō	光明
kongō hokkaigū	金剛法界宮
Kongō yasha	金剛夜叉
Kongōai	金剛愛
Kongōbuji	金剛峰寺
Kongōchi	金剛智
Kongōchō giketsu	金剛頂義訣
Kongōchōkyō kaidai	金剛頂経開題
Kongōchōkyō	金剛頂経
Kongōge	金剛牙
Kongōgō	金剛業
Kongōgo	金剛語 (Skt. *Vajrabhāṣa*)
Kongōgo	金剛護 (Skt. *Vajrarakṣa*)
Kongōharamitsu	金剛波羅密
Kongōhō	金剛宝 (Skt. *Vajraratna*)
Kongōhō	金剛法 (Skt. *Vajradharma*)
Kongōin	金剛因
Kongōkai kuemikki	金剛界九会密記
kongōkai	金剛界
Kongōken	金剛拳
Kongōki	金剛喜
Kongōkō	金剛光
Kongōō	金剛王
Kongōri	金剛利
Kongōsatta	金剛薩埵
Kongōshō	金剛笑
Kongōshū	金剛手
Kongōshuin	金剛手院
Kongōtō	金剛
Konkōmyō saishōōkyō	金光明最勝王経
konpon daitō	根本大塔

Konshōōmyōkyō himitsu kada	金勝王明経秘密伽陀
Kōshōji	興聖寺
Kōya-san	高野山
Kuang-li-ssu	廣利寺
Kūkai	空海
kūshu genkyō	空手還郷
kuwakaku	蝸角
kuyō	供養
kyō	経
Kyōgen Chikan	香嚴智閑
kyōhan	教判
kyokuroku	曲录
kyoō jikki	虚往實帰
Kyōōkyō kaidai	教王経開題
kyōryaku	経歴
kyosaku	警策
kyōsō hanjaku	教相判釋
Leng-ch'ieh ching	See Nyūryōgakyō
Li Chen	李真
Lin-chi	See Rinzai
Ling-yun Chih-ch'in	See Reiun Shigon
Machida Hisanari	町田久成
Makakashō	摩訶迦葉
mandara	曼荼羅
Manzan	卍山
Mikkyō	密教
Miroku	弥勒
Misae	御斉会
Mitsugo	密語
miyako	京;身や子
miyama	みやま;御山;深山;身山
mokugyō	木魚
mon	文
monji	文字
Monju	文殊
Monjuin	文殊院
mudō sanmai	無動三昧
mujō seppō	無情說法
mujō seppō	無情説法
Mumonkan	無門關
munen musō	無念無想

Murōji	室生寺
Muryōju	無量寿
mushikishin sanmai	無識身三昧
musō	無相
myōgaku	妙覺
myōgō honzon	名号本尊
myōkan-zatchi	妙觀察智
myōkan-zatchi	妙觀察智
Myōō	明王
Myōzen	明全
Nagaoka	長岡
Nakatsukasa shō	中務省
Nan-shan	南山
nanten tettō	南天鉄塔
Nan-yang Huichung	南陽慧忠
Nara	奈良
nembutsu	念仏
Nenjū gyōgi emaki	年中行事絵巻
Nichiren	日蓮
nikon	而今
Ning-tsung	寧宗
Ninmei	仁明
Ninnōkyō	仁王経
nōen	能縁
nōyuiyaku nōgō	能迷亦能悟
Nyojō	See Tendō Nyojō
nyokyota	如許多
nyoze	如是
nyūga ganyū	入我我入
Nyūryōgakyō	楞伽經
Onjōji	園城寺
Pei-shan	北山
Pi-yen lu	碧巖錄
Pu-k'ung Chin-kang	See Fukū kongō
Reiun shigon	霊雲志勤
ri	理
richi funi	理知不二
Rinzai	臨済
Rishukyō	理趣経
Rokushu mandara ryakushaku	六種曼荼羅略釈
Saga	嵯峨

Saichō	最澄
Saiji	西寺
saku	作
Sanbō	三宝
Sangō shiiki	三教指帰
sanmistu	三密
Sansuikyō	山水経
sato	里
satori	悟り
Seigen	清源, alt.青原
Seireishū	See *Henjō hakki seireishū*
seisei	清浄
senbutsuko	千仏子
Shakain	釈迦院
shakamuni bodaboji	繹迦牟尼勃陀勃地
Shan Wu-wei	See Zemmui
Shari sōdenki	舎利相傳記
shen-hsin t'o lo	身心脱落
shidosō	私度僧
Shiga	滋賀
shikan taza	只管打坐
shikizō	色像
shimandara	四曼荼羅
Shimotsuke	下野
shin	心
shin	身
shinden	寝殿
shinden	心殿
Shinfukatoku	心不可得
Shingon	真言
Shingon'in	真言院
shinjin datsuraku	心塵脱落
shinjin datsuraku	身心脱落
Shinkō	真興
Shinran	親鸞
Shinzen Daitoku	真然大徳
Shisho	嗣書
shō	声
Shōben	清辯
shōbōgen	正法眼
Shōbōgenzō	正法眼蔵
Shobutsu seiken	諸仏斉肩

shoen	所縁
shōgon	荘厳
Shōji jissōgi	声字実相義
Shōji	生死
shōjō	清浄
Shokanzeon	聖観世音
Shōmu	聖武
Shōrai mokuroku	請来目録
Shōren-in	青蓮院
shosō	諸相
Shōsōin	正倉院
sō	相
sokushin jōbutsu	即身成仏
Sokushin jōbutsugi	即身成仏義
sokushin zebutsu	即心是仏
sokuten	則天
sokuza jōbutsu	即座成仏
Sonkai	尊海
Soshitsujiin	蘇悉地院
sōsho	草書
Sōtō	曹洞
ssu-he yüan	四各院
Sumiyoshi Jokei	住吉如慶
Sung	宋
T'aipai shan	太白山
T'ang	唐
T'ien Tung Ching-te	天童景徳
Tachibana Hayanari	橘逸勢
Ta-chih-tu lun	See *Daichidoron*
tahōtō	多宝塔
tai	體
taimitsu	台密
T'aipai shan	太白山
Taiyūji	太融寺
taizōkai	胎蔵界　胎蔵海
Takaosan	高雄山
Takaosanji	高雄山寺
tanden	丹田
Tan-hsia T'ien-jan	丹霞天然
Tao-sheng	道生
Tendai	天台
Tendō Nyojō	天童如淨

tenkatsu	点瞎
Tenkuraion	天鼓雷音
Tenrei banshō myōgi (alt. meigi)	篆隷万象名義
Te-shan Hsüan-chien	See Tokuzan Senkan
T'ien t'ung Ju-ching	See Tendō Nyojō
T'ien t'ung Ching-te ch'an ssu	天童慶徳禅寺
Tochigi	栃木
Tōdaiji	東大寺
Tofukuji	東福寺
tōgaku	等覺
Tōji	東寺
Tokiwa Mitsunaga	常盤光長
Tokuitsu	徳一
Tokuzan Senkan	徳山宣鑑
tōmitsu	東密
Tōshōdaiji	唐招提寺
totsu	咄
tōzan	東山
Tōzan	洞山
Tōzan Gohon (Ryokai)	洞山悟本 (良价)
tsūshin	通身
Tung-shan Liang-chieh	See Tōzan Gohon (Ryokai)
Tu-shun	杜順
Uji	有時
Ungan	雲巌
Unjigi	迂字義
unsui	雲水
waka	和歌
Wang cheng	王城
Wanshi Shōgaku	宏智正覺
Weiyangong	未央宮
Yakushi	薬師
Yamatokuni masudaike himei narabinijo	大和州益田池碑銘並序
yuibutsu yobutsu	唯仏与仏
yü-lu	語錄
zattaisho	雑体書
zazen	坐禅
Zemmui	善無畏
Zen	禅
Zenki	全機
Zentsūji	善通寺

Zhouli	周禮
Zuigan	瑞巌
Zuiganji	瑞巌寺
Zuimonki	随聞記
zuga	図画
zuzō	図像

Bibliography

PRIMARY SOURCES

DZZ—Dōgen. *Dōgen zenji zenshū*. Edited by Ōkubō Dōshō. 2 vols. Tokyo: Chikuma shobō, 1969–70.

DZZ—Dōgen. *Dōgen zenji zenshū*. Edited by Genryū Kagamishima, Tokyo: Shunjusha, 1988.

KDZ—Kūkai. *Kōbō daishi kūkai zenshū*. Edited by Miyasaka Yūshō. 8 vols. Tokyo: Chikuma shobō, 1983–85.

KZ—Kūkai. *Kōbō daishi zenshū*. Edited by Hase Hōshū. 6 vols. Tokyo: Yoshikawa Kōbunkan, 1909–11.

KZ—Kūkai. *Kōbō daishi zenshū*. Revised edition. 6 vols. Tokyo: Yoshikawa Kōbunkan, 1923.

KZ—Kūkai. *Kōbō daishi zenshū*. 3rd ed., rev., edited by Inaba Yoshitake et al. Mikkyō Bunka Kenkyū-sho, 1965.

T—*Taishō shinshū dai zōkyō*. Revised edition. Edited by Takakusa Junjirō, Watanabe Kaikyoku, et al. 100 volumes. Tokyo: Taishō issaikyō kankōkai, 1924–1932 [–1935]. Also accessed from Robert Buswell's *East Asia Buddhist Studies: A Reference Guide*. http://alc.ucla.edu/refguide/refguide.htm#contents.

SECONDARY SOURCES

Abé, Ryūichi. "Capturing the Dharma at the Margins of Tangibility: On Eikyuji's Two Dharma Transmission Paintings." http://research.yale.edu/eastasianstudies/esoteric/abe.pdf.

Abé, Ryūichi. "Mandala as a Time Machine: Sexual Symbolism and the Figuration of Time in Shingon Buddhist Iconography." Symposium paper delivered for the exhibition *Mandala: Space and Symbols of Enlightenment*. Asia Society, New York. October 1997.

Abé, Ryūichi. *The Weaving of Mantra: Kūkai and the Construction of Esoteric Buddhist Discourse*. New York: Columbia University Press, 1999.

Addiss, Stephen. *The Art of Zen: Painting and Calligraphy by Japanese Monks 1600–1925*. New York: Harry N. Abrams, 1989.

Adorno, Theodor W. *Minima Moralia: Notes from a Damaged Life*. Frankfurt am Main: Suhrkamp Verlag, 1951.

Ames, Robert T. *Focusing the Familiar: A Translation and Philosophical Interpretation of the* Zhongrong. Honolulu: University of Hawaii Press, 2001.

Arnheim, Rudolf. *Visual Thinking*. Berkeley: University of California Press, 1969.

Aurier, Albert. "Le Symbolisme en Peinture: Paul Gaugin." *Le Mercure de France* 2 (March 1891): 155–65. http://gallica.bnf.fr/ark:/12148/bpt6k1051454.zoom.f161.

Bailey, Don Clifford. "Early Japanese Lexicography." *Monumenta Nipponica* 16, no. 1/2 (April-July 1960): 1–52.

Benjamin, Walter. "The Work of Art In the Age of Mechanical Reproduction." In *Illuminations: Essays and Reflections*. Edited by Hannah Arendt, translated by Harry Zohn. New York: Harcourt, Brace, Jovanovich, 1968. 217–52.

Bhattacharyya, Benoytosh. *An Introduction to Buddhist Esotericism*. Delhi: Motilal Banarsidass Publishers Pvt. Ltd., 1980.

Bodiford, William M. *Sōtō Zen in Medieval Japan*. Honolulu: University of Hawaii Press, 1993.

Bogel, Cynthea J. *With a Single Glance: Buddhist Icons and Early Buddhist Vision*. Seattle: University of Washington Press, 2009.

Brinker, Helmut and Hiroshi Kanazawa. *Zen Masters of Meditation in Images and Writings*. Translated by Andreas Leisinger. Zurich: Artibus Asiae Publishers, 1996.

Corbin, Henry. *Temple and Contemplation*. Translated by Philip Sherrard and Liadian Sherrard. London: KPI in association with Islamic Publications, 1986.

d'Acquili, Eugene, Andrew Newberg, and Vince Rouse. *Why God Won't Go Away: Brain Science and the Biology of Belief*. New York: Ballantine Books, 2001.

Davidson, Julian M. "The Physiology of Meditation and Mystical States of Consciousness." In *Meditation: Classic and Contemporary Perspectives*, edited by Deane N. Shapiro and Roger N. Walsh, 375–95. New York: Aldine Publishers, 1984.

deBary, William Theodore. *The Buddhist Tradition in India, China and Japan*. New York: Vintage Books, 1972.

DeConcini, Barbara. "The Crisis of Meaning in Religion and Art." *Christian Century* (March 1991): 223–326.

Delevoy, Robert L. *Symbolists and Symbolism*. Geneva: Editions d'Art Albert Skira S.A. 1982.

Dobbins, James. "Portraits of Shinran." In *Living Images*. Edited by Robert H. Sharf and Elizabeth Horton Sharf. Stanford: Stanford University Press, 2001, 19–48.

Dōmoto Inshō. *Dōmoto Inshō: gushōga hen* Kyoto: Kyoto shoin, 1981.

Duara, Prasenjit. *Culture, Power and The State: Rural North China, 1900–1942*. Stanford: Stanford University Press, 1988.

Dumoulin, Heinrich. *Zen Buddhism: A History, Vol. II Japan*. Translated by James W. Heisig and Paul Knitter. New York: Macmillan Publishing Co., 1990.

Eckel, Malcolm David. *To See the Buddha: A Philosopher's Quest for the Meaning of Emptiness*. Princeton: Princeton University Press, 1992.

Eddington, Sir Arthur Stanley. *The Physical World*. New York: Macmillan Co.; Cambridge: The University Press, 1928.

Eliade, Mircea. *The Sacred and Profane: The Nature of Religion*. Translated by Willard R. Trask. New York: Harcourt Brace Jovanovich, 1959.

Faure, Bernard. *Visions of Power: Imagining Medieval Japanese Buddhism*. Translated by Phyllis Brooks. Princeton, NJ: Princeton University Press, 1996.

Faure, Bernard. *The Rhetoric of Immediacy: A Cultural Critique of Chan/Zen Buddhism*. Princeton, NJ: Princeton University Press, 1994.

Fontein, Jan. *The Pilgrimage of Sudhana: A Study of Gaṇḍavyūha Illustrations in China, Japan and Java*. Netherlands: Mouton, 1967.

Foulk, T. Griffith and Robert Sharf. "On the Ritual Use of Ch'an Portraiture in Medieval China." *Cahiers d'Extrême Asie* 7 (1993–1994): 149–219.

Fowler, Sherry Diane. *Murōji: Rearranging Art and History at a Japanese Buddhist Temple*. Honolulu: University of Hawaii Press, 2005.

Gardiner, David. *Kōyasan*. Kōyasan, Japan: Head Temple Kongōbuji Printing Office of Kōyasan Shuppansha, 1992.

Gardiner, David. "Kūkai and the Beginnings of Shingon Buddhism in Japan." PhD diss., Stanford University, 1995. ProQuest (ATT 9516825).

Gardiner, David. "Mandala, Mandala on the Wall: Variations of Usage in the Shingon School." *Journal of International Association of Buddhist Studies* 19, no. 2 (1996): 245–76.

Gardiner, David. "Transmission Problems: The Reproduction of Scriptures and Kūkai's 'Opening' of an Esoteric Tradition." *Japanese Religions* 28, no. 1 (2003): 5–49.

Gibson, Morgan and Hiroshi Murakami. *Tantric Poetry of Kūkai (Kōbō Daishi), Japan's Buddhist Saint*. Bangkok: Amarin Press, 1982.

Hakeda, Yoshita S. *Kūkai Major Works: Translated with an Account of His Life and A Study of His Thought*. New York: Columbia University Press, 1972.

Harvey, Peter. *An Introduction to Buddhism: Teachings, History and Practices*. Cambridge: Cambridge University Press, 1990.

Heine, Steven. *A Blade of Grass: Japanese Poetry and Aesthetics in Dōgen Zen*. New York: Peter Lang, 1989.

Heine, Steven. *Did Dōgen Go to China? What He Wrote and When He Wrote It*. Oxford: Oxford University Press, 2006.

Heine, Steven. *Opening a Mountain: Kōans of the Zen Masters*. New York: Oxford University Press, 2002.

Heine, Steven. *The Zen Poetry of Dōgen: Verses From the Mountain of Eternal Peace*. North Clarendon, VT: Tuttle Publishing, 1997.

Heine, Steven. *Zen Ritual*. Edited by Steven Heine and Dale S. Wright. New York: Oxford University Press, 2008.

Hershock, Peter. *Liberating Intimacy: Enlightenment and Social Virtuosity in Ch'an Buddhism*. Buffalo: State University of New York Press, 1996.

Hollenbach, Jess Byron. *Mysticism: Experience Response and Empowerment.* University Park, PA: Penn State Press, 1996.

Honmyōji rekishi shiryō sahōkokusho: bijutsu, kōkeihin hen. Edited by the Kumamoto kenritsu bijutsukan. Kumamoto-shi: Honmyōji, 1981. Temple publication.

Horkheimer, Max and Theodor Adorno. "The Culture Industry: Enlightenment as Mass Deception." In *The Cultural Studies Reader,* edited by Simon During. London, New York: Routledge Press, 1999. 31–41.

Inagaki, Hisao, trans. *Kūkai's Principle of Attaining Buddhahood with the Present Body.* Ryūkoku Translation Pamphlet Series 4. Kyoto: Ryūkoku University Translation Center of Buddhist Scriptures, 1975.

Ingram, Paul O. "Nature's Jeweled Net: Kūkai's Ecological Buddhism." *Pacific World 6* (1990): 50–73.

Kasulis, Thomas P. "On Knowing the Mystery: Kūkai and Thomas Aquinas." *Buddhist Christian Studies* 8 (1988): 37–45.

Kasulis, Thomas P., trans. "Uji (Being-Time)." Unpublished manuscript, 1976.

Katz, Steven T. "Language, Epistemology and Mysticism." In *Mysticism and Philosophical Analysis,* edited by Steven T. Katz. Oxford: Oxford University Press, 1978. 27–74.

Kawamura, Kōdō, ed. *Eihei kaisan dōgen zenji gyōjō kenzei-ki, shohon taikō.* Tokyo: Daishūkan Shoten, 1975.

Kim, Hee-Jin. "'The Reason of Words and Letters': Dōgen and Kōan Language." In *Dōgen Studies,* edited by William R. LaFleur, 54–82. Honolulu: University of Hawaii Press. 1985.

Kitagawa, Joseph. *Religion in Japanese History.* New York: University of Columbia Press, 1990.

Kiyota, Minoru. *Shingon Buddhism: Theory and Practice.* Los Angeles: Buddhist Books International, 1978.

Kiyota, Minoru. "Shingon Mikkyō's Twofold Mandala: Paradoxes and Integration." *The Journal of the International Association of Buddhist Studies* 10, no. 1 (1987): 91–116.

Kōbō daishi ten. Kōyasan: Kongōbuji. 1985. Exhibition catalogue.

Kōbō daishi to mikkyō bijutsu. Kyoto National Museum, 1983–84. 1150th memorial exhibition catalogue.

Kodera, Takahashi James. *Dōgen's Formative Years in China: An Historical Study and Annotated Translation of the "Hōkyō-ki."* Boulder: Prajñā Press, 1980.

Kohn, Livia. *Early Chinese Mysticism.* Princeton: Princeton University Press, 1991.

Kokubunji. Nara: Nara National Museum, 1980. Exhibition catalogue.

Komine, Michihiko. "Satori no tenkai: chūtai hachiyōin kara soshitsujiin made." In *Shingon mikkyō to mandara,* edited by Daihōrinkaku henshūbu, 139–61. Tokyo: Daihō rinkyaku, 1997.

Leighton, Taigen Dan and Shohaku Okumura, trans. *Dōgen's Extensive Record: A Translation of the Eihei Koroku*. Somerville, MA: Wisdom Publications, 2004.

Leighton, Taigen Dan. *Visions of Awakening Space and Time: Dōgen and the Lotus Sūtra*. New York: Oxford University Press, 2007.

Mack, Karen. "A Reconsideration of the Goshichinichi mishuhō." In *Esoteric Buddhist Studies: Identity in Diversity. Proceedings of the International Conference on Esoteric Buddhist Studies, Koyasan University, 5 Sept.–8 Sept. 2006*, edited by Executive Committee, IABS, 85–90. Kōyasan: Kōyasan University, 2008.

Mason, Penelope. *History of Japanese Art*. New York: Harry N. Abrams, 1993.

Masunaga, Reihō. *A Primer of Sōtō Zen: A Translation of Dōgen's Shōbōgenzō Zuimonki*. Honolulu: University of Hawaii Press, 1990.

Matsunaga, Daigan and Matsunaga, Alicia. *Foundation of Japanese Buddhism*. 2 vols. Tokyo: Buddhist Books International, 1993–96.

McFarland, H. Neill. "If You Meet the Patriarch, Kill Him! Dispensing With Bodhidharma." *Japanese Religions* 14, no. 1 (December 1985): 13–27.

Morgan, David. *The Sacred Gaze: Religious Visual Culture in Theory and Practice*. Berkeley: University of California Press, 2005.

Nagatomo, Shigenori. "The Logic of the *Diamond Sūtra*: A Is Not-A, Therefore It Is A." *Asian Philosophy* 10, no. 3 (November 2000): 213–44.

Nakata, Yujiro. *The Art of Japanese Calligraphy*. Translated by Alan Woodhull. New York: Weatherhill, 1973.

Nichiei bukkyō daijiten. Tokyo: Daitō Shuppansha, 1965.

Nicholoff, Philip L. *Sacred Kōyasan: A Pilgrimage to the Mountain Temple of Saint Kōbō Daishi and the Great Sun Buddha*. Buffalo: State University of New York Press, 2007.

Nishijima, Gudo Wafu and Chodo Cross, trans. *Master Dōgen's Shōbōgenzō*. 4 vols. London: Windbell Publications Ltd., 1994–99.

Nishiyama, Kōsen and John Stevens, trans. *Shōbōgenzō (The Eye and Treasury of the True Law)*, vol. 2. Tokyo: Nakayama shōbō, 1977.

Okumura, Shohaku. *Realizing Genjōkōan: The Key to Dōgen's Shōbōgenzō*. Somerville, MA: Wisdom Publications, 2010.

Ono, Genmyō. *Bukkyō no bijutsu to rekishi*. Tokyo: Kaimei Shoin, 1977.

Orzech, Charles. *Esoteric Buddhism and the Tantras in East Asia*. Handbook of Oriental Studies. Edited by Charles D. Orzech, Richard K. Payne, and Henrik H. Sørensen. Leiden, Brill Publishers, 2011.

Orzech, Charles. *Politics and Transcendent Wisdom: The Scripture for Humane Kings in the Creation of Chinese Buddhism*. University Park, PA: Penn State Press, 1998.

Osabe, Hideo. *Tenno wa doko kara kita ka*. Tokyo: Shinchōsha, 1996.

Otto, Rudolf. *Mysticism East and West: A Comparative Analysis of the Nature of Mysticism*. New York: The Macmillan Co., 1932.

Payne, Richard K. "*Ajikan*: Ritual and Meditation in the Shingon Tradition." In *Re-Visioning Kamakura Buddhism*, edited by Richard K. Payne, 219–48. Honolulu: University of Hawaii Press, 1998.

Payne, Richard K. *Re-visioning Kamakura Buddhism*. Edited by Richard K. Payne. Honolulu: University of Hawaii Press, 1998.

Payne, Richard K. *Tantras in East Asia*. Somerville, MA: Wisdom Publications, 2006.

Prince, A.J. "The Hua-yen Vision of Enlightenment." *Journal of the Oriental Society of Australia* 15–16 (1984): 137–60.

Rambelli, Fabio. *Buddhist Materiality: A Cultural History of Objects in Japanese Buddhism*. Stanford: Stanford University Press, 2007.

Rambelli, Fabio. "Secrecy in Japanese Esoteric Buddhism," in *The Culture of Secrecy in Japanese Religion*. Edited by Mark Teeuwen and Bernhard Scheid. London and New York: Routledge, 2006, 107–29.

Rambelli, Fabio. "True Words, Silence and the Adamantine Dance: On Japanese Mikkyō and the Formation of the Shingon Discourse." *Japanese Journal of Religious Studies* 21, no. 4 (December 1994): 373–405.

Reader, Ian. *Making Pilgrimages: Meaning and Practice in Shikoku*. Honolulu: University of Hawaii Press, 2006.

Rinne, Melissa M., trans. *The 53rd Annual Exhibition of Shōsōin Treasures*. Nara: Nara National Museum, 2001. Published in conjunction with the exhibition of the same name.

Rosenfield, John. "Prologue: Some Debating Points in Gandhāran Buddhism and Kuṣāṇa History" in *Gandhāran Buddhism*. Edited by Pia Brancaccio and Kurt Behrent. Vancouver: University of British Columbia Press, 2006, 9–40.

Ruppert, Brian. *The Jewel in the Ashes: Buddha Relics and Power in Early Medieval Japan*. Boston: Harvard University Asia Center, 2000.

Sadakata, Akira. *Buddhist Cosmology: Philosophy and Origins*. Translated by Gaynor Sekimori. Tokyo: Kōsei Publishing Co., 1999.

Sawa, Ryuken. *Mikkyō no bijutsu*. Vol. 8 of *Nihon no bijutsu*. Tokyo: Heibonsha, 1964.

Shaner, David Edward. *The Bodymind Experience in Japanese Buddhism: A Phenomenological Perspective of Kūkai and Dōgen*. Albany: State University of New York Press, 1985.

Sharf, Robert H. "Visualization and Mandala in Shingon Buddhism." In Sharf and Sharf, *Living Images: Japanese Buddhist Icons in Context*. Stanford: Stanford University Press, 2001, 151–97.

Sharf, Robert H. and Elizabeth Horton Sharf, eds. *Living Images: Japanese Buddhist Icons in Context*. Stanford: Stanford University Press, 2001.

Steinhardt, Nancy Shatzman. *Chinese Imperial City Planning*. Honolulu: University of Hawaii Press, 1999.

Stone, Jacqueline. *Original Enlightenment and the Transformation of Medieval Buddhism*. Honolulu: University of Hawaii Press, 1999.

Suzuki, D. T. *Zen Buddhism: Selected Writings of D. T. Suzuki.* Edited by William Barrett. Garden City, NY: Doubleday Anchor Books, 1956.

Tanahashi, Kazuaki, trans. and ed. *Moon in a Dewdrop: The Writings of Zen Master Dōgen.* San Francisco: North Point Press, 1985.

Tanahashi, Kazuaki, trans. *Enlightenment Unfolds: The Essential Teachings of Zen Master Dōgen.* Boston: Shambhala, 1999.

Takahashi, Masanobu. *The Essence of Dōgen.* Translated by Yuzuru Nobuoka. London, Boston and Melbourne: Kegan Paul International. 1983.

Tanabe, George. "Kōbō Daishi and the Art of Esoteric Buddhism." *Monumenta Nipponica* 38, no. 4 (Winter 1983): 409–12.

Tanjō garan to okunoin. Kōyasan: Kōyasan Reihōkan Museum, 2001. Published in conjunction with special exhibition no. 22 National Treasures of Mt. Kōya in Commemoration of Being on the Provisional List of Registered World Heritage Sites.

ten Grotenhuis, Elizabeth. *Japanese Mandalas: Representations of Sacred Geography.* Honolulu: University of Hawaii Press, 1999.

Tōji soken issen-nihyakunen kinen shuppan hensan iinkai. *Shin tōbōki: Tōji no rekishi to bijutsu.* Tokyo: Tokyo bijutsu, 1995.

Underhill, Evelyn. *Mysticism: A Study in the Nature and Development of Man's Spiritual Consciousness.* 1st ed. New York: E. P. Dutton, 1911.

Unno, Mark. *Shingon Refractions: Myōe and the Mantra of Light.* Somerville, MA: Wisdom Publications, 2004.

Waddell, Norman and Abe Maso. "Buddha Nature Part I." *The Eastern Buddhist 8*, no. 2 (October 1975): 94–112.

Waddell, Norman and Abe Maso, trans. "Genjōkōan." *The Eastern Buddhist* 5, no. 2 (October 1972): 124–40.

Waddell, Norman and Abe Maso, trans. and ed. *The Heart of Dōgen's Shōbōgenzō.* Albany: State University of New York Press, 2002.

Watson, Burton, trans. *The Lotus Sūtra.* New York: Columbia University Press, 1993.

Weber, Max. *The Sociology of Religion.* Translated by Ephraim Fischoff. Boston: Beacon Press, 1991.

Williams, Duncan Ryuken. *The Other Side of Zen: A Social History of Sōtō Zen Buddhism in Tokugawa Japan.* Princeton: Princeton University Press, 2004.

Williams, Paul. *Mahāyāna Buddhism: The Doctrinal Foundations.* London: Routledge, 1989.

Winfield, Pamela "Mandala as Metropolis." In *Esoteric Buddhism and the Tantras in East Asia,* edited by Charles Orzech, Richard Payne, and Heinrich Sørensen, 719–43. Leiden: Brill Publishers, 2011.

Yamamoto, Chikyō. *Introduction to the Mandala.* Kyoto: Dōhōsha Publishing Company, 1980.

Yamaori, Tetsuo. *Wandering Spirits and Temporary Corpses: Studies in the History of Japanese Religious Tradition.* Translated and edited by Dennis Hirota. Kyoto: International Research Center for Japanese Studies, 2004.

Yamasaki, Taiko. *Shingon: Japanese Esoteric Tradition*. Translated and adapted by Richard and Cynthia Peterson. Edited by Yasuyoshi Morimoto and David Kidd. Boston: Shambala, 1988.

Yampolsky, Philip. *The Platform Sūtra of the Sixth Patriarch*. New York: Columbia University Press, 1967.

Yoritomi, Motohiro and Tachikawa Musashi. *Chūgoku mikkyō*. Tokyo: Shunjusha Publishers, 1999.

Yoritomi, Motohiro and Tachikawa Musashi. *Dainichikyō nyūmon: jihi no mandara sekai*. Tokyo: Daihorinkaku, 2000.

Yoritomi, Motohiro and Tachikawa Musashi. *Indō mikkyō*. Tokyo: Shunjusha Publishers, 1999.

Yuasa, Yasuo. *The Body: Toward an Eastern Mind-Body Theory*. Edited by Thomas P. Kasulis. Translated by Shigenori Nagatomo and Thomas P. Kasulis. Albany: State University of New York Press, 1987.

Yuasa, Yasuo. *Overcoming Modernity: Synchronicity and Image Thinking*. Translated by Shigenori Nagatomo and John W. M. Krummel. Albany: State University of New York Press, 2008.

Index

Lightning Source UK Ltd.
Milton Keynes UK
UKHW010206011118
331570UK00003B/96/P